Lyman Hotchkiss Bagg

Castle Solitude in the Metropolis

Lyman Hotchkiss Bagg

Castle Solitude in the Metropolis

ISBN/EAN: 9783337293499

Printed in Europe, USA, Canada, Australia, Japan

Cover: Foto ©Suzi / pixelio.de

More available books at **www.hansebooks.com**

Taking all things into consideration, strong and weak points alike, we believe that the author has most faithfully kept his promise and that "Ten Thousand Miles on a Bicycle" will always hold the undisputed place of the first great work on the subject of cycling, bearing to all wheelmen that relation that Isaac Walton's Complete Angler bears to fishermen, the world over. —*Wheelmen's Record, Indianapolis.*

An *olla podrida* of endless variety.—*Scientific American.* As comprehensive as a file of newspapers.—*Baltimore American.* Most useful to those wishing such information.—*The Times, N. Y.* Invaluable to one contemplating a tour.—*The Bicycle South.* A valuable encyclopædia, well worth the price asked for it.—*L. A. W. Bulletin.* For the public it seeks it will be a handy volume.—*The Nation, N. Y.* Invaluable to all who follow in his footsteps, or wheel-tracks. — *Lippincott's Magazine.* Those who are just beginning the sport will find it a work of absorbing interest.—*New Englander.* Although a veritable cycling encyclopædia, it is really of especial value to all horsemen who drive for pleasure.—*Spirit of the Times, N. Y.* This manual will prove indispensable to the wheelman. It is most valuable to the bicycler who has time for riding long distances.—*Boston Advertiser.*

The chief characteristic is its comprehensiveness.—*Canadian Wheelman.* Unique in literature and unsurpassed in its line.—*McGregor News, Ia.* The largest and most complete work on cycling ever published.—*The Cyclist, Coventry, Eng.* The most thorough book that any recreative sport has ever had published.—*Boonville Advertiser, Mo.* Not alone unique, but prodigious; this monument of cycling must stand.—*Australian Cycling News.* A really wonderful work, the first classic of cycling literature.—*Wheeling, London.* The work will stand as "the Domesday Book of Cycling."—*Sewing Machine & Cycle News, London.* As an insight into American cycling, the volume is very valuable.—*Irish Cyclist & Athlete, Dublin.* Statistical and historical, amusing and pathetic, it has charms for every reader.—*Saturday Night, Birmingham, Eng.* Whatever has been said in way of praise of this book, by the wheel literature of the world, is well merited.—*New Zealand Referee.*

A masterpiece of egotism.—*Pall Mall Gazette, London.* The most ridiculous book of the season.—*Philadelphia Press.* His individuality has asserted itself, and some of his literary excursions are exquisite.—*Hartford Courant.* A monument only to be compared with Webster's Dictionary or the Great Pyramid.—*The Bookmart, Pittsburg.* One of the most worthless volumes ever written; it is the work of an idiot, not of a sane man.—*Boston Herald.* Cyclists of all nations may get from it many useful "wrinkles." To Americans, especially, it will be invaluable and almost indispensable. The author is a genial and kindly philosopher, who makes no false or undue pretensions of any kind.— *The Saturday Review, London.* An autobiography of a singularly self-sufficient mediocrity; a faddist of the worst order; an egotistical nonentity; a gigantic sham; the self-confessed committer of every literary crime.—*Bicycling News, London organ of "the Coventry ring."*

CASTLE SOLITUDE

IN THE METROPOLIS

A STUDY IN SOCIAL SCIENCE

By KARL KRON

AUTHOR OF "FOUR YEARS AT YALE, BY A GRADUATE OF '69"

PRICE, TWENTY-FIVE CENTS, POSTPAID

———————

———————

PUBLISHED BY KARL KRON

THE UNIVERSITY BUILDING, WASHINGTON SQUARE

NEW YORK

1888

(F)

ADVERTISEMENT OF "CASTLE SOLITUDE."

Competent critics of that monumental volume have given a favorable verdict on this chapter of it, and their comments are now presented as a preface to the present pamphlet. Several of them say, however, that, though interesting enough to deserve buying on its own account, the act of inserting it in such a book was hardly a proper one, because of its irrelevancy to the main purpose thereof. They thus ignore the fact that it could not have been profitably printed in any other way,—since it is too long to be available for magazine use, and too limited in scope for wide circulation as an independent book.

Having, as publisher, staked $12,000 on the first edition of the book (in the hope of so thoroughly pleasing my 3000 " copartners " in all quarters of the globe that they will force a demand for later editions until the total sale reaches 30,000 copies), the main problem before me was to get my money back. If the insertion of a few extraneous chapters seemed conducive to this, —because allowing a readable and amusing style of literary treatment, which the nature of the subject forbade in the bulk of the book,—I certainly had a right to insert them. As I remark in the preface to the companion reprint, " Curl," in answer to a similar criticism of irrelevancy, " A good dog-story is always in order." If Artemus Ward was right in declaring, " It isn't a bad idea for a comic paper to print a joke, once in a while," surely the compiler of a cycling encyclopædia need not be condemned for presuming to enliven it with a few really readable chapters.

" As almost all books are written as a matter of vanity, I fear few people will believe me when I declare that this one is written as a matter of business ; and that its chief significance, so far as concerns the outside world, is as a unique business enterprise rather than as a literary curiosity. I have a right to insist that the solid phalanx of 3000 advance subscribers, representing every State and Territory of the Union and almost every section of Europe and Australasia, shall never be ignored in the judgment of any one who assumes fairly to judge the book which has been produced by their encouragement. Unless denial be made in advance that I have any right to persuade these people to serve me freely as book-agents, my mere attempt to placate them, by showing the sort of person they are serving, cannot be condemned."

Finally, if there is enough of interest in this sketch of the Castle to win the attention of college-bred men, as such, there is a chance of thus indirectly winning them to the cause of bicycling ; and if there is any value in securing newspaper mention of my scheme for pushing a bicycle book round the world, there is an evident economy in sending to reviewers the two "literary " chapters of it (in an easily-read pamphlet edition, containing also specimens of the general text and the indexes), rather than the massive tome itself. Recipients of it have given a sufficiently favorable verdict,—as shown in the appendix of this pamphlet,—but in most cases there is the underlying sentiment: " We cannot really be expected to review an encyclopædia."

THE PUBLISHER.

WASHINGTON SQUARE, N. Y., Jan. 24, 1888.

S2

It must be said that fair warning is given in the Preface, both in the text and conspicuously in the sub-headings, that this book was written for a special class—"for men who travel on the bicycle"—and that in general no effort has been made to make it readable. Whoever is fortunate enough to begin by reading this Preface may thus be prepared and propitiated for what follows; for it is very exhaustive and straightforward. But the usual point of beginning probably is at the first chapter, and that is decidedly well written and amusing—well calculated to hold the reader's attention to the end, and to raise expectations which the succeeding chapters, with two exceptions, will be likely to disappoint. One exception is the engaging story of the dog, and the other an interesting and pleasantly discursive history of the quaint old University Building on Washington Square, New York, a building at present inhabited chiefly by artists and college-bred men who value its remarkable seclusion and peculiar traditions. To many readers who might care little for the rest of the book, these two irrelevant chapters, together with the first,—the only ones which have much literary merit,—would be worth the price of all.—*Boston Advertiser.*

For the general reader into whose hands the book may fall there are two chapters of a more literary character. "Curl, the Best of Bull-Dogs," an old pet of the author's, is honored by a humorous and sympathetic biography; while the chapter entitled "Castle Solitude in the Metropolis" is an interesting study of Bohemian life in New York.—*New Englander.*

We have been reading Karl Kron's great book slowly but surely, and can thoroughly recommend it. There are blemishes, of course, such as the multiplicity of detail introduced, but most of it is excellent, especially the chapter on "Curl." We shall review the volume later..........We have again been dipping into the great book, though the immense size of the monster has as yet prevented us from grappling with the whole. Since we noticed the chapter on "The Best of Bull-Dogs," we have reached another equal to it in interest, styled "Castle Solitude in the Metropolis." What it or the Bull-dog have to say to cycling we know not, but both these chapters are full of interest as literary works.—*Irish Cyclist & Athlete, Dublin.*

A very cleverly written sketch of queer life at the University Building.—*Cape Ann Breeze, Mass.*

Two chapters of the book—one devoted to the biography of Curl, "My Bull-Dorg, the very best dog whose presence ever blessed this planet" (to whose memory the book is dedicated), the other, called "Castle Solitude in the Metropolis," and giving an account of life in the New York University building—seem quite irrelevant to the volume's purpose and to be introduced without sufficient reason.—*The Nation, N. Y.*

Last Tuesday, our Financier became a hopeless ruin, with water welling from his gentle eyes. He loves dogs, does the Financier, and he had read Karl Kron's chapter on "Curl," and after his guffaws had assembled a kind of Derby Day crowd under the windows, he fell a-crying.—*Wheeling, London.*

COMMENTS ON "CASTLE SOLITUDE."

To the non-rider there is much of interest, sometimes whole chapters, such as the one called "Castle Solitude in the Metropolis," and at other points very readable and suggestive pages.—*St. Louis Spectator.*

Kron is careful to assure his readers that he does not crave a "literary" reputation, yet, although he has carried compression to the point of eliminating every "Mr.," he inflicts two long and utterly irrelevant chapters, one about his dog, the other about the University Building.—*The Epoch, N. Y.*

Karl Kron gives a chapter to the cryptic building on Washington Square wherein was laid the scene of "Cecil Dreeme"; and no one can grudge the score of pages devoted to the humors and virtues of a companion of his boyhood, to wit, a bull-dog. This is the only portion of the book done with any literary skill. The rest is in excellent guide-book style, and derives its virtue from its correctness and its mass.—*The Times, N. Y.*

What this extraordinary gem has to do with cycling it is difficult to discover, but those condemned for their sins to peruse this work will welcome the restful pause which it affords. "Castle Solitude" belongs to the same category as "Curl's" biography, though of less merit, as being more labored and artificial. These two chapters are like the much-quoted flies in amber, with a modification :—

"neither rich nor rare,
One only wonders 'how the devil they got there.'"
—*Bicycling News, London organ of "the Coventry ring."*

"Curl" and "Castle Solitude in the Metropolis" are well worth reading, but of doubtful appropriateness in "a book of American roads."—*Wheelmen's Gazette, Indianapolis.*

We have perused three or four of its chapters (from advance sheets) with the greatest pleasure,—being particularly impressed with the one which contains the biography of "Curl," a pet bull-dog to whom the book is dedicated and whose heliotype forms its frontispiece.—*Tricycling Journal, London.*

The author's style may be sampled from the dedication of the book, "To the Memory of My Bull-Dorg," &c.—*Newark Advertiser, N. J.*

The general reader is quite as likely as the cycling reader to be amused by what I have said in these two extraneous chapters concerning the dear dog that I loved and the queer house that I live in.—*Author's Preface.*

The portions of the book that I most particularly liked were, first of all, the opening chapter, "On the Wheel," which I consider the masterpiece; then the chapters on "Curl," "White Flannel and Nickel Plate," "Castle Solitude," "Bermuda" and "Bone-Shaker Days,"—preference given according to the order named. The extraneous chapters are certainly amusing. All lovers of the dog must like to read the chapter on "Curl,"—and who is there that does not love a dog? I think one could find a greater number who do not love their own race. I should have preferred the author's picture instead of Curl's as a frontispiece, but of course acknowledge the author's right to keep his face from becoming familiar to the public.—*J. J. B., San Francisco.*

(M)

The unique frontispiece of "Ten Thousand Miles on a Bicycle,"—a clip-ped-eared bull-dog, done by the new process called photogravure,—is something of a surprise in a book on such a subject, and the question as to its meaning is not answered by reference to some 20 pages of the dog's biography to which attention is called. The volume is inscribed to the memory of "the very best dog whose presence ever blessed this planet." Well, he certainly does not look it, but the account of his life—and death—is the very best thing, from a literary point of view, in a volume of 900 pages. It is capital in itself, but its excellence must be the chief reason for its appearance in the midst of a tedious record of roads and journeys with which it has no sort of connection. That the dog thus immortalized was a great favorite of the author's in his youth, and that the author himself is popular with wheelmen and now avowedly wishes to make money upon his popularity, are facts hardly sufficient to justify the insertion of such a sketch in the body of a work so different in style and purpose. It is a piece of egotism that by no means stands alone. Yet, in view of the great quantity of matter here condensed and classified, the picture of the bull-dog which embellishes the first page, would seem to be a fitting emblem of the perseverance with which the author has pushed to completion his three years' task.—*Boston Advertiser.*

The extraordinary author dedicates his work to "The Memory of My Bull-Dorg."—*Boston Post.*

The dedication of the book to the author's bull-dog may have merit as a sentimental freak, but it is a literary execration.—*McGregor News, Ia.*

The author is possessed of a vein of smart American humor, which illuminates the dry text of his book from beginning to end. In places, such as the inimitable chapter devoted to his bull-dog "Curl," he soars to a pitch which reminds the reader very forcibly of Mark Twain and Max Adeler; and the cyclist who loves his dog will read this chapter over more than once. To "Curl," whose noble and expressive features act as frontispiece, the book is dedicated, and there is a certain pathos in the selection.—*Wheeling, London.*

Admirers of dogs, and of out-door sports, will take kindly to the book.—*New Orleans Picayune.*

"Curl" and "Castle Solitude in the Metropolis" are well worth reading, but of doubtful appropriateness in "a book of American roads."—*Wheelmen's Gazette, Indianapolis.*

A frontispiece, representing the head of a particularly ill-favored bull-dog, to whose memory the book is lovingly dedicated, forewarns the reader that the intellectual rambles of a bicycler did not necessarily share in the directness and regularity of his routes. The claim of this pet dog to public notice is not clearly established; but his interesting physiognomy, confronting the reader, in some measure compels a perusal of the chapter devoted to the uneventful career of the animal; and the theme apparently draws out the author's best literary powers.—*Alta California, San Francisco.*

TITLES OF THE 41 CHAPTERS.

"**Ten** Thousand Miles on a Bicycle" (908 pages of 675,000 words; pub. May 25, 1887; price $3) is characterized as "A Gazetteer of American Roads in Many States; an Encyclopædia of Wheeling Progress in Many Countries." Of its 20 local indexes, the chief one gives 8413 references to 3482 towns; and its chief personal index gives 3126 references to 1476 individuals. There are 1555 subjects catalogued in its general index, with 3330 references, and its table-of-contents shows 557 descriptive head-lines to principal paragraphs. An idea of the book's general scope, and of the regions and subjects to which it gives greatest prominence, may be gained by inspecting the titles of its 41 chapters, which stand as follows:

ON THE WHEEL (essay) — AFTER BEER (verse) — WHITE FLANNEL AND NICKEL PLATE — A BIRTHDAY FANTASIE (verse) — FOUR SEASONS ON A FORTY-SIX — COLUMBIA NO. 234 — MY 234 RIDES ON "NO. 234" — AROUND NEW YORK — OUT FROM BOSTON — THE ENVIRONS OF SPRINGFIELD — SHORE AND HILLTOP IN CONNECTICUT — LONG ISLAND AND STATEN ISLAND — COASTING ON THE JERSEY HILLS — LAKE GEORGE AND THE HUDSON — THE ERIE CANAL AND LAKE ERIE — NIAGARA AND SOME LESSER WATERFALLS — ALONG THE POTOMAC — KENTUCKY AND ITS MAMMOTH CAVE — WINTER WHEELING — IN THE DOWN EAST FOGS — NOVA SCOTIA AND THE ISLANDS BEYOND — STRAIGHTAWAY FOR FORTY DAYS — A FORTNIGHT IN ONTARIO — FROM THE THOUSAND ISLANDS TO THE NATURAL BRIDGE — THE CORAL REEFS OF BERMUDA — BULL RUN, LURAY CAVERN AND GETTYSBURG — BONE-SHAKER DAYS — CURL, THE BEST OF BULL-DOGS — CASTLE SOLITUDE IN THE METROPOLIS — LONG-DISTANCE ROUTES AND RIDERS — STATISTICS FROM THE VETERANS — BRITISH AND COLONIAL RECORDS — AUSTRALASIAN REPORTS — SUMMARY BY STATES — THE TRANSPORTATION TAX — THE HOTEL QUESTION — THE LEAGUE OF AMERICAN WHEELMEN — MINOR CYCLING INSTITUTIONS — LITERATURE OF THE WHEEL — THIS BOOK OF MINE, AND THE NEXT — THE THREE THOUSAND SUBSCRIBERS — DIRECTORY OF WHEELMEN — THE LAST WORD (verse). These chapters cover 800 pp. of 585,000 words; the PREFACE and ADDENDA, 33 pp. of 27,000 words; and the INDEXES, 75 pp.

"**Ten Thousand Miles on a Bicycle**" has been produced at an expense considerably in excess of $12,000 (representing a cash outlay of $6200, and four years' all-absorbing work). It will not be exposed at the bookstores, but an ultimate sale of 30,000 copies will be enforced by the unpaid efforts of the 3000 "co-partners" whose subscriptions combined to cause its publication. In more than 150 of the 852 towns represented on the subscription list, volunteer agents of this sort have consented to serve regularly as depositaries. A circular containing their names will be mailed on application. The chief agencies are as follows: New York, 12 Warren st., 313 W. 58th st., 49 Cortlandt st.: Boston, 79 Franklin st., 509 Tremont st., 107 Washington st.; **Baltimore**, 2 & 4 Hanover st.: Buffalo, 565 Main st.: Chicago, 291 Wabash ave., 222 N. Franklin st., 108 Madison st., 77 State st.; Cincinnati, 6 E. 4th st.; Cleveland, 1222 Euclid ave.; **Indianapolis**, office of Wheelmen's Gazette, Sentinel Building; Newark, Broad & Bridge sts.; **New Orleans**, 115 Canal st.; Philadelphia, 811 Arch st.: Portland, Or., 145 Fifth st.; **St. Louis**, 310 N. Eleventh st.; San Francisco, 228 Phelan Building; Washington, 1713 New York ave. Booksellers wishing to fill orders from their customers will be allowed a deduction of 25 c. on each volume purchased at these places (merely to cover the cost of handling), but there will be no other "trade discounts," nor will the book be mailed to any one for less than $2.

The volume is bound in dark blue muslin, smooth finish, with beveled edges and gilded top (size, 8 by 5½ by 1½ inches; weight, 2 pounds), and is not disfigured by advertisements. Its only ornament is a photogravure portrait of the distinguished bull-dog (b. 1856, d. 1872), to whose memory the entire work is dedicated, and whose biography forms its most readable chapter. Copies will be sent for $2, post-paid to any post-office, or express-paid to any office of the American Express Co. and many connecting expresses which allow the 15 c. mail-rate.

Requests for forwarding the volume "on approval" (to be paid for subsequently or returned, — a month's inspection thus costing but 20 c.) can be granted only by the Publisher, "KARL KRON, AT THE UNIVERSITY BUILDING, NEW YORK CITY, D."

Subscribers' Autograph Edition.

"*Nulla non donanda lauru* is that Building : you could not —
Placing New York's map before you — light on half so queer a spot."

This May Certify that

Pledge No.

To pay One Dollar in support of the publication of

"Ten Thousand Miles on a Bicycle"

Was made to me by

Mr.

Author and Publisher

XXIX.

CASTLE SOLITUDE IN THE METROPOLIS.[1]

THAT subtle essence which, in lack of a more graphic term, we call "character," though it is sufficiently rare among men, and rarer yet among women, is rarest of all among the buildings which the human race erect for their habitations. However greatly the houses of men may differ in size or architecture,—in outward appearance or inner arrangement,—one house is apt to be very much like another in its lack of inherent distinctiveness. The reader must be a very exceptional and widely-traveled person if he can recall as many as a dozen abodes which have impressed him as endowed with a genuine individuality,—as having a nature essentially different from that of every other house in the world. It is within the experience of almost every one to occasionally meet with a man whose peculiar traits and endowments create this impression, that he is the only one of his kind that ever existed or ever could exist; but an inanimate building possessed of this indescribable attribute of "character" is so rare an object—especially in a new country like America—that I presume a great majority of the people whose lives have been spent here have never formed the acquaintance of even one such specimen. Grotesque and singular mansions, whose exact types of grandeur or ugliness or absurdity are known to be unique, may be found on both slopes of the continent; but they all afflict the nostrils with so strong an odor of fresh paint and varnish as to render them in a moral sense quite colorless. "Character" is a product of age and experience, and it can no more be attached to a house by artificial process than a "moss-grown, historic ruin" can be incorporated into a landscape by contract with the nearest stone-cutter.

London is to me the most interesting city in the world, because of the amount of "character" which seems to have accumulated there as a gift of all the ages. It is this, I take it, which gives the touch of truth to Dr. Johnson's oft-quoted remark to the effect that it is all things to all men; that each individual's conception of it reflects his own nature; that it is a city of banks, or a city of book-shops, or a city of taverns, or a city of horse-markets, or a city of theaters, or a city of a hundred other things, according to one's personal point-of-view. The Modern Babylon is certainly the only inhabited spot in Europe where a man may mind his own business, and isolate himself almost as completely from observation as if in a desert solitude. The fact that it contains more people than the cities of Paris, Berlin, Vienna,

[1]Copyrighted, 1884, as Chapter XXIX of "Ten Thousand Miles on a Bicycle."

Rome, Dresden and Turin combined, suggests "the boundless contiguity of shade" that renders possible a degree of seclusion which is quite unattainable in those lesser cities. The immensity of London was the characteristic of it which never left my consciousness during the half-year that it was my good-fortune to be hidden there,—without once setting eyes upon a single personal acquaintance ; and I do not pretend that my persistent explorations of its mysteries revealed to me a one-hundredth part of them. I know that there are secret chambers, in the "inns-of-court" and other secluded buildings, where men may live peacefully for years without having their existence or their daily movements known to more than a very few people. But I am confident that there is no place in London where the habit of bodily self-suppression can be maintained with such a degree of completeness as is possible to tenants of a certain Building in America whose phenomenal queerness it is my present object to exhibit and explain.

The two millions of people who dwell upon Manhattan Island and the opposite shores—though equal in number to the combined inhabitants of Philadelphia, Chicago, Boston and Baltimore—form but a twenty-fifth part of the nation's population, whereas a fifth of all the people of England are concentrated at London. Nevertheless, New York is the exact counterpart of the latter city in respect to the obliteration of the sense of locality. It is certainly the only inhabited spot in the western hemisphere where a man is allowed to live as he likes, without question, or criticism or notice from his next-door neighbor. I have visited all but two of the other twenty cities here which have a population in excess of a hundred thousand ; and I know it is not possible for even the obscurest person to live as much as a week in any one of them without attracting remark or recognition. No visitor who walks along Broadway, or any other great thoroughfare of the metropolis, can fail to feel impressed, if not oppressed, by his own relative insignificance to the mass, in a far more intense degree than he is ever conscious of when elsewhere. An entire change in the moral atmosphere,—a subtle sense of greater strangeness, and remoteness, and "unhumanity" in the active life around him,—must be perceptible to any one who comes here after visiting a smaller city. This metropolitan characteristic of indifference and impersonality is appreciatively shown by a certain accomplished Bostonian, when he describes, as a part of his "midsummer day's dream of 97° in the shade," the business-like and effective, but entirely unsympathetic, way in which the wants of a victim of sun-stroke were attended to in a Broadway drug-store :

"Did you see how the people looked, one after another, so indifferently at that couple, and evidently forgot them the next instant ? It was dreadful. I should n't like to have *you* sunstruck in New York." "That's very considerate of you ; but, place for place, if any accident must happen to me among strangers, I think I should prefer to have it in New York. The biggest place is always the kindest as well as the cruelest place. Amongst the thousands of spectators the Good Samaritan as well as the Levite would be sure to be. As for a sun-stroke, it requires peculiar gifts. But if you compel me to a choice in the matter, then I say, give me the busiest part of Broadway for a sun-stroke. There is such experience of calamity there that you could hardly fall the first victim of any misfortune. Probably the gentleman at the apothecary's was merely exhausted by the heat, and ran in there for revival. The apothecary has a case of the kind on his hands every blazing afternoon, and knows just what to do. The crowd may be a little *ennuyé* of sun-strokes, and to that degree indifferent, but they most likely know that they can only do harm by an expression of sympathy, and so they delegate their pity as they have delegated their helpfulness to the proper authority, and go about their business. If a man was overcome in the middle of a village street, the blundering country druggist would n't know what to do, and the tender-hearted people would crowd about so that no breath of air could reach the victim."—"Their Wedding Journey," by W. D. Howells, 1871, pp. 53, 54.

Now, in just the same unique degree that New York is distinguished above all other American cities for the lightness of its "social pressure," so is the particular Building which I have in mind to describe distinguished above all other abodes in New York. It offers the nearest approximation to a home of perfect individual liberty that has ever been heard of outside of a wilderness. I have said that nothing comparable to it is contained in London,—which is the only European city where the existence of its counterpart could be conceived of as possible,—and I insist upon again designating it as the freest place to be found anywhere—not simply in free America but on the whole habitable globe. So singular a structure could not well survive the storms of fifty years without attracting the notice of the story-tellers; and one of them made it serve effectively as the scene of a society novel. I quote his descriptions, written a quarter of a century ago, as showing with almost literal truthfulness the facts of to-day :

"There's not such another Rubbish Palace in America," said he, as we left the Chuzzlewit [New York Hotel] by the side door on Mannering [Waverley] Place and descended from Broadway as far as Ailanthus Square. On the corner, fronting that mean, shabby enclosure, Stillfleet pointed out a huge granite or rough marble building.

"There I live," said he. "It 's not a jail, as you might suppose from its grimmish aspect. Not an Asylum. Not a Retreat. No lunatics, that I know of, kept there, nor anything mysterious, guilty, or out of the way."

"Chrysalis College, is it not ?"

"You have not forgotten its monastic phiz ?"

"No; I remember the sham convent, sham castle, modern-antique affair. But how do you happen to be quartered there? Is the college defunct?"

"Not defunct ; only without vitality. The Trustees fancied that, if they built roomy, their college would be populous ; if they built marble, it would be permanent ; if they built Gothic, it would be scholastic and mediæval in its influences; if they had narrow, mullioned windows, not too much disorganizing modern thought would penetrate."

"Well, and what was the result ?"

"The result is that the old nickname of Chrysalis sticks to it, and whatever real name it may have is forgotten. There it stands, big, battlemented, buttressed, marble, with windows like crenelles ; and inside they keep up the traditional methods of education."

"But pupils don't beleaguer it ? "

"That is the blunt fact. It stays an ineffectual high-low school. The halls and lecture-rooms would stand vacant, so they let them to lodgers."

"You are not very grateful to your landlords."

"I pay my rent and have a right to criticise."

"Who live there besides you ? "

"Several artists, a brace of young doctors, one or two quiet men-about-town, Churm, and myself. But here we are, Byng, at the grand portal of the grand front."

"I see the front and the door. Where is the grandeur ? "

"Don't put on airs, stranger. We call this imposing, magnifique, in short, pretty good.

Up goes your nose! You have lived too long in Florence. Brunelleschi and Giotto have spoilt you. Well, I will show you something better inside. Follow me!"

We entered the edifice, half college, half lodging-house, through a large doorway, under a pointed arch. The interior was singularly ill-contrived. A lobby opened at the door, communicating with a dim corridor running through the middle of the building, parallel to the front. A fan-tracery vaulting of plaster, peeled and crumbling, ceiled the lobby. A marble stairway, with iron hand-rails, went squarely and clumsily up from the door, nearly filling the lobby. Stillfleet led the way upstairs. He pointed to the fan-tracery. "This of course reminds you of King's College Chapel," said he.

"Entirely," replied I. "Pity it is deciduous!" and I brushed off from my coat several flakes of its whitewash.

The stairs landed us on the main floor of the building. Another dimly lighted corridor, answering to the one below, but loftier, ran from end to end of the building. This also was paved with marble tiles. Large Gothicish doors opened along on either side. The middle room on the rear of the corridor was two stories high, and served as chapel and lecture-room. On either side of this a narrow staircase climbed to the upper floors.

By the half-light from the great window over the doorway where we had entered, and from a single mullioned window at the northern end of the corridor, there was a bastard mediævalism of effect in Chrysalis, rather welcome after the bald red-brick houses without.

"How do you like it?" asked Stillfleet. "It's not old enough to be romantic. But then it does not smell of new paint, as the rest of America does."

We turned up the echoing corridor toward the north window. We passed a side staircase and a heavily padlocked door on the right. On the left was a class-room. The door was open. We could see a swarm of collegians buzzing for such drops of the honey of learning as they could get from a lank plant of a professor. We stopped at the farther door on the right, adjoining the one so carefully padlocked. It bore my friend's plate. Stillfleet drew a great key, aimed at the keyhole and snapped the bolt, all with a mysterious and theatrical air.

"Shut your eyes now, and enter into Rubbish Palace!" exclaimed he, leading me several steps forward before he commanded "Open sesame!"

"Where am I?" I cried, staring about in surprise. "This is magic, phantasmagoria, Harry. Outside was the nineteenth century; here is the fifteenth. When I shut my eyes, I was in a seedy building in a busy modern town. I open them, and here I am in the Palazzo Sforza of an old Italian city, in the great chamber where there was love and hate, passion and despair, revelry and poison, long before Columbus cracked the egg."

"It is a rather rum old place," said Stillfleet, twisting his third mustache, and enjoying my surprise.

"You call it thirty feet square and seventeen high? Built for some grand college purpose, I suppose?"

"As a hall, I believe, for the dons to receive lions in on great occasions. But lions and great occasions never came. So I have inherited. It is the old story. *Sic vos non vobis ædificatis ædes.* How do you like it? Not too somber, eh? with only those two narrow windows opening north?"

"Certainly not too somber. I don't want the remorseless day staring in upon my studies. How do I like it? Enormously. The place is a romance. It is Dantesque, Byronic, Victor Hugoish. I shall be sure of rich old morbid fancies under this ceiling, with its frescoed arabesques, faded and crumbling. But what use has Densdeth for the dark room with the padlocked door, next to yours?—here, too, in this public privacy of Chrysalis?"

"The publicity makes privacy. Densdeth says it is his store-room for books and furniture."

"Well, why not? You speak incredulously."

"Because there's a faint suspicion that he lies. The last janitor, an ex-servant of Densdeth's, is dead. None now is allowed to enter there except the owner's own man, a horrid black creature. He opens the door cautiously, and a curtain appears. He closes the door before he lifts it. Densdeth may pestle poisons, grind stillettos, sweat eagles, revel by gas-light there. What do I know?"

"You are not inquisitive, then, in Chrysalis?"

"No. We have no *concierge* by the street-door to spy ourselves or our visitors. We can live here in completer privacy than anywhere in Christendom. Daggeroni, De Bogus, or Mademoiselle des Mollets might rendezvous with my neighbor, and I never be the wiser."—
"Cecil Dreeme," by Theodore Winthrop, 1861, pp. 32-42 (N. Y.: H. Holt, 1876, pp. 360).

That final paragraph is the most significant one of the entire quoted description, for it can be applied with similar truthfulness to no other habitation on the planet; but, before attempting any commentary on the words of the novelist, I wish to compare with them the words which other well-informed writers have printed, beginning with those of the present editor of the *Atlantic Monthly.* They appeared a half-decade later than the novel, in a series of sketches which he prepared concerning the young artists of New York for a youths' magazine. He was then not quite thirty years old. An ill-drawn northwest view of the University accompanied one of his articles, and a well-drawn picture of an artist's chamber therein embellished the other:

Trades of a feather, like the birds, are fond of flocking together, and have a habit of lighting on particular spots without any particular reason for so doing. Our friends, the artists, possess the same social tendencies, and, in the selection of their studios, often display the same eccentricity. We shall never be able to understand why eight or ten of these pleasant fellows have located themselves in the New York University. There isn't a more gloomy structure outside of one of Mrs. Radcliffe's romances: and we hold that few men could pass a week in those lugubrious chambers without adding a morbid streak to their natures,—the present genial inmates to the contrary notwithstanding. There is something human in the changes which come over houses. Many of them keep up their respectability for a long period, and ripen gradually into cheery, dignified old-age; even if they become dilapidated and threadbare, you see at once that they are gentlemen, in spite of their shabby coats. Other buildings appear to suffer disappointments in life, and grow saturnine, and, if they happen to be the scene of some tragedy, they seem never to forget it. Something about them tells you,

" As plain as whisper in the ear, the place is haunted."

The University is one of those buildings that have lost their enthusiasm. It is dingy and despondent, and doesn't care. It lifts its machicolated turrets above the tree tops of Washington Square with an air of forlorn indifference. Summer or winter, fog, snow, or sunshine,—they are all one to this dreary old pile. It *ought* to be a cheerful place, just as some morose people ought to be light-hearted, having everything to render them so. The edifice faces a beautiful park, full of fine old trees, and enlivened by one coffee-colored squirrel, who generously makes himself visible for nearly half an hour once every summer. As we write, his advent is anxiously expected, the fountain is singing a silvery prelude, and the blossoms are flaunting themselves under the very nose, if we may say it, of the University. But it refuses to be merry, looming up there stiff and repellant, with the soft spring gales fanning its weather-beaten turrets,—an architectural example of ingratitude. Mr. Longfellow says that

" All houses wherein men have lived and died are haunted houses."

In one of those same turrets, many years ago, a young artist grew very weary of this life. Perhaps his melancholy spirit still pervades the dusty chambers, goes wearily up and down the badly-lighted staircases, as he used to do in the flesh. If so, that is what chills us, as we pass through the long uncarpeted halls, leading to the little nookery tenanted by Mr. Winslow Homer. The University is not monopolized by artists, however. The ground floor is used for a variety of purposes. We have an ill-defined idea that there is a classical school located somewhere on the premises, for we have now and then met files of spectral little boys, with tattered Latin grammars under their arms, gliding stealthily out of the somber doorway, and disappearing in the sunshine. Several theological and scientific societies have their meetings here, and a literary club sometimes holds forth upstairs in a spacious lecture-room. Excepting the studios there is little to interest us, unless it be the locked apartment in which a whimsical *virtuoso* has stored a great quantity of curiosities, which he brought from Europe, years ago, and has since left to the mercy of the rats and moths. This mysterious room is turned to very good dramatic account by the late Theodore Winthrop, in his romance of "Cecil Dreeme." (A friend informs us that this "antiquary's collection" has been removed within a year or two.)—"Among the Studios," by T. B. Aldrich (*Our Young Folks*, Boston, July, 1866, pp. 394-395).

In the September issue of the magazine (p. 573) the same writer added : "A little boy— we know he must be a spectral little boy, and are sure he has a tattered Latin grammar under his arm—has written us a dispiriting missive, in which he finds fault with us because we called the University a gloomy building, and wondered how people could live in it and not grow morbid. Now the tone of our sinister little friend's letter is an evidence of the deteriorating effect which the cheerless architecture of the University exercises on the youthful mind. Figuratively speaking, he has thrown down the tattered Latin grammar, taken off his little jacket, and dared us to meet him in mortal combat on the threshold of the haunted castle. For our part, we shall avoid that spectral little boy." Mr. Aldrich also tells a story (p. 397) concerning a negro boot- black called Bones, who, after having been persuaded with great difficulty to enter one of the studios, in order to serve as a model ("at the foot of each stairway he evinced a desire to run away"), was so alarmed when the artist locked the door upon him that he shrieked aloud and bounced furiously around the room until permitted to escape : "The cause of this singular conduct on the part of Mr. Bones was afterwards accounted for. It appears the simple fellow had somehow conceived the idea that the artist was 'a medicine man' (*i. e.*, an army surgeon), and that he had lured him, Mr. Bones, into his den, for the purpose of relieving said Mr. Bones of a limb or two, by way of practice. This is one solution of our friend's terror. My own im- pression is, however, that the profound gloom of the University turned his brain."

A much more recent article concerning "The Young Artists of New York" (By W. H. Bishop, in *Scribner's Monthly*, January, 1880, p. 362), accompanied by a good wood-cut of one of the chambers alluded to, said: "If something odd in the way of a studio be demanded, it may be found in the old-fashioned Tudor pile known as the University building, more singular now than when Winthrop found it an appropriate place for the location of his romance of 'Cecil Dreeme.' The chapel has been divided by a floor at half its height, and this again by a few partitions. In the spacious upper chambers thus formed, which command picturesque views of Washington Square, the Hudson River and the New Jersey hills beyond, the ribs and pendentives of the vaulted roof still show, with a most ancient and baronial effect." With this may be compared the remarks, of the same date, in "Appletons' Dictionary of New York" (p. 221): "The University building was formerly a place in which the best known members of the artistic and literary world had their chambers, which were used both as studios and lodgings. Some of them still remain as tenants of their old apartments, but the prevalence of lodging and apartment houses of late years has drawn the majority of them away. Theodore Winthrop's clever novel of 'Cecil Dreeme' gives a capital idea of the buildings as they were in the ante- war period, and among his characters will be recognized a well-known *littérateur* and editor, who is still a tenant of the University, and whose elegantly decorated apartments and fine collec- tion of bric-a-brac form one of the attractions there."

A metropolitan correspondent of the *San Francisco Chronicle*, who said he himself had once occupied the historic little room, in the southwest turret of the Building ("historic" because there Professors Draper and Morse, in 1839, made the first American experiments in photography, simultaneously with Daguerre's discovery of it in France), offered the following testimony in that paper of June 6, 1880: "The most interesting feature of this locality is a ponderous pile at the eastern end of the Square, built of gray stone, and frowning, like a gloomy ancient castle, upon the trees and greensward of the park. There is no building in the city that resembles it in any particular. Its architecture is of a Gothic type, its windows, walls, massive doors and all, being in keeping. Along the edge of its roof are heavy battlements, and battle- mented turrets rise at the four corners. A venerable air of age hangs over it. It is one of the few buildings in the metropolis that awaken curiosity in a stranger, and give his fancy an opportunity to roam. The structure has an evil repute with the servant-girls of the neighbor- hood. At night they pass it on the other side of the street, and they whisper about it with dilated eyes. They have a notion that deep in sub-cellars lie corpses, skeletons and other dreadful things; for they believe that among the many institutions and persons quartered in the building is a medical school, frequented by a large number of heartless young doctors."

The square itself, covering eight acres of ground, is the largest one in the city, — excepting Central Park, whose area is just a hundred times greater, and whose lower boundary is two and a half miles to the northward. The deed of the transfer of the eight acres in 1797, when the city purchased them from the Smith estate to form a Potter's Field, called for "ninety lots on Sandy Hill lane." Thirty years later, when the place was converted into Washington Parade Ground, burials there had been for a long time unknown. The novelist whom I have first quoted called it (1860) "a mean, shabby enclosure. Ailanthus Square was indeed a wretched place, stiffly laid out, shabbily kept, planted with mean twigless trees; and in the middle stood the basin of an extinct fountain, filled with foul snow, through which the dead cats and dogs were beginning to sprout, at the solicitation of the winter sunshine. A dreary place, and drearily surrounded by red brick houses, with marble steps monstrous white, and blinds monstrous green,—all destined to be boarding-houses in a decade." The prophecy was not fulfilled, however, for a recent chronicler has truthfully said: "The whole neighborhood was formerly one of the most quiet and fashionable in the city, and along the north front of the park it is so still." A view of this "north front," and of the northwest turret of the University, is impressed upon the cover of Henry James's novel called "Washington Square" (N. Y.: Harpers, 1881, pp. 223), into which he inserts a "topographical parenthesis" as follows (p. 23):

The ideal of quiet and of genteel retirement, in 1835, was found in Washington Square, where the Doctor built himself a handsome, modern, wide-fronted house, with a big balcony before the drawing-room windows, and a flight of white-marble steps ascending to a portal which was also faced with white marble. This structure, and many of its neighbors, which it exactly resembled, were supposed, forty years ago, to embody the last results of architectural science, and they remain to this day very solid and honorable dwellings. In front of them was the square, containing a considerable quantity of inexpensive vegetation, enclosed by a wooden paling, which increased its rural and accessible appearance; and round the corner was the more august precinct of the Fifth Avenue, taking its origin at this point with a spacious and confident air which already marked it for high destinies. I know not whether it is owing to the tenderness of early associations, but this portion of New York appears to many persons the most delectable. It has a kind of established repose which is not of frequent occurrence in other quarters of the large, shrill city; it has a riper, richer, more honorable look, than any of the upper ramifications of the great longitudinal thoroughfare—the look of having had something of a social history. It was here, as you might have been informed on good authority, that you had come into a world which appeared to offer a variety of sources of interest; it was here that your grandmother lived, in venerable solitude, and dispensed a hospitality which commended itself alike to the infant imagination and the infant palate; it was here that you took your first walks abroad, following the nursery maid with unequal step, and sniffing up the strange odor of the ailanthus trees which at that time formed the principal umbrage of the Square, and diffused an aroma which you were not yet critical enough to dislike as it deserved.

Elsewhere the novelist says of his heroine: "She preferred the house in Washington Square to any other habitation whatever, and * * * the middle of August found her still in the heated solitude of Washington

Square." When the palings were taken down, and the park otherwise "improved," more than a decade ago, the mistake was made of cutting it in two by a roadway,—under the pretense of a necessity for giving a direct outlet to the traffic of Fifth Avenue into the two streets obliquely opposite. Since then, two more-serious assaults on the integrity of the park have been made and decisively baffled. One plan contemplated using it as an approach to the Hudson River Tunnel, and the other sought to erect upon it a regimental armory. From a journalistic protest against the latter desecration, I extract this sympathetic and accurate account of the Square as it appears to-day :

The park is one of the oldest and prettiest in the city. With the picturesque University buildings on the east side, and to the north the old-fashioned, substantial dwelling-houses—not a wooden row of "four-story, high-stoop, brown-stone fronts," but a quiet row of well-built houses, suggesting a life within of a different sort from that led by the McGillicuddys and the Potiphars—removed from the roar and bustle of Broadway, it seems, what in fact it is, a quarter of an older and pleasanter town which luckily has escaped the ravages of contractors and street-openers, and survives to remind us that city life is not necessarily ugly and repulsive. Washington Square, too, is one of the few public parks in the older parts of the city in which rich and poor meet on common ground. The south side of the square and the streets near it are inhabited by people of the poorer class who have looked upon the park for years as their children's play ground, and on Sundays and public holidays in the spring and early summer it is pleasant to notice that the shade of the fine old trees and the cool breezes are not monopolized by the rich at the expense of the poor, nor by the poor to the exclusion of the rich, but are really democratically shared by both classes. For a democratic city it is singular how little this is the case in most of the old parks. They generally fall prey to some distinct class, as with Tompkins Square, or else become mere thoroughfares, like Madison and Union Squares. But Washington Square has preserved this characteristic of a bygone time, and with its fountain, and its broad walks and shady seats, filled with merry children, nurses with their white caps, and here and there a group of enterprising householders spending the morning *al fresco* with their neighbors, it suggests faintly the pictures of life in New York handed down to us by our grandmothers, when the Bowling Green was in all its glory, and the Von Twillers and Stuyvesants used to take their afternoon stroll upon the Battery.—*The Nation*, March 7, 1878, p. 169.

I have taken pains to present this great variety of citations, as a preliminary to my own story, in order that their united testimony, concerning the phenomenal amount of "character" concentrated upon this particular point in the metropolis, may convince the reader that the tale is worth the telling. The legal style and title of the institution is "The University of the City of New York." Its corner-stone was laid in July, 1833, and its rooms were first occupied for purposes of instruction in 1835. Meantime its erection had been the cause of a "stone-cutters' riot," arising from the fact that the material used to form its walls had been chiseled and worked by convicts of the State at Sing Sing ; and one of its walls had to be rebuilt, at great expense, because, as originally misplaced, it intruded upon ground belonging to the city. These initial mischances seem almost like portents of the executive misfortunes which have ever since connected themselves with the problem of management. The great and irremediable misfortune, as I understand it, was the business panic or revulsion of 1837, which financially crippled the men of wealth upon whose generosity, public-spirit and local-

pride the trustees had confidently counted for the proper endowment of
professorships. Neither Harvard nor Yale possessed at that period a single
building which could claim any architectural attribute beyond what attaches
to a rectangular pile of red bricks (or of white stone—for Harvard had one
such structure); and though Princeton could point with pride to the brown
sandstone front of Nassau Hall, against which Washington fired his cannon,
—and which was, when erected in 1756, "the finest building between New
York and Philadelphia"—the first really massive and imposing collegiate
pile put up on this continent was that of the New York University. It was
one of the very largest, if not the largest, of all the big buildings then to be
found within the limits of America's biggest city; and marvelous as has been
the growth of that city within the intermediate half-century, there are not
many of its monster buildings of to-day which cover a greater superficial area
or make a greater impression upon the memory of the casual passer-by.[1]

The dream of the founders doubtless was to endow their professorships
on a proportionately magnificent scale,—to make the emoluments of service
in this great "university" as much superior to those of the poorly-paid in-

[1] A picture of Washington Square, surmounting similar ones of Union and Madison squares,
may be found on the 554th page of the second volume of "Picturesque America" (N. Y.:
Appleton, 1872), accompanied by this remark: "The castellated-looking building on its eastern
border is the University, a Gothic pile of considerable age and quaint aspect, suggestive of the
mediæval structures that lie scattered through the European countries." The sketch gives the
Building a squatty appearance, however, quite different from its actual loftiness; and no proper
conception of this is afforded by the little wood-cut in "Duyckinck's Cyclopædia" (ii., 755).
The picture which I have had printed on the fly-leaf of subscribers' copies of this book, though
equally small, is fairly satisfactory, and is taken from the southwest. That also is the frontage
shown by the larger and better cut in Mrs. Martha J. Lamb's "History of the City of New York"
(ii., 719), which says : "It was a Gothic structure of white freestone, modeled after King's College, England, and was esteemed a masterpiece of pointed architecture, with its octagonal turrets rising at each of the four corners. It was a fine edifice, 180 feet long by 100 feet wide, on
Washington Square, which was then (the corner stone was laid in 1833) quite a long distance
from the city, whose population was about 200,000. It was opened in 1835, and publicly dedicated May 20, 1837. The rooms of the upper story adjacent to the chapel on the north side
were occupied by Professor S. F. B. Morse and his pupils ; and in the following September,
having completed the first crude telegraph recording apparatus, he exhibited to a select assembly
at the University the operation of the new system, showing his ability to communicate between
points five miles apart (p. 742). In the 'stone-cutters' rebellion' the men paraded the streets with
incendiary placards and even went so far as to attack several houses. The troops were called
out and, after dispersing the malcontents, lay under arms in Washington Square four days and
four nights." Biographical details concerning the professors and other people interested in the
enterprise cover more than two pages in "Duyckinck's Cyclopædia of American Literature"
(1850), already alluded to, but the only remarks that seem worth my quoting are these : "The
erection of the building, and the period of commercial depression which followed its commence-
ment, weighed heavily on the fortunes of the young institution. It was the first introduction,
on any considerable scale, of the English collegiate style of architecture." The "Supplement
of 1866" to the work just quoted offered this additional fact about the University : "Its debt
of $70,250 was paid June 14, 1854. Immediately afterwards the council proceeded to carry out
the great aim of the institution by measures for organizing the School of Art, the School of
Civil Engineering, and the School of Analytical and Practical Chemistry."

structors in mere "colleges" like Harvard and Yale, as this pretentious academic palace of the metropolis was superior to the mean rectangular barracks which sheltered their students in the little provincial cities of Cambridge and New Haven. No "dormitory system " was to be tolerated here; no undergraduates whatever were to be lodged in this latest temple of learning; all of its apartments were to be devoted to purposes of instruction and government; and professors and students alike were to make their homes where they pleased, throughout the city, as is the custom of university life in Germany. The Chancellor and the Vice Chancellor, however (so common a title as "President" naturally seemed inadequate for the executive chief of so grand an institution!), were to occupy the two houses which are attached to the flanks of the main edifice, on parallel streets, and which justify the occasional designation of it in the plural. The second part of the founders' dream—or perhaps I may better say the second original feature in their scheme—concerned the attraction of endowments by the device of so constituting its governing board as to "represent no single religious denomination," though at the same time "keeping the University under distinct religious and evangelical influence." All the earlier colleges had been started by sectarians avowedly as feeders for some particular church denomination; and I believe the University of Virginia (which had been got into operation hardly half-a-dozen years before, just as its famous founder, Thomas Jefferson, drew his latest breath) was the first important academic experiment ever attempted in America without the aid and control of the clergy.

The theory, therefore, seemed then sufficiently plausible, that, as the clerical influence of a single religious order had been able to attract enough funds for founding and endowing many a fairly prosperous college, such influence in several powerful denominations combined might suffice for creating and maintaining a colossal university, of a scope and dignity commensurate with the wealth and splendor of the metropolis. The practical difficulties in the way of making a combination of that sort really effective to-day are generally recognized as insuperable; and I am probably not alone in believing that they were insuperable in 1830. I do not think that, at the best, the trustees could have collected money enough to make their professorial chairs the "softest" seats of the sort attainable in America,—money enough to have finally formed a Faculty outranking in fame and influence the educational staff of every other college. But except for the business disaster of 1837, they might very likely have secured sufficient endowments to have given the institution a prosperous start and allowed it to make a fair test of whatever distinctive merits really attached to the plans of its organizers. I have called that initial misfortune an irremediable one, because, although the rich men of America often give their money in support of educational enterprises with a lavishness that seems incomprehensible to a foreigner, they almost always prefer to act as "founders," even when they do not insist on attaching their family names to their gifts. The common human desire to create, to originate, to figure among the first, controls the course of their generosity. The argument which demonstrates that all money added to the endowment of an old college does ten times as much good as the same amount spent in founding a new one, has never been seriously disputed ; but the new schemes, nevertheless, are the ones to which the wealth of the wealthy may be most easily attracted. Fifty years ago, furthermore, the sense of locality was as strong here as it now is in the lesser American cities, so that the pride of citizenship could be successfully appealed to for stirring a man's generosity in behalf of any project calculated to ennoble the name and fame of his native town. But to-day this feeling is so completely obliterated that, to the minds of most of the two millions of people here congregated, the name " New York City " means just what the name " London " did to the mind of Dr. Johnson ; —it means simply " the world." One's personal pride in the present planet—as distinguished from the sun or the moon, or any less familiar member of the universe— may be very sincere and hearty, but it is too vague a sentiment to prompt the loosening of one's purse-strings ; it cannot be traded upon as can the Western man's fierce desire to see Chicago exalted above St. Louis. The existence of " the Board of Regents of the University of the State of New York " (a body having a sort of visitorial power in respect to the institutions of higher education chartered by the State, but authorized also to itself confer academic degrees), and of " the College of the City of New York " (which was formerly called " the Free Academy," and which is carried on by the city government as a sort of crown to the free public school system, being the only American college maintained by municipal taxes), are two facts which serve to impair still further the local significance of the title of the institution which I am describing ; because its identity is often confused with those others in the popular mind. The friends of Columbia College also insist that the efforts of that wealthy corporation, in enlarging the number and scope of its courses and departments, have won for it the position of the real university of the metropolis.

All these things prove the hopelessness of ever attracting an endowment adequate to the plans of the founders. A conviction of this truth has so disheartened such sanguine souls as have in recent years made zealous attempts in that direction, that some of them have been driven to the other extreme and have urged that, in lack of funds for its full development, the undergraduate department ought to be suspended or abolished. The indignant negative which checked a serious attempt of this sort in 1881, following the lesser attempts of three and four years earlier, demonstrated the perpetuity of the University. Its entire suppression is just as impossible as its magnificent enlargement. No man or body of men will ever give money enough to effect the latter, but hundreds of its graduates will always contribute a sufficiency of their dollars to prevent the former, when the pinch really comes. There is a very creditable trait in the American character which ensures an enormous amount of latent vitality to even the poorest one of our colleges that has managed in some way to outlive its infancy. Almost every alumnus takes pride enough in his bachelor's degree to be willing to help away from the verge of bankruptcy the institution which conferred it. He may not be generous enough to help it achieve success, but he will rally to its rescue when he sees it approaching actual dissolution. Such a prospect makes a very strong appeal to his self-love, for no man likes to confess that "the college where he graduated" is really defunct. The admission seems a sort of personal stigma upon his early life. It may be too poor an affair to boast about, or to send his sons to, or to help push into prosperity; but he is not quite willing to see it die.

The New York University, however, is very far from being the poorest one among our four hundred American colleges. On the contrary, as soon as a dozen or twenty of the oldest and richest of them have been passed by, it can easily stand comparison to almost any one of the others. The contemptuous tone with which its educational advantages are belittled by the novelist whom I have quoted, and by others, is not based upon justice,—however much it may add to the literary effect of their remarks. The half-century catalogue of instructors and alumni exhibits as large a proportion of noteworthy names as any similar collection which is known to me. The professors who have distinguished themselves in science and literature; the graduates who have won fame and recognition as leaders in the various walks of active life, are as numerous as those whom any other college of its size can boast of. The circumstance which obscures this truth is the overshadowing immensity of the city itself, which seems to dwarf whatever comes into comparison with it. *Stat magni nominis umbra.* Situated elsewhere, the University might easily overshadow its surroundings, and give tone and distinction to some quiet village which would otherwise remain obscure. Many a lesser school has done this, and thereby ensured for itself the respect and deference of casual writers, who carelessly sneer at the University as if it were of smaller consequence. It is its fate to be misjudged and condemned in popular repute, not for lack of merits of its own, but because it has the misfortune to take the name of the great city in vain. Even Columbia College, ranking fourth in age and almost first in wealth among such foundations in America, is hardly recognized as a factor in the active life of the metropolis. This was well shown by the remark which its most authoritative newspaper made, a few years ago, in commenting on the great gains that had resulted to Harvard from the policy of absolute publicity with respect to the college finances: "Our own Columbia treats its affairs as if they were the affairs of a private business partnership,—that is, keeps the details of its management more secret than the law allows any banking corporation to keep theirs. * * Columbia is suffering, and must always suffer, from this mistaken policy. There is about as much known, and as much interest felt, about her by the ordinary New Yorker as about Trinity Church or the Sailors' Snug Harbor." —*The Nation*, July 7, 1881, p. 2.

I believe that the Medical School of the University has always been conducted at a distance of a mile or more from the Square; and the School of Pharmacy has also, in recent years, been removed from the University Building; but the Law School still flourishes there, as well as the Department of Science and Arts, with its four undergraduate classes of Seniors, Juniors, Sophomores and Freshmen. It happens, therefore, that, for five days of the week, between ten in the morning and two in the afternoon, something like two hundred people frequent the corridors in the lower part of the Building, and the lecture-rooms which open out from them. Several societies likewise have their halls and offices there, and the chapel in the center is usually rented to some religious organization which holds service in it on Sundays, and occasionally on the evenings of other days. The janitor and his family, and the servants in his employ, live upon the ground floor. His office or reception-room is not adjacent, however, to either one of the five entrances of the Building; and as these entrances face upon three different streets, and are left unlocked from daybreak until ten o'clock at night, whoever pleases may visit the Building without attracting any one's observation, either outside or inside. Tenants may of course gain admission by their latch-keys at any hour of the night, and they also know how to arouse the janitor by rapping on a certain secluded window; but that worthy is freed from the attacks of the general public, after his hour of locking-up, for no bell-pull or other device exists by which any casual visitor may interrupt the nightly quiet of the University. He might kick and pound for an hour upon its ponderous portals without being heard inside, and without arousing any one's protest except, perchance, that of a passing policeman. There is no other house in the world where the conditions of management combine so completely to protect each individual inhabitant from casual observation or deliberate espionage. The identity of the forty or fifty people who live there is merged in the mass of two hundred or more who daily visit there; and the attempt to watch the incomings and outgoings of any particular one of them would be extremely difficult, even if all passed through a single doorway. But as all may in fact choose between five doorways,—opening on three separate streets, to the north, west and south,—no effective watch can be kept except by the establishment of a spy system so elaborate as to defeat its own object by attracting notice to itself.

This peculiarity of the place was put into prominence by the novelist whom I have quoted, because the plausibility of his story of "Cecil Dreeme" depended entirely upon the degree of his success in convincing his readers of the singular fact. He caused the heroine of the tale to live for a long time, disguised as a man, in a solitary chamber of the University, to which she had taken flight in order to escape marriage with the villain of the tale (who also had a room there, though he resided elsewhere), to whom she had been pledged by her wealthy but mercenary father. This father believed she had committed suicide, and he buried with due solemnity the body of another unfortunate young woman, which was found floating in the river, and was identified as his daughter's. The daughter, living in disguise as "Cecil Dreeme, artist," never ventured into the open air except by night, and thus escaped recognition by her kindred and fashionable friends whose mansions were in the immediate neighborhood. Now, there is no other habitation in the city where such singular conduct could fail to attract suspicious observation to the person who practiced it; and such observation would necessarily mean discovery when the person to whom it attached was a woman in disguise. But no conduct of dwellers in the University is accounted singular, or suspicious or noticeable. No one of them pretends to know or care about any other one,—whether he be in or out, ill or well, rich or poor, alive or dead! I may have troops of friends call upon me daily, or I may seclude myself for months without letting a creature cross my threshold, and no outsider need be aware of either circumstance; not even the janitor need know whether I am enjoying a sociable or a solitary life. The novelist told the simple truth in saying: "*We can live here in completer privacy than anywhere in Christendom. Daggeroni, De Begus, or Madamoiselle De Mollets might rendezvous with my neighbor, and I never be the wiser.*"[1]

---

[1] The main incident of the story turns upon the disguise of a woman as a man, and we are bound to say that we remember no instance of a like success,—perfectly pure, modest and spirited,—short of Viola and Rosalind. * * * He has invested this building with a mysterious, romantic interest far beyond anything hitherto attained by our local writers. We must protest against some of the charges of shabbiness, decay and flimsiness he has brought against an edifice of very fair architectural pretensions. The marble staircase would be a very respectable flight of steps in any college edifice of the old world, and you can ascend without any fear of flakes of whitewash. Mr. Winthrop should have known that the boys did not mob their professors and that such men as * * * are not mullein stalks. An occasional injustice must, however, be pardoned to the satirist. His hits are in the main as well deserved as they are sharp.—Sketch of Winthrop, in "Supplement to Duyckinck's History of American Literature" (1866: p. 151).

"The Life and Poems of Theodore Winthrop" edited by his sister, with portrait (N. Y.: H. Holt & Co., 1884, pp. 313), is a book which I hoped might supply much quotable material, but it really contains no allusion whatever to the fact of his living in the University, and it accredits the writing of "Cecil Dreeme" to the year 1860 only by implication. That sketch shows such intimate knowledge and sympathetic appreciation of the Building's queerness, however, as to force the conviction that the author must have resided in it during some part of the thirteen years which he lived after graduating at Yale. If not, he must have been on intimate terms with some of the residents, and made frequent visitations at their chambers. Winthrop was born at New Haven, September 22, 1828, and was killed at Great Bethel, Virginia, June 10, 1861, in the earliest skirmish of the civil war. "He fell nearer to the enemy's works than any other man went during the fight." If fame is worth dying for (which I doubt), he was singularly fortunate in his death. It made him the representative man of an era. It gave a strange stir and intensity to the patriotic passion for Union. It proclaimed that the very best youth of the North were bound to do battle in its defense. As his biographer truly says, "his memory was idealized and worshiped by the young men of that day." Even the youngest of us gave him reverent recognition as the typical hero of a troublous time. Thus, the books which appeared soon after his death (for he had won no wide literary reputation while living) assumed a factitious importance, and were ensured a remarkably wide circulation. I say nothing against their fully deserving this as pieces of literature. I merely record the fact that their great vogue was due to

Why, then, is this not an ideal haunt for the assassin, the counterfeiter and the adventuress? What has prevented its becoming a very Alsatia of disreputable refugees and enemies of society? What protection exists for the tenant's property or life, if unobserved access may be had by every one to these solitary corridors until ten o'clock at night, and no police supervision whatever is maintained? The answer to the latter question easily is, that, as robbers and murderers seek those places which are most promising of spoils, they avoid the University because of a belief that it contains nothing worth the trouble of stealing. Its appearance is altogether too prison-like for attracting any escaped jail-birds who may chance to be fluttering beneath the trees of the Square. To the minds of the ignorant, the word "college" or "university" is often synonymous with or suggestive of "medical-school"; and, as the chief function of such schools is believed to be the dissection of a vast quantity of human bodies, the walls which conceal this uncanny work are looked upon with a good deal of superstitious dread and abhorrence. The casual sneak-thief has a healthy fear of prowling for plunder in the dark and dingy halls of the University, lest "the medical students," who are presumably secreted there with their carving-knives, shoul' seize upon and devour him. The story already quoted concerning the terror shown by the negro boot-black in the artist's studio, illustrates this same tradition, as to the dangers of entering the Building, which has wide currency in all the region round about it. Another theory in reference to its occupants was disclosed to me as I sat in the Square, one Monday evening, near the bench where two washerwomen were resting with their bundles. The subject of their conversation was the then newly-built apartment-house called "The Benedick," whose red-brick front is on a line with the University's, and not many rods to the south of it, and whose chambers were designed and advertised for the occupancy of men only. "It's all the same as the big stone buildin' where they keeps the old bachelors," said one of the women, gravely. "You see the popilation has growed since the city built it for 'em, long ago, and so they got too crowded like. That's why the new brick house was built to put some of 'em in." This conception of an infirmary or retreat for "the old bachelors," as a sort of class apart, under municipal protection and authority, doubtless has less vogue than the notion of a vast dissecting-room or chamber-of-horrors; but I think it probable that most of such evil-disposed frequenters of the locality as may know that there are other lodgers in the University besides "the medical students," believe those others to be bachelors. They believe them to be impecunious ones also, for they cannot conceive of a man's living in so funereal a pile except under

the "blood and iron" behind them. We felt that the pen which traced them had been dipped in gunpowder; that the pages smelled of the cannon smoke. We had a fierce longing to share somewhat in the personality of this fine gentleman and scholar who had been fated first to fall. We were proud to read an author of whom we could rightly say, in sad and wrathful defiance:

"A better or a braver man never rode in battle's van."

pressure of poverty. Furthermore, even if an adventurous thief managed to break into a half-dozen apartments without detection, he might not find anything better than empty recitation-benches, or dusty laboratory apparatus, or full-length "portraits of the chancellors," or ponderous law tomes,—for most of the doors of the public rooms bear no labels, and they look exactly like those of the adjoining private rooms, which also, in many cases, make no showing of the tenants' names. But if a thief had the luck to avoid the collegiate chambers, and penetrate a private room in the owner's absence, the chance for plunder would still be much poorer than in a private house. It may fairly be assumed, of men who live alone, that the personal possessions with which they surround themselves—even when they have the ability to indulge in a good degree of splendor and luxury—are not of that compact and portable sort dear to the heart of the housebreaker. A bachelor, if he likes to have good furniture about him, may buy a costly sideboard to gratify that liking; but his ideal of lavishness in fitting it up will be more apt to take the shape of potables than of silver-plate. Hence the intelligent burglar's chief interest centers upon family life; for well he knows that, where the wife is, there shall the solid silver-ware be found also. I am not forgetful of the wide advertisement that the newspapers gave in 1883 to the public auction of pictures and bric-a-brac which netted $50,000 to a departing tenant of the University (though some of the choicest of the treasures accumulated in his chambers, rumor said, were reserved from the sale); but I do not think the prevalent belief as to the unwealthy character of the other tenants was thereby diminished at all. If the thieves read about the auction, they must also have read that the owner of the collections which brought such "big money" was the chief editor of a prominent daily newspaper, and that he kept a body-servant continually guarding his door. They must have rated him as an entire exception to the ordinary inhabitants of such a prison, whose possessions offer, ostensibly as well as actually, no real temptation to a robber. It would be hard to name another lodging-house in the city where the very nature of things makes the danger of sneak-thievery so slight.

Some of the same considerations which deter the lower order of criminals from attempting to prey upon the tenants of the Building deter also the higher order of criminals from becoming tenants there, as a means of more secretly concocting their schemes for preying upon society in general. Such birds-of-a-feather, however much they may like to hide themselves from the observation of the police, are very generally inclined to flock together; and they are undoubtedly wise in believing that such procedure offers them the best chance of individual concealment. A man of evil-conscience looks upon solitude as a supreme terror; he cannot endure continued isolation; "the profound gloom of the University would turn his brain." It is about the last place in the world, therefore, where a bad woman would consent to seclude herself; though the entire truthfulness (so far as practicability goes) of the story of "Cecil Dreeme's" concealment there shows that no other place exists in the world where such seclusion could be made so complete. This peculiar possibility often gives rise to considerable verbal banter, representing each bachelor tenant as the proprietor of a sort of harem; and a disreputable daily newspaper once went so far as to publish silly stories of this kind, with the serious "business" purpose of impairing the influence of a rival sheet in local politics. As a matter of fact, however, there is probably no other public house in the city where the conditions of existence offer so few temptations to indulgence in that particular sort of "immorality." Such women as are encountered here exhibit in a pre-eminent degree the supreme virtue of minding their own business. They give no occasion or pretext for any gossip or tittle-tattle or scandal, like that which is continually cropping out in every hotel or boarding-house. If, therefore, a bachelor resident of the University is disposed "to sport with Amaryllis in the shade," the chosen scene of such indulgence seems more likely to be the hotel or boarding-house than his own mysterious home. Since, not being at hand, she must definitely be sought, it is manifestly more easy as well as more prudent thus to meet her on neutral ground, or even in her personal and private haunts, than to escort or summon her to his own grim chambers. No difficulty exists, in any city where a million of the human race are herded, to prevent a man and woman from living together, though unmarried, with entire privacy and concealment; and no city of that size can maintain a hotel—whether large or small, magnificent or humble, fashionable or exclusive—in the possession of machinery powerful enough to exclude such unwedded pairs. "The nature of things," on the other hand, seems sufficient to exclude them from the University; for I can conceive of no place where the mutual wearisomeness which always ends that sort of relationship would be more quickly developed.

Nevertheless, though a most unsuitable place for the keeping of a mistress, the Castle might conceivably supply an acceptable home for the shelter of a wife, provided her tastes were unconventional enough to be in sympathy with such solitary surroundings. Many a lonely dweller here has doubtless dreamed wistfully of these as a charming background for some new Paul-and-Virginia business, wherein he himself might play a most delighted and devoted part,—"the world forgetting, by the world forgot." Indeed, the dream may have been realized, for aught that I know to the contrary. I possess a vague impression that one or two married pairs have at times had a place among my contemporaries in the Building; but, if this were so, they must have tired of it quickly, for I think that all the long-term stayers are single men. I recall, too, the fact that an acquaintance of mine, who came back to live here in his bachelor chambers, during the summer months while his wife took an outing in Europe, spoke regretfully of the hopeless gap between the two kinds of existence. He was happy in his married life, and was too generous to wish to deprive his wife of such happiness as she found in "society"; but, he thought, "if madame might really be inspired to throw it all overboard, in order to share a free life with me in this peaceful solitude,—ah!

that *would* be fine !" His notion was that such existence might continuously supply the same sort of zest which a man briefly secures by dragging his wife off to some remote mountain or wilderness or mining-camp, "where there are no other women around, to keep her neck tightly chained beneath the yoke of conformity." The fun and freedom of the mining-camp experience are somewhat impaired, however, by the wife's consciousness of eccentricity : she attracts too much attention, and is gazed at too curiously, as the only present specimen of her sex. But in the solitude of the University she would attract no notice at all, for a great many other women are to be seen there, silently going their own separate ways. "They never speak as they pass by." The tomb-like atmosphere of the corridors does not encourage loitering or sociability. People hasten through them as speedily as possible and disappear into their several chambers. No one wastes time in looking at any one else, or curiosity in speculating about any one else. No decently-dressed visitor, whether man or woman, who goes directly along, as if on business bent, is ever questioned by the janitor.

That worthy, however, makes vigorous warfare on all evident intruders ; and it is unusual for beggars, tramps, pedlars or other pests to get beyond his office. His wife and family dwell with him upon the ground floor, as well as two or three female servants. Washerwomen regularly call for clothes in all parts of the Building. In the artists' studios at the top, women and girls often pose as models. A charitable society has an office, presided over by a woman, which is frequently visited by the lady managers. Another apartment has been honored, I believe, in times past, by fashionable maidens attending their music lessons. More women than men are attracted to the public religious services which are held in the chapel on Sundays, and on the evenings of certain other days. A physician's office, long established here, doubtless has its due proportion of feminine patients. The storage of household effects in the basement is sometimes superintended by the women who own them. The professors' wives and daughters presumably make the University an occasional rendezvous. Serious argument has been offered in favor of opening its lecture and recitation-rooms to lady students, or of having the professors instruct them in private classes; while, on the other hand, "the annual reception of the graduating class" draws hither the sisters and cousins and other girl friends thereof, to make the grim corridors gay for a few hours with music and dancing. Thus, for one reason or another, a great variety of womankind have proper business within the walls of the University; and the going or coming of any individual woman is no more noticed nor thought of than the going or coming of a man. The peculiarity of the place is that its atmosphere forces every one to stick strictly to business; to maintain a personal isolation and reserve; to be solitary, exclusive, unobservant and self-absorbed. In the same way that, as Winthrop said, "its publicity makes privacy," so does its unique capacity for the complete concealment of a woman keep it singularly free from scandal. A bachelor resident has a serene consciousness that the inquisitive eyes which would watch his movements in any lodging-house or hotel, and the idle tongues which would there set afloat silly stories of his " undue attentions " to any women of the place towards whom he showed a chance kindness or civility, cannot exist in the University. A married resident knows likewise that here his wife is protected not only from all such invidious gossip, but from all contact with or suggestion of the sort of social evil which that gossip represents.

I have quoted the published testimony of many witnesses to show that the outward appearance of the Building is apt to suggest the notion of a castle to the mind of a stranger; but I do not consider this circumstance of any great importance except as a coincidence. " Walls do not a prison make "; and it is not because of its stone turrets and battlements that I account my home a castle. *Domus sua cuique est tutissimum refugium.* " Every man's house," as Lord Chatham said, "is called his castle. Why? Because it is surrounded by a moat, or defended by a wall? No. It may be a straw-built hut; the wind may whistle around it, the rain may enter it,—but the king cannot." Personal freedom, in other words, is what is distinctively predicated by the " castle " simile ; and the place where the largest amount of this is attainable by any one is inside his own doorway. The largest amount which he actually obtains there is apt to be small, however; for, though it is the general habit of people to speak of individual liberty as a thing supremely desirable, they are not generally willing to pay the price which it costs. They may occasionally make sacrifices for a brief taste of it, but, as a regular diet, there are other things which better suit their digestion. The ordinary ambition of people is to complicate rather than to simplify the machinery of their lives, and the ordinary result of success is that they become slaves to the machine. They welcome to the control of the castle a tyrant more relentless than any law-defying king could ever have been, and they pay him most liberally for robbing them of the last shred and atom of privacy and independence. " Custom " is the admired Juggernaut under whose wheels they long to be rolled until they become as flat and undistinguishable as a row of postage stamps. Instead of the old, heroic, "*Ave! Cæsar, Imperator! Morituri te salutant!*" these self-immolating moderns seem to cry :

> " Hurrah for the Brother of the Sun! Hurrah for the Father of the Moon!
> In all the world there's none like Quashiboo.
> Buffalo of buffaloes! Bull of bulls! He sits on a throne of his subjects' skulls.
> And if he needs more to play at foot-ball, ours all for him—all! all!
> Huggabejee! Huggabajoo! Hail, Lord and Emperor of Bugaboo!"

The perfection of creature-comfort—the highest imaginable ideal of purely physical well-being and material ease—may be found in the great country houses and the London mansions of the wealthy men of England. "No set of tellurians at least can affect to despise them. The descendants of Adam, the world over, can show nothing better." As machines for the dispensing of hospitality, nothing so complete exists elsewhere on this planet.

The visitor is charmed and delighted with the admirably effective devices by which his personal ease and tranquillity are at all times ensured. Yet the chief feeling left upon my mind, by a contemplation of these wonderfully fine establishments, has always been one of pity for the mental serfdom which the elaborateness of their management necessarily entails upon the proud proprietors. The "castle" ideal is completely obliterated. The ostensible owners have no right of initiative,—no power to gratify any personal freak or whim. The real rulers are the so-called servants, who lord it over the master and mistress with a rod of iron. The movements of the latter must be as unvarying as the movements of automatons, or the smoothness and harmony of the play will be spoiled. If the chief actors attempt to vary the monotony by interpolations in the traditional text, the people behind the scenes ring down the curtain, and the show is stopped. The lives of the wealthy seem generally like a sort of clock-work, run for the benefit of a vast body of vassals and retainers, whose comfort depends upon the regularity of that running. No matter, therefore, how pronounced an individuality a man may have been given by nature, he is powerless to assert it in the presence of this pervasive and uncompromising opposition. The mere dead-weight of numbers is against him. The combined interest which all his hirelings have, in keeping him moving inside the conventional groove, finally conquers any impulse of his own to move out of it. Their opposition—though silent, and passive, and respectful and decorous—is irresistible because of its supreme stolidity. Having no heat nor passion, it never flags nor tires; and, after the master's collisions with it have been numerous enough to produce intellectual weariness, he always abandons the game as not worth the candle, and submits to the inevitable necessity of living in strict accordance with the ideal which his servants have marked out for him as correct. The certainty of such ultimate submission is shown by the old story of the coachman who, when asked to bring his master a pitcher of water, respectfully urged that such service was the proper function of the butler. "Being a reasonable man, the master admitted the conventional justice of this, and ordered him to harness the horses and transport the pitcher-bearing butler to the well which was a few rods distant." If people laugh at the coachman's punishment, it is because they lack the philosophy to see that the master was the worse punished. The mental wear of thus asserting himself was far more annoying to him than the slight physical labor was to his coachman; and it is to be presumed that he either changed his policy or ended his life in an asylum.

The highly-organized social system of England, with its strictly-defined grades and "classes," produces various creditable results; but one of its most obtrusively characteristic results is the prominent development given to that unlovely trait in human nature which causes a man to fawn on those of his race who are classed above him, and to spurn those who are classed below. This is why the English are so stilted and strait-laced in their manners and personal behavior. "Self-suppression is the lesson which the system constantly inculcates, by precept and by very strong example." If a man expects to "get on," he must adapt his notions and conduct as closely as possible to those of "the class just above"; and he is under the constant pressure of temptation to so conduct himself as to deceive others into thinking that he *has* "got on," in advance of the fact. No scheme could be better devised for producing artificiality and uniformity, and for concealing every trace of "nature"; and if any Englishman, from the highest to the lowest, professes that he is not in some degree affected by this fundamental fact of his environment, he declares that he is more than human. In every civilized country the struggle to "keep up appearances" absorbs most of the energy of the human race; but the conditions of existence in England cause the struggle to rage there with phenomenal intensity and obtrusiveness. The inevitable compulsion under which each class imitates "its betters," results, of course, in the transfer of the same ideal from the richest to the poorest. As the chief ambition of the wealthy is to own an establishment so vast that the machinery for managing it obliterates the owner's personality, the chief vanity of the very poor is to boast the ability to hire some one still poorer, for a "slavey," and to put their necks under the yoke of her caprice and inefficiency. No Englishman feels that he is quite respectable unless he makes his life in some way dependent upon a social inferior whom he can nominally command,—unless he occasionally postures, in one guise or another, as "an employer."[1] The universal prevalence of this habit-of-mind is illustrated by the story (otherwise pointless) of a certain "literary discussion" in which the first speaker indignantly asks : "Do you suppose there's any truth in the rumor that Lord Suchaplace didn't really write his recently published book of poems?" and the second speaker says, with languid surprise : "Write 'em? Why should he? I never heard that he was such a stingy man. Of course he employed a servant to make the book for him." The joke implied in this matter-of-fact stripping off of the last shred of responsibility, in a case essentially personal, is relished by everybody, because

---

[1] There is no nation in the world that has so acute a sense of the value, almost the necessity, of wealth for human intercourse as the English nation. They silently accept the maxim, " A large income is a necessary of life "; and they class each other according to the scale of their establishments, looking up with unfeigned reverence to those who have many servants, many horses, and gigantic houses where a great hospitality is dispensed. An ordinary Englishman thinks he has failed in life, and his friends are of the same opinion, if he does not arrive at the ability to imitate this style and state, at least in a minor degree. I think it deeply to be deplored that an expenditure far beyond what can be met by the physical or intellectual labor of ordinary workers should be thought necessary, in order that people may meet and talk in comfort. The big English house is a machine, which runs with unrivaled smoothness ; but it masters its master, it possesses its nominal possessor. George Borrow had the deepest sense of the Englishman's slavery to his big, well-ordered dwelling, and saw in it the cause of unnumbered anxieties, often ending in heart-disease, paralysis, bankruptcy, and in minor cases sacrificing all chance of leisure and quiet happiness. Many a land-owner has crippled himself by erecting a great house on his estate,—one of those huge, tasteless buildings that express nothing but pompous pride.— " Human Intercourse," by P. G. Hamerton, p. 145 (Boston: Roberts Bros., 1884, pp. 430).

each one is secretly conscious of the many cases where he himself feels constrained, for appearance's sake, "to employ a servant," in doing what might be more pleasantly and decently done by his own hands. I believe it was President Lincoln who remarked, in reference to the expressed amazement of some titled foreigner, over a newspaper statement that the President sometimes expedited matters by blacking his own boots: "Well, I've always noticed that the folks who are ashamed of doing any such proper act for themselves never have any scruples about blacking other people's boots!" Perhaps the unpleasant necessity of continually "truckling to the class above" needs the counter irritant of rigid adherence to the custom of "employing some one below," as a means of preserving to the Briton his self-respect. At all events, he is apt to look with contempt upon all fellow-beings who habitually perform certain personal offices without paid assistance. Poverty or penuriousness is the only explanation which he can assign for such conduct,—or for the use of water as a beverage. The drinking of "something better" seems, in its way, to the minds of "the lower classes," a token of affluence and "respectability." That belief, therefore, helps intensify their resentment of legal restrictions upon such indulgence, and to give political potency to their cry:

"Damn your eyes, if ever you tries to rob a poor man of his beer!"

The "globe-trotting" proclivities of the well-to-do English, which have won for them the title of "a nation of travelers," seem to me perfectly explained by the necessity they labor under of seeking abroad an antidote for their continuous self-suppression at home. "The great distinction which rank and money obtain in England must at times grow unspeakably irksome to those who spend their lives in the midst of its society." Unless they had the outer world to wreak themselves upon—unless they could occasionally break away from the self-imposed and ever-present thralldom of living in subjection to their servants—they would simply die from the cumulative pressure of their own eminent respectability! When last I sojourned in the shadow of this, a decade ago, I had for a companion an excellent little book (newly published then, by a Yale graduate of '64) from which I've already adapted a phrase or two, and from which I will now extract a longer paragraph, as well representing my own observations on the spot. I have italicized the sentence which seems to best formulate the reason for the personal colorlessness of "society people," in all climes and countries:

I found everywhere an excessive respect of the individual for the sentiment of the mass—I mean in regard to behavior. In matters of opinion there is greater latitude than with us. Nowadays a man in England may believe anything he chooses; the reason being, I suppose, that beliefs have not much root or practical importance. Authority seems to have left the domain of thought and literature, and to have invaded that of manners. Of the two sorts of tyranny, I think I should prefer the first. I should rather be compelled to write my poetry in pentameters, and to speak with respect of the Church and the Government, than to be forever made to behave as other people dictate. I know Englishmen do not accept this as true of themselves. One of them, to whom I had hinted something of the sort, said, "Oh, I don't know; we do about as we please." Precisely; but they have lived so constantly in the eyes of other people, have got so used to conforming, that they never think of wanting to do what society would disapprove of. *They have been so in the habit of subduing whatever native individuality they possess, that they have at last got rid of it.* Of course, it would be impossible to make them believe this. They mistake their inattention, the hostile front they present to the world, and their indifference to the strictures of foreigners when they are abroad, for real independence and a self-reliant adherence to nature. But there seems to me to be something conventional even about the rude and lounging manners of which they are so proud. It is like the "stand-at-ease" of soldiers. It would be highly improper and contrary to orders to do anything else. Englishmen appeared to me to be criticising themselves away; but the age everywhere partakes of the tendency. It has come to attach great importance to proper externals, to seemliness, to a dignified and harmonious behavior. We all devote an exceedingly particular and microscopic care to our outward walk and conversation. This is true of Americans, and it is true of all educated English people; but the disease reaches its extremest form among Englishmen of fashion and quality.—"Impressions of London Social Life," by E. S. Nadal, pp. 10-12 (New York: Scribners, 1875).

The final words of the same book (pp. 217-223) seem also worth quoting here, as a correct showing of the social conditions which exist in the American metropolis. How such conditions are affected by aristocracy and by democracy seems to me excellently shown by thus contrasting the two greatest cities of the English-speaking race:

There is no society in New York which corresponds to that of London or Paris, and any writer who attempts to make the idea that there is the key-note of his work will be likely to produce a silly, vulgar book. Whether or no there should be such societies, or whether, where they exist, they do good or harm, I do not say. I only say that there is no such society among us, and that novelists should not write as if there were. There are yet some unreasonable discriminations concerning employments among us, but it is certain that the movement of public sentiment has been strongly and rapidly towards democracy. There was, during the early years of our existence, an approach to a national aristocratic society. A governor or a senator, a judge, a commodore, or a general, was an aristocrat. Anybody who reflected or represented the dignity of the government was an aristocrat. This feeling continued till near the middle of the century, or until the second generation of statesmen had disappeared. It has now gone "where the woodbine twineth" to use the significant expression of the significant Jim Fisk. The extreme weakness of the aristocratic element among us at present is in part—in very small part—to be explained by the want of respect in our people. A plain man in this country cares nothing for the man who is above him; is rather proud, and believes it to be a virtue, that he does not care. Nor does it appear a thing to be regretted that such a state of mind exists in the humbler citizen towards the greater one. It is well to have A admire B, if he is a person of superior rectitude, energy and intelligence. But what advantage will it be to society to have A admire B because B lives in a better house and may have a better dinner than A? There is no need to put the cart before the horse. The value of veneration among the masses of men is obvious where they have anything to venerate. And there can be no want of the capacity for respect among our people. It is absurd to call this "a country in which superiorities are neither coveted nor respected." The contrary is the fact; the few real superiorities that we have are, perhaps, respected too much. The bulk of our reading public know enough to recognize what is excellent, but have not the critical self-confidence which is the property of educated men. They therefore fail to insist that the greatest men have their limitations and cannot include everything; but, in a kind of dazed reverie, accept whatever is told them.

The national aristocratic society has disappeared with the disappearance of respect for the politician. What is called "position" is in this country now altogether local. This is necessarily true. A is known among his neighbors as a rich and decent person; his wife and daughters are " nice " (the American for " noble "), either absolutely or relatively to the people around them. A has position therefore in his own town; if he moves elsewhere he does not inevitably take it with him. Now, in very little and very simple communities, these ideas of position and precedent are most important. In a very great place, on the other hand, few men are large enough to be seen over the whole town. As a consequence, we see that New York is perhaps the most democratic town in the country. It has become so during the years in which it has been shooting into a position of such national and cosmopolitan importance. It is now quite as democratic a place as the inevitable varieties of accident and talent among men will permit it to be. The artifice of exclusiveness, which is sure to succeed in a smaller place, will not do here. People greatly desire to do what they find difficult to do. They do not care at all to do what they know they may do. Accordingly, in a town or city of moderate size, the people who wish to be thought better than their neighbors, and who have some little advantage to start with, are wise to keep to themselves. They thus prevent their neighbors from finding out that the excluded and the exclusives are just alike. They have for their ally that profound want of confidence of ordinary people in their own perceptions. But this is a device which will not do in a city of the size and wide-reaching importance of New York. What will the mover of commerce or politics over the face of the country care for the opinion of the gentlewoman around the corner, who thinks him vulgar ? Thus we see it to be impossible that any dominant society may exist in this country. The recognition of this fact should teach quiet to people inclined to be restless. It need not be unwelcome to the friend of man, for he will remember that democracy does not mean the triumph of utility over dignity and refinement, but that it means dignity and refinement for the many. Writers of fiction may regret the want of diversity and picturesqueness which the fact involves, but it is always well to know the truth ; if they desire to avoid vulgarity and the waste of such opportunities as they have, they must heed it. To make men and women interesting as members of society is denied them ; but should these writers have the wit to paint men and women as they are, the field is wide enough. There are on all sides people who are charming to contemplate, and whom it should be a pleasure to describe.

The social life of America is ruled by the servants, just as relentlessly as that of England, but the tyranny takes a somewhat different shape, on account of the changed environment. They rule here by their insolence and worthlessness (the result of a happy-go-lucky consciousness of ability to earn a livelihood, and "perhaps better their chances," whenever discharged by an employer), and not, as in England, by the mechanical perfection of their deportment. An Englishman's servants are so proper and punctilious that they constrain him to perform his appointed function in the social machine with similar correctness and solemnity; but an American's are so pert and untrustworthy—so likely to desert him as soon as he has drilled them to a fair degree of efficiency, or stands in special need of their services—that they prevent the construction of any elaborate social machine whatever. I am aware, of course, that the non-existence of such a thing in the Western World is due, in a broad sense, to the sweep of democracy. There is simply no place for it in our free system of living, as is well shown by the writer whom I have just quoted. But as the impossibility of procuring a permanent retinue of personal servitors—a set of well-trained menials who can always be depended upon to operate a complicated system of housekeeping, without jar or friction—is itself a direct result of the one-man's-as-good-as-another axiom, I think it right to make a point of asserting this one immediately practical part of the argument, in preference to the whole general truth. I know that, among the wealthy, there may be occasionally found a family whose womankind are gifted with such an unusual amount of executive tact, combined with kindness of heart, that they compel "the servant question" to assume much the same settled phase which it has in the home of a well-to-do Englishman. I know that, among the multitude of luxuriously-appointed houses in this rich city, a few may be found whose smoothness of "movement" seems permanently assured, in spite of the democratic restlessness which pervades the very atmosphere. Nevertheless, I believe it may be safely assumed that, wherever two American matrons meet together under conditions favorable to an unreserved conversation, a prominent place in it will almost always be given to the trials and tribulations experienced at the hands of their "help." Like "politics" in the case of a pair of men similarly situated, this is one of the stock subjects to talk about,—a topic which may be presumed to challenge the interest and sympathetic attention of every housekeeper,—a "burning question" which in some degree embitters every such woman's life. If hotels and boarding-houses here attract a larger proportion of families than in England, it is not because the privacy and comforts of a home are prized less here than there. It is simply because our womankind break down under the strain and serfdom resulting from the effort to get any efficient service out of the only class available for household hire: the ignorant and ill-trained domestics of an alien race. Whether the scale of the *ménage* implies the presence of only one servant, or of a full dozen, the result is the same : the mistress of it is subjected to constant annoyance and anxiety, until at last she "gives it up," and takes her husband and children to a hotel.[1]

Hotel-life, in its turn, produces a sort of constraint analogous to that which crushes an English householder in the presence of his servants, but without the compensation which he enjoys in dignity and privacy and repose. Whoever inhabits a house to which another family besides his own may have access is always exposed to the danger of contact with people whose presence is disagreeable, whose acquaintanceship is undesirable, whose evil tongues produce gossip and backbiting, and whose evil acts result in

---

[1] A few days after this paragraph was put in type, I came across a confirmation of it in a letter concerning "South-Coast Living in England." It was written in Devonshire, August 8; and, as New Yorkers will generally recognize the writer as an entirely competent witness, on account of his extensive international experiences, I am glad to quote the paragraph which concerns my argument : " In America we are very fond of boasting of our superior comfort, but this consists in our having houses provided with every convenience and structural facility for comfort, in which, except for large incomes, real comfort is out of the question, for want of good service. In our own homes the miserable dependence on wretched servants makes life only diluted woe. In exceptional cases, and at great cost, people in America can enjoy comfort in their own houses ; but when we go away for the summer the comfort of the poorest watering-place in England is not to be had for love or money. It is a great mistake to suppose that we have the maximum of domestic comfort in America ; say what we will, that is reserved for England."—W. J. Stillman, in the *Nation*, Aug. 27, 1885, p. 169.

public scandal. These and its other evident disadvantages render hotel-life necessarily restless and transitory. It is a make-shift; a temporary device for "getting along" until the arrival of some happier day when a better and more permanent mode of living can be sought elsewhere. A methodically-minded person, whose sense of locality is so strongly developed that he takes pleasure in thinking of his home as a fixture and finality, and hates to consider the possibility of "changing his spots like the leopard," sees in advance that every hotel continually threatens to utter the command, "Move on!" This edict may come not only in the form of an outbreak of any one of the evils specified as latent in the situation, but in the form of increased rent, or of a transfer of the building to other owners or uses. These transfers in New York are so continuous,—the ebb and flow of particular classes of the population is so erratic,—that even if a man purchase a mansion, instead of merely hiring apartments, "in a genteel neighborhood," the fact of proprietorship gives no pledge of an extended stay there. A band of railway robbers may suddenly despoil him of his repose, or other invincible invaders may obliterate every trace of "gentility" from his surroundings.

An additional social danger (which threatens the pride of permanent tenancy, if not the fact itself) results from the great length of the residence streets, which stretch across the island in unbroken east-and-west parallels, from river to river,—a distance of two full miles. I have already explained, in describing the topography of the city (p. 65), that there are more than fifty such streets (numbered successively northward from 7th st. to 59th st.) between Washington Square and Central Park, a distance of two and a half miles, but that distinctive residential "character" attaches chiefly to the longitudinal thoroughfares of the island, which are called "avenues," and which are also parallel (in a north-and-south direction, at distances varying from a fifth to a tenth of a mile), and which therefore intersect the "streets" at right angles. Fifth Avenue, the center or backbone of the system, has none but wealthy people for residents, while the houses of Twelfth Avenue, its westernmost parallel, and of Avenue D, its easternmost, on the opposite water-fronts, shelter none but very poor people. Each of the fifteen other parallel avenues between these extremes has a more-or-less generally recognized "character" of its own; though there are, of course, great contrasts between specific sections of the same avenue, that lie four or five miles apart. Nevertheless, the numbered east-and-west streets of the metropolitan "gridiron" are the ones that contain the vast bulk of our well-to-do people; while, as the "character lines" are drawn across them at right angles by the "avenues" (of greatly varying reputations), no single "street" can hope to have a uniform "character" for its whole two miles,—such as is accredited to Fifth Avenue's straight stretch of thrice that distance, from Washington Square to the Harlem. Hence results the social peril alluded to in the opening words of my paragraph: that the numerous people quite the reverse of "nice," who must of necessity occupy numerous houses at the river ends of each of these streets, will so conduct themselves as to give its distinctive numeral "a bad name." New Yorkers themselves may know, in such a case, that the central section of the street (to which the bisecting line of Fifth Avenue gives character and dignity) has a longer row of handsome houses, than are usually comprised in the whole of a fashionable street in London; and that none but the most eminently respectable of residents are to be accredited to those houses. New Yorkers may know that proximity of a doorway to Fifth Avenue is denoted by the lowness of its number (1, 2, 3 and the like), and proximity to the water-side by a high number, like 600 or 700. But outsiders do not know these things, nor make any discrimination when they read the newspapers' appetizing stories of metropolitan vice and crime. A given street sometimes gets a sudden shove into national notoriety in this manner; and though fashionable folks may not feel forced to change their abodes on account of the evil deeds done in another neighborhood, many blocks away, the fact that such things are proclaimed as happening in "our street" must prove a bar to the development of much affection or enthusiasm for the particular numeral which represents it. "Thirtieth Street," for example, is rather endeared to me personally because of a certain fine house there whose elegant hospitality has for twenty years been extended to me with unvarying kindness. The owner had built and occupied it, ten years or more before I knew him, at a time when the site seemed very far "up town." At first, indeed, I believe the house stood almost isolated between the Avenue and Broadway, though its individuality was soon swallowed up in the undistinguishable mass of "solid front" which has long connected the two. No doubt, the other houses in this front may be filled with treasures just as fine, and possibly some of the owners may have lived there nearly as long, in spite of the temptation to follow the wave of fashion that through all these years has been ever receding northward. But though "Thirtieth Street" thus privately appeals to me as a shining example of the truth that the possession of wealth does not inevitably debar a New Yorker from having a permanent home of his own, "Thirtieth Street," as projected on the mind of a casual reader of the newspapers, carries a definite suggestion of crime and ill-repute. In the western section of that street stands the "police station-house of the 29th precinct," and the captain in command thereof is more talked about, for whatever reason, than any similar officer of the entire force. This exceptional notoriety he is said to attribute to the exceptional difficulties inherent in his position,—as a result of the fact that within the limits of the region under his sway are included a majority of the great hotels and theaters, and (as their inevitable accompaniment) a large number of those resorts where the people who have been attracted to the hotels and theaters, from all parts of America, like to go "in search of whom they may be devoured by." Thus it happens that, as a vast floating population, of the sort which practitioners of "the profitable vices" best like to prey upon, always demand police attention, either for control or defense, within the boundaries of "the 29th,"

the name of the street containing its station-house suffers somewhat by fall-
ing under the shadow of their wickedness. But the name of the great central artery of the street system stands superior to all its offshoots, and the
fact that it alone is held so high above reproach tempts me to quote the following description, recently written by Joseph H. Howard, jr.:

Whenever a house is for sale or rent in Fifth Avenue its residents feel a profound interest
in the character of the inmates that are to be. They dread lest the mansion may be converted
to unworthy uses; lest they may be hourly shocked by a plebeian neighbor who is what they
themselves were twenty years, or five years, or perhaps a few months before. Their vigilance
is sleepless in this regard; still they have often been compelled to buy out common tradesmen
and ambitious courtesans, and enterprising blacklegs, who had purchased an abiding place in
the socially sacred vicinage. It is the habit of New Yorkers to style Fifth Avenue the first
street in America. So far as wealth and extent and uniformity of buildings go, it probably is.
Beginning at Washington Square, it extends above Harlem; and as far as Fifty-ninth Street, it
is almost an unbroken line of brownstone palaces, while from that point up its magnificence is
marvelous. The architecture is not only impressive, it is oppressive. Its great defect is in its
monotony, which soon grows tiresome. A variation, a contrast—something much less ornate or
elaborate—would be a relief. Its lack of enclosures, of ground, of grass-plats, of gardens, is a
visual vice. Block after block, mile upon mile, of the same lofty brownstone, high stoop,
broad-staired fronts wearies the eye. It is like the perpetual red brick, with white steps and
white door and window facings for which Philadelphia has become proverbial. One longs in the
avenue for more marble, more brick, more iron, more wood even—some change in the style and
aspects of the somber-seeming houses, whose occupants, one fancies from the exterior, look,
think, dress and act alike. One might go, it appears, into any drawing-room between Central
Park and the old Washington Parade Ground, and he would be greeted with the same forms,
see the same gestures, hear the same speeches. The stately mansions give the impression that
they have all dreamed the same dream of beauty the same night, and in the morning have found
it realized; so they frown sternly upon one another, for each has what the other wished, and
should have had alone. The slavish spirit of imitation with poverty of invention has spoiled
the broad thoroughfare, where we should have had the Moorish and Gothic, Ionic and Doric
order, Egyptian weight and Italian lightness, Tudor strength and Elizabeth picturesqueness.
It is a grievous pity that where there is so much money there is so little taste. The sum of
Fifth Avenue wealth is unquestionably far beyond that of any street in the country. The
dwellings cost more; the furniture and works of art are more expensive; the incomes of the inmates are larger and more prodigally spent than they are anywhere else on the continent. The
interior of the houses is often gorgeous. Nothing within money's purchase, but much that perfect taste would have suggested, seems omitted. There are few of the mansions that do not re-
veal something like tawdriness in the excess of display. The outward eye is too much addressed. The profusion is a trifle barbaric. The subtle suggestions of complete elegance are
not there. Still, to those who have suffered from the absence of material comfort, or to those
whose temperaments are voluptuous and indolent, as most poetic ones are, a feeling akin to
happiness must be born of the splendid surroundings that belong to the homes of the Fifth
Avenue rich. What soft velvet carpets are theirs; what handsome pictures; what rich cur-
tains; what charming frescoes; what marbles of grace. The people who live side by side in the
pretentious avenue know each other not. Knickerbocker and parvenu, the inheritor of wealth
and the architect of his own fortune, the genuine gentleman and the vulgar snob, reside in the
same block. One house is visited by the best and most distinguished; the house adjoining by
men who talk loud in suicidal syntax, and women who wear hollyhocks in their hair, and
yellow dresses with pink trimmings. Here dwells an author whose works give him a large
income; over the way, a fellow who has a genius for money-getting, but who cannot solve the
mysteries of spelling. Some of the most spacious and expensive mansions on the avenue

always have a deserted look. Only the occupants and servants appear on the high, carved stoop; only the carriages the master of the establishment owns stop before the door. That family purchased a house in the avenue, but society has not accepted its members. They have nothing but a new fortune to recommend them. They must bide their time. The first generation of the unrecognized fares hard. The second is educated and the third claims lineage—prates of "gentility," and frowns upon what its grandparents were. To get into the avenue and into its society are different things. They who struggle to enter certain circles are not wanted. Those who are indifferent to mere fashion are in request; for not to seek, socially, is usually to be sought. Fifth Avenue is, indeed, one of the phenomena, and its growth one of the extraordinary developments of this peculiar age.—N. Y. cor. of the *Philadelphia Press*, May 14, 1885.

Thus, through this famous Avenue, my pen at last comes back to the curious Castle which stands at the head of it, and which I wish to celebrate for the contrast which the freedom attainable within its walls offers to the "servitude to servants" that generally prevails elsewhere. Though there may be some who actually enjoy personal contact with that sort of people, it can be fairly assumed that the majority would prefer to employ any practicable mechanical appliance to effect the same results. The majority recognize that the employment of the human machine is an evil, but they resort to it as an inevitable necessity,—because no substitute is obtainable for properly performing the drudgery of civilized life. When their servitude to this "necessary evil" grows absolutely unendurable from long continuance, they "make a break for the woods," and adopt a savage life for a while,—camping out and "doing their own work,"—or else they resort to travel, which, though it implies a great deal of dependence upon menials, at least frees the relationship from the personal element : no single one of them wields supreme power. A variety of gains, of course, results both from "the visiting of many cities" and from "roughing it in the wilds"; but the chief gain possible from either experience is the relief offered from wearing the yoke of conformity. It is only while freed from the routine tyranny of his own house that a man can afford to be his simple self, to live naturally, to do just what he likes, to speak his own mind.

When I assert, therefore, that a tenant of the University may there secure for himself continuously either the absolute isolation of a savage in the wilderness, or the relative isolation of a traveler through the cities,—that he may there approximate the ideal of intellectual independence exactly according to the degree of his willingness to sacrifice creature comforts and conventional luxuries,—I assert what can be truly said of no other house in the world. This statement of its distinctive quality shows, of course, why the Building makes so strong an appeal to those who can sympathize with the cry of Shelley : "I will submit to any other species of torture than that of being bored to death by idle ladies and gentlemen." The conventional escape which is allowed an active young New Yorker of wealth and fashion from this sort of conventional torture, is "the running of a cattle ranch out in Montana." His frivolous friends do not resent as a personal affront such scurrying away for "the plains," and he may even print a book like "Hunting Trips of a Ranchman" without rousing their languid consciousness to the fact that its existence is a significant tribute to their own utter uninteresting-ness. They will be apt to act differently, however, if, instead of hiding from them amid the mountains of Washington Territory, "where rolls the Oregon, and hears no sound save his own dashings," he ventures to pitch his lonely camp upon the castled crag that frowns o'er the wide acres of Washington Square. There, his seclusion seems rendered more profound by the muffled roar of a mighty city's traffic which ceaselessly rolls its human tide along the great thoroughfares beyond; and there, without the expense, and waste, and discomfort demanded by a sojourn in the Far West, he may "rough it" to his heart's content. But there, also, such unsocial conduct will be stigmatized as "crankiness" by the fine ladies and gentlemen who may chance to hear of it;—for the notion of his permanently "camping out" in the midst of a great city, and leading the free and unsophisticated life of a gentle savage, in preference to taking part in their own "chromo civilization" which surrounds him, is a notion of such direct and unequivocal contempt for their authority that the sting of it has power to penetrate even the dense vanity and stolid self-complacency of such "social leaders."

I entertain a theory as to a certain little room in the University, which is of about the size and shape of a hunter's hut, that the bachelor owner thereof never lets another human being enter it; that he has no carpet, nor easy chairs, nor bed nor bed-clothing; and that, when he spends a night in the den, he throws himself into a hammock, pulls a bear-skin or buffalo-pelt over his usual attire, for the sake of warmth, and, with a pistol-holster under his head for a pillow, gazes at the stars above the tree-tops until his closed eyes bring dreams of "old times among the Rockies." I imagine that he has a few grimy paintings and dusty war-relics for ornaments, and a few well-worn books for companions; and that he takes pride in the cobwebs and dirt and disorder which characterize his abode,—rejoicing daily at the tangible testi-mony which they give of the uninterruptedness of his occupancy, and of the powerlessness of any menial intruder to "arrange" his possessions accord-ing to some cast-iron system of propriety. I *know* nothing at all of the life led by this man, or by any other one of my co-partners in the Castle. I only say that the sort of existence which I have attributed to him would be entirely practicable here, and would attract no notice or comment. If a "society man" never really indulges in it, it is merely because he does not esteem such indulgence worth the sacrifice of all his fashionable affiliations;—be-cause he deems it cheaper to get the same kind of thing by "roughing it" under the conventional conditions which do not arouse the resentment of the stay-at-homes of Fifth Avenue. He knows that "on the plains of the Far West" he can "run his own ranch" without seeming to them ridiculous or "cranky"; but he hardly has nerve enough to attempt the same experiment in their immediate presence, on the plains of Washington Square.

Most men, however, even among those who hate conformity, do not care to make the sacrifice implied in securing complete independence from the employment of household servitors. They are satisfied if they can hold the latter at arm's length, in an impersonal relationship, such as results from the constant changes implied in traveling. The resources of modern science allow a resident of the University to do this with a near approach to completeness. If he is willing, at the outset, to expend as much upon the fittings and permanent machinery of his apartments as would suffice to purchase a good-sized house in the country, he may enjoy a fair degree of comfort or even luxury, without the loss of liberty which such enjoyment usually implies. If he is willing to put in water-works, telephones, electric-lights, fireplaces, chimneys, elevators, floorings, doors, windows and walls (all these, without any written lease, and without any assurance, save the mere *vis inertia* of the place, that his " improvements " will not be made a pretext for an increase in his rent, or the transfer of his chambers to some one else), he may fairly supply the more obtrusive physical deficiencies of a house that has been standing for a half-century, that was built chiefly with a view to securing impressiveness of outward aspect, and that was not designed to be lived in at all. A man may readily arrange that a washer-woman shall bring and take his clothes without entering his door, or even setting eyes on him personally. He may adopt a similar scheme in reference to the waiters whom he summons by telephone from a restaurant to bring him food or drink. He may likewise keep a valet " on call," who never sees his face, or oppresses him with attentions that are not desired. The police, the fire alarm and the messenger service may be brought to his immediate command by the touching of a knob. In other words, if a man of wealth thinks it worth while, it is entirely practicable for him to arrange here a scheme by which he may employ a great many people to help him carry on quite an elegant and elaborate system of living, but in a quite impersonal way,—I mean without the friction and annoyance of direct contact and acquaintanceship. Perhaps no such man ever does in fact lead such a life here. All I insist upon is that the conditions exist here for leading it, as they exist nowhere else, and that the fact of leading it would excite no observation or comment.

Pungent fumes from the chemical experiments in the laboratories may sometimes ascend the stairways, but nothing so suggestive of ordinary human life as the odor of food will often be encountered there or in the connecting corridors. No cooking goes on in the Building, except that of the janitor's small *ménage*, in the subterranean regions; and it is only on great occasions that this is rank enough to smell to heaven. Hotels, restaurants, and boarding-houses, of all styles and prices, may be found within a half-mile radius, and in these the tenants of the Castle may be presumed to take most of their solitary repasts. Breakfasts are regularly brought in to the chambers of some of them, however; and such as possess telephone connection no doubt use it to summon in the more extensive meals of the day, whenever bad weather or indolence disposes them to avoid the trouble of going out. The janitor, in addition to his regular salary for general services, is paid a certain small percentage on the rents, as a device for stimulating his activity and promptness in making the quarterly collections thereof; but the power of this stimulus is more than offset by a stimulus of the opposite sort,—an incentive to dilatoriness,—which attaches to the fact that the janitor's income is much more largely affected by his success in persuading' tenants to employ his servants. He generally succeeds in impressing each new-comer that it is an unwritten law of the place that they should be thus employed; and, as it is easier for the new-comer to submit to the existing scheme than to devise a substitute for it, I suppose that most of the lodgers' rooms are cared for in this way: that is, the janitor is paid a fixed monthly stipend for the services of his servants, and is held responsible for their efficiency and honesty. At a certain hour of the day they have access to the tenant's rooms and "put things in order" there; but he exercises no personal authority over them, and, if their routine work is not satisfactory, his complaint is not made to them personally but to their employer. The wages which the janitor agrees to pay his servants being necessarily a fixed quantity, whether they have many or few rooms to care for, it is evidently for his interest that the number should be many rather than few. Thus it comes about that the janitor's percentage on the promptly-paid rent of a tenant who renders no tribute to him for servants, is of much less account than his profits in leasing these servants to a tenant who promptly pays the monthly stipend agreed upon, but who indefinitely postpones the payment of the rent due to the trustees of the University.

I entertain a dreadful suspicion that, when the natural effects of this enlightened system are unpleasantly obtruded upon the minds of the latter, they are apt to decide that the exaction of increased rents, against those permanent tenants who can be depended on to pay, is an easier device for "bringing up the average receipts" than the pursuit of hopelessly delinquent "transients." Perhaps I am wrong in this suspicion, as well as in the one on which it is based (that the janitor's zeal in enforcing the law against such delinquents is apt to be somewhat modified by the natural human desire "not to take the bread out of his own mouth"); but, in any case, I must accredit the janitor with a great gift, akin to genius, for persuading people of the appalling dangers which overhang the existence of a tenant who declines to employ the regular servants of the University. Even the traditional Philadelphia lawyer never rendered himself a more perfect master of the trick, which Demosthenes used to tell us about, as the characteristic one of the legal fraternity in his time, of "making the worse appear the better reason." If a prospective tenant finally forces out the unwelcome truth that private servants are not positively prohibited from entering these walls, the admission is coupled with such significant shruggings of shoulders, such dark hints of past misdeeds, and such dreadful suggestions of future peril, as to make a man feel that the employment of them here would be a sort of impious defiance of Providence,—a fool-hardy exposure of his life, his fortune and his sacred honor. He is somehow given to understand, without any exact verbal formulation or assertion of the idea, that the pervasive gloom of the University has a subtle power to develop a morbidly thievish—not to say murderous—tendency in the minds of such servitors as he might elsewhere rely upon as trustworthy and kind ; and that no comfort or safety can, therefore, be expected, unless he entrusts his chambers to the care of those competent domestics who are under the responsible rule of the janitor, and who have been trained by this, and by habit and custom and experience, to resist the evils which are inherent in so peculiar an atmosphere. There is enough truth on the surface of this theory to make it plain that a majority of the tenants act wisely in refraining from the introduction of a troop of special servants into the Castle, to prey upon themselves and their neighbors. I should regret the general adoption of any such system and should deprecate its dangers. The present plan ensures as good service as the average man is willing to pay for ; and I would not recommend any new-comer to depart therefrom. It will certainly be wise for him, at the outset, to " make himself solid with the janitor," even though he may not share that worthy's conviction that the robberies, suicides and sudden deaths, sometimes noted in the newspapers as happening at the Building, are, in some occult way, ultimately due to the non-exclusion from its walls of all valets, body-servants and " private sweeps " except those controlled by himself.

" The mighty concierge " is classed *hostis humani generis*, by the writers of all highly-civilized countries, just as universally as the subscription-book agent, or the patent-medicine pedlar ; and the extract given below from the testimony of a recent witness (who prints more than a solid column to show " why the Parisian press sneer and mock at the candidacy of M. Aube, because he is a concierge ") would be fairly applicable to the janitors of the fashionable apartment-houses in New York.[1] It would be quite unjust, how-

---

[1] Do not mistake this for a pleasantry. The concierge rules as autocratically over his kingdom as ever did any Russian Czar over his empire before the emancipation of the serfs and the invention of Nihilism. A great change has been made from the olden time when Cerberus inhabited a hole in the wall, as it were ; mended old boots and pieced ancient garments, while his spouse did odd jobs for tenants, and his olive-branches went of errands. While all the rest of Paris tends toward democratization, the concierge goes in for " aristocratization." Like all functionaries, he has a supreme contempt for the public. He considers the tenants of the dwelling which he " manages " as his subordinates, and you need no more expect civility from him than you can from a hotel clerk, or the conductor of an omnibus, or a railway official, or an employé at the Paris Post Office. Nothing can convince him that he is not the absolute master of every lodger. I represent, he says, the landlord, and as such have full authority to let the premises, to raise the rent, and to give warning. It is he who elaborates the " rules of the house," and it is he who has invented the interdiction of dogs, children, and canary birds, an interdiction which is only revocable at his good pleasure. And try to be on good terms with him, for he has at his disposal ways and means by which, if your *entente* be not *cordiale,* your life will become a burden. He will keep the door unopened for you on a rainy day, he will invariably tell your friends that you are not at home, he will shake his carpet over your head as you descend the staircase, and inflict upon you a thousand petty annoyances against which you have no redress,

ever, to confound with them the janitor of the University Building; and my quotation concerning the insolence and tyranny which must be submitted to at the hands of the others is chiefly designed to point by contrast his own relative politeness—and powerlessness. Though I have hinted on a previous page that he may not always rise entirely superior to the distinguishing trait of his class, I am bound to add that he seems to be about as unique a phenomenon among janitors as the Building is among buildings. At all events, he is the only one I ever heard of, in any part of the world, in whom the usual strictly sordid and mercenary motives are sometimes supplanted by sentimental considerations as a basis for conduct. The janitor takes a personal pride in the place, not merely because he has for fifteen years personally helped maintain it " in the front rank of American universities " (with his name in the annual catalogue), but because he is vaguely conscious that its queerness as a lodging-house reflects a sort of personal distinction upon himself. He feels that no other janitor lives in so scholarly and mysterious and historic an atmosphere, or comes in such close contact with so many curious and remarkable characters. According to the familiar principle, *omne ignotum pro magnifico*, he learns to reverence those who will not submit to him. He points with a kind of hushed and awe-struck pride at those tenants who have asserted complete independence of his authority, as if he would say, " What other janitor in New York can exhibit such fine specimens of crankiness and eccentricity? " He exalts no one to this pantheon, however, until the last conceivable device for holding him down to the level of ordinary mortals has been tried in vain. Reversing the maxim of Richelieu, his policy might perhaps thus be fairly formulated :

" First, employ all means to crush! "   " Failing these? "   " All methods to conciliate! "

The janitor is quite loyal to the undergraduates; and when each departing class of them (after having been for four years summoned to their daily recitations by his hourly beatings of the gong; and after having, for that period, tormented him by the tricks and skylarking customary with such youth) present him or his wife with a gift of silver-ware or jewelry, as a final

---

for to your complaint he will reply that it was " purely an accident independent of his will." True, you can retaliate, but I am not sure that you will come off first best. And it is not the concierge's ability to cause petty annoyances which constitutes his importance. In his hands he holds your credit, your reputation, your fortune, and your honor. Should you undertake any business enterprise it is of the concierge that is asked information of your standing ; should you have any difficulty with Dame Justice, he is the first authority appealed to for proofs of your honorableness ; should you change your tailor, it is your concierge to whom will be put the question of your solvency. Everything depends upon your relations with this autocrat, who will give a certificate for the Prix Montyon to the blackest of scoundrels, or ruin the standing of an honest man, according to the degree of generosity of the individual. Last week, a concierge was sentenced to a heavy fine and sixteen days in jail for defamation of character, but few persons are brave enough to risk the scandal which that suit caused, when the plaintiff's character was torn to shreds by the defendant's counsel ; and so people go on and let themselves be bled and blackmailed.— Paris correspondence (Sept. 25) of the *New York Times*, Oct. 12, 1884, p. 5.

testimonial of good-will, he is always equal to the occasion. I mean that he makes it an excuse for "treating" the class to a "reception" whose expensiveness must considerably exceed the mere money value of their gift, and whose chief feature is a "speech of acceptance," glorifying this latest class as superior to all its distinguished predecessors. The janitor rather prides himself, indeed, on his oratorical powers, and as these have given him a sort of reputation among the local political managers, he not unfrequently figures at their autumn "campaign rallies" in the thickly-settled region below the Square. I believe this is the only vanity he ever indulges in outside the Building; and except during these brief seasons of shouting the praises of his party (which is the "G. O. P.," opposed to "R. R. R."), he may always be found there at evening time, ready to bar its doors against the outside world, promptly on the stroke of 10. Portraits of his admired political leaders form a prominent feature in the adornment of the walls of his office, but he is not an "offensive partisan" to any such extent as the Parisian concierge, who suppresses all political circulars and newspapers which he does not wish his tenants to read, and who takes care to keep them fully supplied with the literature of his own party. Dwellers in the University, on the other hand, need not allow any of their mail-matter to be submitted to the janitor's inspection, for the government postmen are instructed to make direct deliveries at the separate chambers of all who express a wish to that effect. In this way also it is distinguished from an ordinary apartment-house or hotel, for there the postal deliveries are all made at the main office.

In enumerating the physical shortcomings of the place, which the tenant must remedy at his own expense if he wishes to live with much comfort or elegance, I have noted by implication the general absence of what are called "modern improvements." The absence of any general means for heating or "elevating" serves the good purpose, however, of lessening the dangers of fire. These are already so considerable that the underwriters attach a high rate of insurance to the Building; and if it were to be "improved" by steam pipes and an elevator shaft, its dry wooden floors and staircases would doubtless soon disappear before the flames. Such a disaster would not be likely to imperil the life of a tenant in the main structure,—for, in the improbable case of both its stairways burning simultaneously at the bottom, with such suddenness as to forbid descent, he could still ascend to the roof, and thence easily jump down to the roofs of the houses which adjoin each wing. If, however, a fire should start at the foot of the narrow stairway of either of these wings, it would be apt to leap almost instantly to the top of the tower (induced by the draft which a window kept constantly open there would ensure), and thus shut off all chance of the tenants' escape, unless they were able to lower themselves from the outer windows to the street below. In other words, these wings are distinctively death-traps, though they were originally designed to serve as elegant abodes for the Chancellor and Vice Chancellor of the University, and were the only parts of it thought fit to live in.

I myself would not sleep in one of them for a single night without a fire-escape by my bedside (I keep one, in fact, even in my own much safer chambers); and the general hopelessness of saving any property from destruction, in case a fire should once get fairly started in any part of the Castle, may well serve as a barrier to prevent a cautious man from risking his treasures in it. A lazy one will likewise do well to think twice before he pitches his camp where access can only be gained by the ascent of nearly one hundred steps; for the best apartments—like so many other best things in life—are those at the top.

In direct contrast to the practice of other American colleges and universities (the latter word has been so generally misused here that it is now synonymous with the former in ordinary usage), where the president is expected to be the chief motive power in the management, and to bring great things to pass by that personal capacity to properly grasp and combine details which is called executive ability—the Chancellor of the University is excused from all attention to its finances. The present incumbent of the office is the pastor of one of the largest congregations in the city, and his immediate predecessor held a similar position. Hence, as the duties directly pressing upon every such man must always be beyond his power of fulfilment, even when he devotes every atom of energy to the work of his church alone, the business management of the University is of necessity abdicated to others. The trustees, of course, are the legal managers, in whom all ultimate authority rests; but, as active men of the world, absorbed in their own affairs, they like to avoid the irksomeness of attending to petty details, by putting as much as possible of responsibility for them upon the shoulders of the two senior professors. These in turn, being already overburdened with their own proper duties as instructors, are inclined, when such matters cannot easily be referred back to the trustees, to leave them to the janitor; who thus becomes, in effect, the executive chief of the institution. A chronic want of funds for its proper maintenance adds to the interestingness of this curious situation, so far as casual tenants are concerned. If one of these objects to a leaky roof or broken window, an overcharge of rent or inefficient service, and gets tired of talking to the janitor on the subject, perhaps he may nerve himself up to the point of bringing his grievance before one of the professors, who may very likely refer him to one of the trustees. The trustee doesn't want to be bored with the case, and refers him back to another professor, who perhaps refers him to the janitor as final authority. A great many days having been wasted in getting the matter as far along as this, a great many more go by before anything is done,—even assuming that the tenant's prayer is granted. After the average man has been badgered for a while in this way,—bandied back and forth between the representatives of a divided and practically unapproachable authority,—he of course goes off in despair to seek some house where less chaotic conditions prevail; and a new tenant follows in his footsteps and in due time undergoes the same exasperations. If the new tenant chances to have more philosophy than "the average man," he will learn to accept these exasperations as natural concomitants of an exceptional situation; he will quietly pay for such "repairs and improvements" as he wants; he will see that if the whole establishment were to be "modernized and run on business principles," the peculiar charm of it would disappear.

This charm attaches to one's individual ability to run his own part of the Castle in his own way; and "his part" is practically "the whole," for all the rest of the tenants are in effect his vassals and servitors: their presence is essential to his own safety and happiness, though they ensure this without personal contact. Like the retinue of an old feudal castle, they give a human attractiveness to the few chambers which the lord thereof really uses as his own. Like the lord thereof, on the other hand, each resident of this Castle may always feel reflected upon himself the dignity of its entire ownership. The fact of such residence makes his life a mystery to every outsider. It conveys no notion of whether he is rich or poor; whether he occupies one room or many; whether he lives in entire isolation with the simplicity of a savage, or with body-servants at his nod and beck to supply him with all the luxuries of an epicurean. There is no general *camaraderie* among the residents; no cohesiveness between the independent atoms; no visits exchanged between rooms unless the occupants have known each other elsewhere. It is tacitly understood by all that the object of a man's making his home in such a place is not to form new acquaintances, but to escape from those already formed,—to simplify the machinery of life rather than to complicate it. The inspiring fiction of "sole ownership by each" would be sadly impaired if the presence and partnership of the others were formally recognized. For my own part, I feel the utmost friendliness and good-will towards my co-proprietors of the Castle; but I believe that the most acceptable manifestation I can make of the sentiment is the negative one of letting them entirely alone while within its walls. Were I to be met in a remote part of the world by some man who had lived long in the University, his mention of that fact would be the best possible passport to my favor. I should feel in advance that he would make an interesting companion, because no one without great resources in himself could long survive a stay here. The capacity to endure solitude with cheerfulness is a crucial test of character, so far as concerns showing that it is above the commonplace; and though a man *may* lead here a very social life of the strictly conventional sort, it is fairly to be presumed that, unless he were fully competent to enjoy a lonely one in his own wigwam, he would not long submit to the limitations which residence here imposes. Their lack of *camaraderie* ensures a sort of placid feeling in the janitor's mind that the tenants will not conspire to accomplish his overthrow, as is often done in other places where individual resentments of slight injuries and shortcomings are combined, by conversation and interchange of experiences, into a general hostile sentiment which has power to remove the object of it. On the other hand, there is a fair offset to this in the uncertainty that the janitor necessarily has concerning the possible "influence" of any given tenant with some unknown member of the board of trustees. This fact that he is employed by a mysterious body of far-extending and undiscoverable connections, instead of by a single owner whose friends could be easily identified, is evidently a fact that tends to secure good treatment for the tenants. There is always a dreadful possibility that each one of these may have a "friend at court," with power to work the guillotine remorselessly, if things go wrong!

In explaining how "its publicity makes privacy," I have said that the habitual passing of many men and women through the corridors renders the presence there of any additional man or woman quite unnoticeable; yet I think that a chance visitor, late in the day, after the departure of the students and their instructors, would be apt to get the idea that the Building was quite uninhabited. It is certainly exceptional when the long halls re-echo any other tread than my own, on my passage through them. During the seven years while the apartments adjoining mine were held by two college acquaintances, with whom I exchanged many calls, I am sure that I never met them on the stairways a dozen times. During an equally long interval while the editor-in-chief of the daily newspaper which employed me had apartments here which I used to pass two or three times each day, and which I knew that he emerged from each day, I never saw him seven times, except inside his chambers or the editorial rooms. Reflecting upon these curious reversals of probability, one might almost be pardoned for a superstitious belief in the existence of some subtle influence which impels each owner of the Castle to enter or leave it only at times when he is least likely to be confronted by any living reminder of the truth that he is not really the sole proprietor of its magnificent solitude. As the chances of casual contact between tenants who are acquainted is so slight, it follows that a man may live here for years before the faces of non-acquaintances become familiar enough to impress themselves upon him as belonging to residents rather than to the ever-changing mass of visitors. Of the latter, as of tenants who stay but a year or two, it may be said: "Come they and go, we heed them not, though others hail their advent." Names of residents become fixed in mind sooner than faces, for they are seen accredited to the Building in newspapers and directories, or noticed at the janitor's post-office, or reported through mutual acquaintances. Indeed, there formerly existed a lonesome-looking bulletin-board where a new-comer sometimes nailed up his "card," as a guide to those who might wish to discover the exact number of his room; but no old-resident ever encouraged a device so inharmonious with the spirit of the place, and this miscalled "directory" has been wisely obliterated. Unless a visitor "gets his bearings," and exact information, at the janitor's office, he may now wander about, as in a labyrinth, for an indefinite period, without finding the person whom he is in search of, or without being confronted by any obtrusive sign whatever. The corridors, I may add, are lighter at night than at any other time; for gas jets burn there continuously until dawn.

Though a master of the Castle soon grows familiar, in these several ways, with certain names as belonging to its retinue, and, ultimately, with certain faces, he may be a still longer time in connecting the faces with the names. Thus, the existence of the Nestor of the place never happened to be revealed to me until, in preparing for print "a directory of Yale men living in New York and its environs" (1879), I had occasion to unearth his name. Were it not for the conventional ban which rests upon each resident, against impairing the freedom of the place by forming any acquaintanceships there, I should be tempted to intrude upon the privacy of this venerable man, and beg him to tell me about some of the interesting people who have been hidden here with him behind these walls, at one time or another, during the half-century (for the tradition is that he began as a tenant, among the very first, as soon as his undergraduate days were over). I recall a rumor that Sam Colt was a resident during the years while he was perfecting the idea of the "revolver" which gave him fame and fortune; and I know that quite a long catalogue might be made of men who have attained distinction as painters, or lawyers, or politicians, or authors, as a sequel to obscurity here in earlier days. That obscurity seems to me to have had in it more likelihood of happiness, however, than the celebrity of later date. "As a man thinketh, so is he." I know nothing of the thoughts of the man who has lived here longest; but in the fact of his long residence here I account him outwardly fortunate. When he went up to New Haven as a Freshman in 1833 he joined a class of young fellows from whom have since been elected a President of the United States, a Chief Justice of the Supreme Court (the officer of greatest dignity in America), a United States Senator of New York, a Minister to England, a member of two Presidential Cabinets, a Governor, a General, a College President, and a long line of professors, clergymen, lawyers, and other dignitaries whose names have attained wide repute in their several States, if not in the nation at large. Yet this veteran, who has kept secluded in Washington Square, during all these years, not even reporting to the class secretary the fact of his existence, appears to me to have been happier in his "environment" than any of those more distinguished classmates who have flaunted themselves in the fierce light that beats about the great dome in Washington City. Not a single one of these eminent people possesses my personal admiration; for even the Chief Justice has forbidden me to hold him in high honor since that lamentable day when he decided that neither the Constitution nor the Supreme Court should any longer serve the citizen as a barrier against the confiscating powers of Congress.

Indeed, I am free to say that, of all the men who have made any public stir in the world during the years in which I have been breathing its air, I can recall only two who have done anything which I myself should have taken supreme pleasure in doing: pleasure enough, I mean, to compensate for the loss of personal freedom implied in the notoriety necessarily accompanying such public acts. One was an English playwright; the other an American naval officer. When the former paused from his routine work in London and listened to the mirthful echoes coming back from every city and town and hamlet in the world that spoke his mother-tongue, assuring him that the praises of "Pinafore" were being simultaneously chanted in a continuous chorus which encircled the planet,—when he reflected that no mortal's pen had ever before been given power thus to enliven the broad countenance of the whole mighty English-speaking race with such a burst of "vast and inextinguishable laughter,"—I think the sensation must have been worth having. Likewise, when the other man laid his right hand on the Obelisk at Alexandria and with his left set it up again in New York,—when, having quietly accomplished, by means of his own invention, a unique enterprise which all well-informed persons had ridiculed as "impossible," he saw the mighty monolith swinging majestically into position on its pedestal in Central Park,—I think that he, too, on that icy midday of midwinter, must have felt entirely "good."[1] It is the private, subjective sensation, in each of these cases, which appeals to me as exceptionably admirable,—not the public, objective celebrity attaching thereto. Indeed, I do not suppose that either man has won any permanent fame, since that is usually reserved for those who are appointed to do something of universal human interest,—such as successfully superintending the slaughter of a vast multitude of the human race, as Lincoln and Grant were appointed in our day. Finer far than that, however, seems to me the sensation of having secretly commanded Castle Solitude during all this troublous half-century; though whether any resident has really lived here as its commander, or only as one of its retinue, can of course be known to his own heart alone. It is an intangible essence whose quality depends upon the intellectual bent of the individual,—upon his willingness to accept exclusively one half or the other of this double-definition:

> Name and fame? "To fly sublime through the courts, the camps, the schools!"
> "'Tis to be the ball of Time, bandied in the hands of fools!"

Aside from the artists, for whom this has always been a recognized haunt, I think that a majority of the tenants have always been college-bred men, and that Yale has always had more graduates here than any other one college. This has certainly been the fact during the last decade; and Yale has also been continuously represented in the Faculty by eminent and influential professors. There existed at New Haven in my time, twenty years ago (manifesting itself most tangibly in the region of "the fence," on lazy summer evenings), a sort of halo of sympathetic respect for the memory of the unknown genius to whom tradition had accredited the apothegm: "Yale College would be the ideal place for an education, if the Faculty would only dispense with the literary and religious exercises!" Perhaps the influence of that ancient but ever-appetizing jest accounts in part for the preponderance of

---

[1] I feel proud to record that, after erecting the Obelisk (Jan. 22, 1881), Lieutenant Commander Henry H. Gorringe lived for two or three years in the University Building. He died before completing his 45th year (July 6, 1885), in a house that fronts upon Washington Square.

the college in respect to the number of graduates who have sought to realize on Washington Square this delightful dream of an academic Utopia, by enrolling themselves as honorary members in this real University of Cockagne.[1] To me, at all events, a special zest is given to life here by a consciousness of the "literary and religious exercises" which are raging on all sides of me, and which others are compelled to take part in while I myself escape such thralldom. The dim strains from the chapel organ add to my tranquillity by reminding me that no Faculty any longer have power to haul me from bed, by that signal, to an unwilling and unbreakfasted participation in the formality called "morning prayers." Even the howlings and fights and rushes and miscellaneous horse-play with which the younger classes of collegians sometimes render the halls uproarious, serve an excellent moral purpose. Like the constant demands which a troop of active children make upon their father, the turmoil and tomfoolery of these academic children help prevent the resident bachelor from becoming entirely self-absorbed. Their antics help keep him in accord with the fun and freshness of the new generation, by the force of the reminiscence which they awaken in his own more frolicsome days. "When I was imbibing classic culture," he reflects; "when I used to 'sock with Socrates, rip with Euripides, and mark with Marcus Aurelius,' this same sort of nonsense pleased me too. As the dear, departed Calverley hath it,

> When within my veins the blood ran, and the curls were on my brow,
> I did, O ye undergraduates, much as ye are doing now! '"

"Anything for a quiet life" is a rendering I like to make of Algernon Sidney's famous phrase, "*Ense petit placidam sub libertate quietem*," which winds its Latin length around the historic Indian on the coat-of-arms of Massachusetts; or, as I sometimes expand the idea, when I gaze upon the full-sized figure of that noble savage, frescoed upon the ceiling of my hallway, "He'll fight to the last gasp, if need be, but he *will* have peace." The unique advantage of Castle Solitude seems to me to be this : that peace may here be had for the least possible amount of fighting,—that a quiet life may here be led without the sacrifice of an "anything" which is of supreme value. I do not extol the place as a hermitage, but rather because it allows those

---

[1] Such a tendency has even gained recognition in current fiction, as shown by this extract from a Yale professor's tale, contrasting the expectations of certain imaginary classmates, on graduation night, with the stories of their actual lives, as reported twenty years later : " Armstrong and you have changed places in one respect, I should think," said I. " He is keeping a boarding-house somewhere in Connecticut. And instead of leading a Tulkinghorny existence in the New York University Building, as he firmly intended, he has married and produced a numerous offspring, I hear."—" Split Zephyr : an Attenuated Yarn Spun by the Fates," by Henry A. Beers, p. 79 (Scribners' Stories by American Authors, Vol. viii., 1884, pp. 206). The allusion, of course, is to one of the characters who plays so prominent a part in " Bleak House," and who is described in the index to Charles Dickens's works, as follows : " Mr. Tulkinghorn, an old-fashioned old gentleman, legal adviser of the Dedlocks; 'an oyster of the old school, whom nobody can open.'"

things which cannot elsewhere be had except amid the discomforts of a hermitage. As "the happiness of sympathetic human intercourse seems to me incomparably greater than any other pleasure,"—as the companionship of my friends seems by far the finest enjoyment that existence has to offer,—so do I value this curious Castle where I can assert my own nature without cutting myself off from the presence of the people whom I like, and can lead my own life without arousing the resentment of the people whom I regard with indifference. "The condition in which a man does not pay formal calls, and is not invited to state dinners and dances, may be very lamentable and deserving of polite contempt, but it need not be absolute solitude, as society people assume. Such is not the condition of any one in a civilized country who is out of a prison cell." In a large city, the social instinct can be gratified by chance acquaintanceships, which are continually changing, like those formed on a journey. All sorts and patterns of "the human various" can be studied off-hand, and without need of introduction. Plenty of people worth talking to are always obtainable at every nook and corner. What fashionable folks really mean when they stigmatize a city man as "solitary" is not that he really leads the lonely life of a hermit, but that he refrains from those social relationships of a formal and permanent sort which would subject him to the inflexible conventions of "good society." In other words, the solitude of the Castle results not from its standing "out of the world" (for it is in the very center of a densely-peopled and most interesting world), but only "out of the fashion." Its situation seems to combine many of the advantages of both the places described in the opening words of the extract which I now give from a favorite author, who has already supplied me with a phrase or two, and whose remarks about solitude and independence show so well the value and the cost of each that I should like to quote even more extensively:

The solitude which is really injurious is the severance from all who are capable of understanding us. The most favorable life would have its times of open and equal intercourse with the best minds, and also its periods of retreat. My ideal would be a house in London, not far from one or two houses which are so full of light and warmth that it is a liberal education to have entered them, and a solitary tower on some island of the Hebrides, with no companions but the sea-gulls and the thundering surges of the Atlantic. One such island I know well, and it is before my mind's eye, clear as a picture, whilst I am writing. It was a dream of my youth to build a tower there, with three or four little rooms in it, and walls as strong as a lighthouse. There have been more foolish dreams, and there have been less competent teachers than the tempests that would have roused me and the calms that would have brought me peace.

It is a traditional habit of mankind to see only the disadvantages of solitude, without considering its compensations ; but there are great compensations, some of the greatest being negative. The lonely man is lord of his own hours and of his own purse ; his days are long and unbroken ; he escapes from every form of ostentation, and may live quite simply and sincerely in great calm breadths of leisure. I knew one who passed his summers in the heart of a vast forest, in a common thatched cottage with furniture of common deal, and for this retreat he quitted very gladly a rich fine house in the city. He wore nothing but old clothes, read only a few old books, without the least regard to the opinions of the learned, and did not take in a newspaper. Though he cherished a few tried friendships and was grateful to those who loved him and could enter into his humor, he had acquired a horror of towns and crowds. This was not from nervousness, but because he felt imprisoned and impeded in his thinking, which needed the depths of the forest, the venerable trees, the communication with primæval nature, from which he drew a mysterious but necessary nourishment for the peculiar activity of his mind. His temper was grave and earnest, but unfailingly cheerful and entirely free from any tendency to bitterness. On the walls of his habitation he inscribed with a piece of charcoal a quotation from De Sènancour : " In the world a man lives in his own age ; in solitude, in all the ages."

He who has lived for some great space of existence apart from the tumult of the world, has discovered the vanity of those things for which he has no natural aptitude or gift—their *relative* vanity, I mean, their uselessness to himself, personally ; and at the same time he has learned what is truly precious and good for him. Surely this is knowledge of inestimable value to a man : surely it is a great thing for any one, in the bewildering confusion of distracting toils and pleasures, to have found out the labor that he is most fit for, and the pleasures that satisfy him best. Society so encourages us in affectations that it scarcely leaves us a chance of knowing our own minds ; but in solitude this knowledge comes of itself, and delivers us from innumerable vanities. The man of the world does not consult his own intellectual needs, but considers the eyes of his visitors ; the solitary student takes his literature as a lonely traveler takes food when he is hungry, without reference to the ordered courses of public hospitality.

The life of the perfect hermit, and that of those persons who feel themselves nothing individually, and have no existence but what they receive from others, are alike imperfect lives. The perfect life is like that of a ship of war, which has its own place in the fleet and can share in its strength and discipline, but can also go forth alone in the solitude of the infinite sea. We ought to belong to society, to have our place in it, and yet to be capable of a complete individual existence outside of it. I value society for the abundance of ideas which it brings before us, like carriages in a frequented street ; but I value solitude for sincerity and peace, and for the better understanding of the thoughts that are truly ours. We need society and we need solitude also, as we need summer and winter, day and night, exercise and rest. Society is necessary to give us our share and place in the collective life of humanity ; but solitude is necessary for the maintenance of the individual life.—"The Intellectual Life," by P. G. Hamerton, pp. 332-333, 324-327 (Boston : Roberts Bros., 1873, pp. 455).

Shelley was a lover of solitude ; which means that he liked full and adequate human intercourse so much that the insufficient imitation of it was intolerable to him. It is in this as in other pleasures, the better we appreciate the real thing, the less we are disposed to accept the spurious copy as a substitute. By far the greater part of what passes for human intercourse is not intercourse at all, but only acting, of which the highest object and most considerable merit is to conceal the weariness that accompanies its hollow observances. Steady workers do not need much company. To be occupied with a task that is difficult and arduous but that we know to be within our powers, and to awake early every morning with the delightful feeling that the whole day can be given to it without fear of interruption, is the perfection of happiness for one who has the gift of throwing himself heartily into his work. This is the best independence,—to have something to do and something that can be done, and done most perfectly, in solitude. Many of us would rather live in solitude and on small means at Como than on a great income in Manchester. As there is no pleasure in military life for a soldier who fears death, so there is no independence in civil existence for the man who has an overpowering dread of solitude. What the railway is to physical motion, settled conventions are to the movements of the mind. There are men whose whole art of living consists in passing from one conventionalism to another, as a traveler changes his train. They take their religion, their politics, their education, their social and literary opinions, all as provided by the brains of others. For those who are satisfied with easy, conventional ways, the desire for intellectual independence is unintelligible. What is the need of it ? Why go, mentally, on a bicycle or in a canoe, by your own toilsome exertions, when you may sit so very comfortably in the train, a rug round your lazy legs, and your softly capped head in a corner ? Independence and originality are so little esteemed in what is called " good society " in France, that the adjectives " *indépendant* " and " *original* " are constantly used in a bad sense. The French ideal of " good form " is to be one of the small crowd of rich and fashionable people, undistinguishable from the others. Bohemianism and Philistinism are the terms by which, for want of better, we designate two opposite ways of estimating wealth and culture. The Bohemian is the man who with small means desires and contrives to obtain the intellectual advantages of wealth, which he considers to be leisure to think and read, travel, and intelligent conversation. The Philistine is the man who, whether his means are small or large, devotes himself wholly to the attainment of the material advantages of wealth,—a large house, good food and wine, clothes, horses and servants. The Bohemian makes the *best* advantages his first aim, being contented with such a small measure of riches as, when ingeniously and skilfully employed, may secure them; and the art and craft of Bohemianism is to get for that small amount of money such an amount of leisure, reading, travel and good conversation as may suffice to make life interesting. Its asceticism, on the physical side, is not a severe religious asceticism, but a disposition, like that of a thorough soldier or traveler, to do without luxury and comfort, and take the absence of them gayly when they are not to be had. Indeed, there may be some connection between Bohemianism and the life of the red Indian who roams in his woods and contents himself with a low standard of physical well being. I sometimes wonder, as regards a certain loved and respected Philistine friend of mine, if it ever occurred to him to reflect, in the tedious hours of too tranquil age, how much of what is best in the world had been simply *missed* by him; how he had missed all the variety and interest of travel, the charm of intellectual society, the influences of genius, and even the physical excitements of healthy out-door amusements. A true Bohemian knows the value of mere shelter, of food enough to satisfy hunger, of plain clothes that will keep him sufficiently warm; and in the things of the mind he values the liberty to use his own faculties as a kind of happiness in itself. His philosophy leads him to take an interest in talking with human beings of all sorts and conditions, and in different countries. He does not despise the poor, for, whether rich or poor in his own person, he understands simplicity of life; and, if the poor man lives in a small cottage, he too has probably been lodged less spaciously still, in some small hut or tent. He has lived often, in rough travel, as the poor live every day. I maintain that such tastes and experiences are valuable both in prosperity and in adversity.—"Human Intercourse," by P. G. Hamerton, pp. 47, 27, 31, 15, 298, 314, with sentences re-arranged (Boston : Roberts Bros., 1884, pp. 430).

As more than four hundred British subjects have subscribed for this book, there may be some truly loyal souls among them who will be proud to know that a remote suggestion of royalty, as well as an odor of sanctity, attaches to the scene of its composition. I think it quite improbable that any other American book has ever been written in a room that has known the presence of the future King of England; but it is a fact that the apartments inhabited by me were constructed in 1875 in a part of the space that formed the chapel of the University at the time when the royal Oxford collegian, Albert Edward, was forced to do penance there, a quarter-century ago. The following report of the ceremonial was published soon afterwards in the students' *Quarterly Magazine*, and was reprinted as a curiosity in its issue of October, 1878, from which I now quote it. The story has an independent interest to home readers, as throwing a strong side-light on the simplicity of social manners and customs in that remote era "before the war." Except the cemetery at Greenwood, and the prisons on Blackwell's Island, it seems that the chapel of the University was the only show-place the city then had for the entertainment of distinguished visitors whom it was desirable to impress with an idea of the grandeur and superiority of things metropolitan :

When the royal visitor arrived in New York he was immediately besieged with numberless invitations to visit our public institutions. But few of these, of course, could be honored with a second thought, owing to want of time; but that of Chancellor Ferris was promptly accepted, and the honor of his first visit in this city was awarded to our University. As soon as the Prince had signified his acceptance, a plan of reception was adopted, and Professor Wedgwood, then at the head of the Law Faculty, appointed to carry it into effect, assisted by the students in the collegiate department. The visit was to take place on Friday, October 12, 1860, at half-past ten A. M., and the Prince was to be received in the large chapel. This chapel, rising through three stories of the building, had a capacity for comfortably seating twelve hundred persons, and its rich ornamentation and beautiful windows gave it a very venerable appearance, quite in contrast to the small chapel in which we now worship every morning. Invitations were issued to the wives and daughters of the professors and members of the council, and to the mothers, sisters and "lady friends" of the students, and a stage was erected sufficiently large to accommodate the Prince and his suite, the officers of the University, and other invited guests.

On the morning of the appointed day, long before the arrival of the Prince, the chapel was densely filled with as brilliant and fascinating an audience as ever assembled within its walls. The council, professors, and judges of the courts assembled in the Chancellor's room; while the students, arrayed in their college gowns, and wearing the insignia of their various societies, were arranged in double columns from the sidewalk along the various halls through which the Prince was to pass in his visit to the several departments of the University. The Prince and his suite left the Fifth Avenue Hotel at half-past ten o'clock and drove rapidly down Fifth Avenue to Washington Square, where a fine view of the University Building at the head of the Square was presented to them. Alighting at the main entrance on University Place, the Prince was met by Prof. Wedgwood, and conducted up the marble stairway to the main hall, where he was received by Chancellor Ferris in his official robes. Arm in arm the Chancellor and the English student proceeded to the large chapel, followed by Lord Lyons, the Duke of Newcastle, Earl St. Germains, General Bruce, the British Consul Archibald, and other members of the Prince's suite, with the officers of the University and the judges of the several courts. As the procession passed along through the lines of students to the chapel, the Prince was greeted with the utmost respect and deference. As he entered the chapel, the band struck up England's national anthem, and the whole audience rose to receive the Prince, and greeted him with the waving of handkerchiefs and half-suppressed words of welcome. The procession, led by the venerable Chancellor and the young Prince, ascended the platform and passed to the places assigned to them. The Prince, with his suite, took a position on one side of the platform, and the council, professors and invited guests occupied the other side. A short consultation was then held, at the termination of which a signal was given, the music ceased, and the audience was hushed to profound silence, while the Chancellor pronounced an address of welcome. The Prince, the Duke of Newcastle and Lord Lyons had each expressed a wish to meet on the occasion of their visit three of the professors, who were personally known to them, and who had attained a European celebrity—Prof. Valentine Mott, at that time acknowledged to be the first surgeon in America; Prof. John W. Draper, who first applied photography to the taking of portraits from life, and in his room in the University Building made the first picture of the human face by the light of the sun; and Prof. Samuel F. B. Morse, who invented the electro-magnetic telegraph, and performed his first successful experiment within the walls of N. Y. U. Accordingly they were now specially introduced, and Prof. Morse expressed his most hearty thanks for the kind attentions shown him by the Duke of Newcastle on his first visit to London with his infant telegraph.

A neatly engrossed copy of the Chancellor's address, with the resolutions previously adopted by the council, was then presented to the Prince, who received the same and made an appropriate reply. The Chancellor then presented to the Prince the members of the council, the professors of the several Faculties, the judges of the courts, and the ladies. The Prince mingled freely with the gentlemen upon the platform for some time, and then, taking the arm of the Chancellor, he left the chapel and passed into the law library and lecture-room. Here he noticed a large number of valuable books presented to the University by King William IV. and Her Majesty Queen Victoria, among which are the entire publications of the Record Commissioners. Mr. John Taylor Johnston's gift, a complete modern law library, seemed to attract especial attention. From the law library the Prince was conducted to the council chamber, and thence to the marble stairway, where the Chancellor took leave of his royal guest. As the Prince and his suite entered their carriages, the students formed in front, and, joined by thousands of spectators there assembled, gave three times three hearty cheers for the Oxford student.

Five days later, when the train which carried the Prince from Albany to Boston passed through Springfield, and that much-admired youth, standing on the rear platform thereof, lifted his little beaver hat, in acknowledgment of the acclamations of the populace, I recollect that the heavy hand of a hackman swept me and my school-fellows from the places of vantage we had gained on the wheels of his vehicle,—so that we saw nothing but the princely hat. The next afternoon, however, enthroned safely upon a stool in the window of Little & Brown's bookstore, on Washington street, I gazed squarely upon the red-coated scion of royalty, as his carriage rolled along in the great procession which the Bostonians arranged in his honor. I mention these facts for the sake of saying that though I was an "ordinary, human boy enough" to take a keen interest in any sort of a show that commanded universal popular attention, I recall my personal feeling towards the central figure in it as one of pity rather than envy. It seemed to me that such a boy could have no fun. I felt that I was more fortunate in the possession of a frolicsome bull-dog, and in the liberty to play with him to my heart's content, after school hours were over, than this resplendent British boy could ever hope to be. Long years afterwards, in '76, a similar sentiment possessed me, when I gazed upon the Prince's mother, as she made a royal "progress" through London, to signalize the opening of some charitable institution at the East End. Looking into the face of this most distinguished woman in the world, the uppermost thought in my mind was one of speculative curiosity as to what real pleasure there could conceivably be to her in the magnificent boredom of all such pomp and pageantry. It seemed to me as if she were owned absolutely, as a sort of toy, by the mighty mob that surged in loyal waves around her. I wondered, too, if she ever, in changing about from one castle or palace to another, felt any longing for that unattainable sort of castle, whose impossible solitude and privacy would make it truly her own.

After all, however, the founders of the University, a half-century ago, builded better than they knew; and their successors of a quarter-century ago acted wiser than they knew when they dragged in the Prince to admire it. The founders failed in their ostensible object, because the stars in their courses fought against it as impracticable; but their very failure was a part and parcel of a unique achievement, which, while I live, shall at least in one heart keep their memory green. All unwittingly, they were the instruments for accomplishing what no one else has ever done,—what no mortal men could conceivably by design and premeditation ever have power to do. If "the noblest study of mankind is man," this temple of learning which they built offers unexampled advantages for studying him most nobly. From its towers, whoever possesses "the vision and the faculty divine" may clearly overlook the

universe.   Like as a London cabman looketh with critical and impersonal interest upon the tendered coin which represents no more than his legal fare, so
here the philosophic observer may hold at arm's length, as if it were no possible concern of his, that mysterious gift called Life.   If America is indeed distinctively a land of liberty, that place in it where the quality reaches its highest development ought specially to interest the foreign visitor.   Thus, though
the "Chancellor" of twenty-five years ago had no possible conception of it,
there was a certain poetic appropriateness in forcing the future King of
England to do his earliest homage in America at what seems to me the most
sacred shrine in the habitable globe because it is the chosen abode of
Freedom.   My pen may not have had power to paint all its peculiarities with
a graphic touch; but I am sure that they deserve such painting.   I am sure
that I rightly use the superlative when I characterize it on my letter-heads
by adapting these lines from Calverley :

> "'Nulla non donanda lauru' is that Building : you could not—
> Placing New York's map before you—light on half so queer a spot."

I am sure, too, that the seemingly strange act of giving to such a subject
the longest chapter in a long book on bicycling, will not go unsupported by
the sympathy of my three thousand subscribers.   Understanding as they do
the supremely exhilarating sense of independence which the whirling wheel
imparts to the motion of the body, they will appreciate the appropriateness
of my describing to them the machinery of a unique habitation whose "simple
shelter" allows a like liberty to the movement of the mind.   They will
readily recognize, I doubt not, the subtle analogy which exists between the
Building and the bicycle, and will clearly comprehend why the two must
needs be coupled in my admiration.   Yet, as the great majority of them are
much younger than myself, they will perhaps be thankful for the reminder
that, while I admire the two, my book recommends to them only the one ;
while I account freedom a very fine thing, I do not urge their general pursuit
of it, to the exclusion of the other fine things which this world contains.   My
own experience is that Renan was right in deprecating the common talk
which ridicules the generous "illusions of youth," and in declaring rather
that its only real illusion is a disbelief in the brevity of life.   When a sense
of this finally comes upon a man, I may name to him not only the bicycle for
balm but the Castle for consolation ; but for his earlier and brighter days my
preferable pointer must always be this famous old poem of Robert Herrick's :

> "Gather the roses while ye may !   Old Time is still a-flying ;
> And this same flower that smiles to-day, to-morrow will be dying.
> The glorious lamp of heaven, the sun, the higher he's a-getting,
> The sooner will his course be run, the nearer he's to setting.
> That age is best which is the first, when youth and blood are warmer ;
> But, being spent, the worse and worst times shall succeed the former.
> So, be not coy, but use your time, and while ye may, go marry,
> Lest, having lost but once your prime, you may forever tarry."

NEWSPAPER NOTICES

AND

SUBSCRIBERS' OPINIONS

OF

"TEN THOUSAND MILES ON A BICYCLE"

["A Gazetteer of American Roads in Many States; an Encyclopædia of Wheeling Progress in Many Countries" 1908 pages, of 675,000 words; 200 contributors of records; 3400 subscribers' names and addresses; photogravure frontispiece but no advertisements), bound in blue muslin, with beveled edges and gilded top; sent by mail or express, boxed and prepaid, on receipt of $2 by the Publisher, KARL KRON, *at the University Building, Washington Square, New York City, D.*]

TOGETHER WITH

SPECIMEN PAGES OF ITS MAIN TEXT,

CONTENTS TABLE, PREFACE AND INDEXES

ALSO THE

INSTRUCTIONS AND ARGUMENTS OF THE PUBLISHER

TO HIS

THREE THOUSAND COPARTNERS

———

PUBLISHED BY KARL KRON
THE UNIVERSITY BUILDING, WASHINGTON SQUARE
NEW YORK
JULY XXXI—MDCCCLXXXVIII

D. C. Crocker, Printer

(G)

CONTENTS OF THIS PAMPHLET.

The remainder of the pamphlet consists of ADVERTISEMENT OF "CURL", 8 pp.; ADVERTISEMENT OF "CASTLE SOLITUDE", 8 pp.; and reprints from 48 pp. of "Ten Thousand Miles on a Bicycle", as follows : TABLE OF CONTENTS, pp. ix to xx ; PREFACE, pp. iii, iv, vii, viii; TITLES OF THE 41 CHAPTERS ; ON THE WHEEL, p. 9 ; WHITE FLANNEL AND NICKEL PLATE, p. 17 ; MY 234 RIDES ON " No. 234," p. 63 ; KENTUCKY AND ITS MAMMOTH CAVE, p. 225; IN THE DOWN-EAST FOGS, p. 275; STRAIGHTAWAY FOR FORTY DAYS, p. 305; LONG-DISTANCE ROUTES AND RIDERS, p. 473; STATISTICS FROM THE VETERANS, p. 502; BRITISH AND COLONIAL RECORDS, p. 531; THE THREE THOUSAND SUBSCRIBERS (alphabetical), p. 734; DIRECTORY OF WHEELMEN (geographical), p. 765; INDEX OF PLACES, p. xxxv; INDEX OF PERSONS, pp. lxv, lxxi, lxxxiii; VERSES OF GREETING, p. cviii; GENERAL INDEX, pp. xxi to xxxiv; INFORMATION FOR BOOKSELLERS; NOTICE TO THE POSTMASTER. Whole number of pages in the pamphlet (including cover and the Stevens lithograph facing p. 65) is 150; and the first 96 of these are reproduced as the central feature in the "Publishers' Trade-List Annual" for 1888.

"My best discount" is occasionally enquired after by some representative of the book-trade who has heard of "Ten Thousand Miles on a Bicycle," but is not familiar with its peculiar mode of publication. This peculiarity ensures directly to each buyer the full discount of $3 (by rating at $2 what would ordinarily cost him $5 if sold through the bookstores), and therefore forbids any further commission to middlemen. Even with selling-agents thus serving me without pay, in all parts of the world, the first edition is practically a gift of mine to the public; for I have shown elsewhere in this pamphlet that no profit can really *begin* to accrue to me until after the first 6000 copies shall have been sold. Hence, I will deliver the book to no man for any lower rate than the $2 plainly stamped upon its cover and title-page,—whether he be "in the trade" or outside it. Nevertheless, if a bookseller will personally apply at one of my agencies where copies are already deposited, he shall be allowed a deduction of 25 cents on each volume paid for there,—merely to cover the cost of delivering it to his customer. I shall also be glad to grant "the usual trade discount" to any dealer who wishes to attempt the sale of the following pamphlets reprinted from the book, on heavy paper, tinted and calendered, and bound in olive-green covers. The price named upon the cover and title-page is 25 cents, but I will sell them for 15 cents each to any bookseller who will pay his own expressage:

CURL, THE BEST OF BULL-DOGS: *a Study in Animal Life.* Twenty-eight pages of 14,000 words, with photogravure frontispiece; appendix of 132 pages giving specimens of the text and newspaper notices of "Ten Thousand Miles on a Bicycle." Sent postpaid to any country in the world, on receipt of 25 cents' worth of the lowest denomination of postage-stamps locally current. KARL KRON, *Publisher, at the University Building, N. Y. City.*

CASTLE SOLITUDE IN THE METROPOLIS: *a Study in Social Science.* Fifty-six pages of 34,000 words, with small picture of the Castle; appendix of 132 pages, the same as the above. Sent to any address for 25 c.

I repeat below, from the page which contains the full prospectus of "My Second Ten Thousand," the application-form, which will ensure to a bookseller—the same as to any one else—the chance of buying the volume "at the usual 33 per cent. off," in case it is ever published. The act of signing does not bind a person to buy the book at any price; it merely binds the Publisher to give a month's option of buying it at two-thirds the retail rate:

I hereby authorize Karl Kron to print my name in the list of supporters of his proposed second book (to be called "My Second Ten Thousand," containing not less than 300 pages of large type, with at least 250 words to the page, and retailing at $1.50); and I agree that, if at any future time I receive notice from him that such a book has been published, I will reply within a month, and either enclose a dollar to pay for a copy, or else give notice that I resign the privilege (which K. K. ensures to me in return for the present pledge) of securing one from him at two-thirds the regular rate.

[Name, address, date and occupation to be plainly written below. Prepay by a 2-cent stamp.]

R3

"TEN THOUSAND MILES ON A BICYCLE."

A GAZETTEER OF AMERICAN ROADS, BY KARL KRON.

Forty-one chapters; 908 pages; 675,000 words; photogravure frontispiece; bound in dark blue muslin, smooth finish, with beveled edges and gilded top. The appendix has 3400 subscribers' names and addresses, but no advertisements. Local index gives 8418 ref. to 3482 towns, and personal index 3126 ref. to 1476 individuals. Contents-table and indexes cover 75 pages, showing 10,468 titles, and 22,800 references. Pamphlets of 48 pages, containing specimens of these and of the main text, mailed free to any applicant by postal card. The book itself (size 8 by 5½ by 1¾ inches; weight 2 pounds) is sent for 82, postpaid to any post-office, or express-paid to any office of the American Ex. Co. and many connecting expresses which allow the 15 c. mail-rate. Remittances may preferably be made in money-orders of the same company. (The 1st ed. of 6200 was pub. May 25, 1887, and the ultimate sale is to be 30,000 copies.)

Each recipient will favor the Publisher by sending notice of the book's arrival.

For Mz.

This volume is not on sale at the bookstores, but may be bought at designated depositories in more than 150 towns. A list of them will be mailed on application, and the chief ones are as follows: New York, 12 Warren st.; 313 W. 58th st.; Boston, 70 Franklin st., 509 Tremont st.; Baltimore, 2 & 4 Hanover st.; Buffalo, 535 Main st.; Chicago, 291 Wabash ave., 222 N. Franklin st., 108 Madison st., 77 State st.; Cincinnati, 6 E. 4th st.; Indianapolis, office of Wheelmen's Record, Sentinel building; Newark, Broad & Bridge sts.; Philadelphia, 811 Arch st.; Portland, Or., 145 Fifth st.; St. Louis, 310 N.Eleventh st; San Francisco, 228 Phelan Building; Washington, 1713 New York avenue.

It will be mailed to any province of Canada, for $2, by A. T. Lane, of 1421 St. Catherine st., Montreal; and to any colony of Australia, for 8s. 8d., by W. J. Parry, of Wills st., Sandhurst, Vict. Residents of Great Britain who send 8s. 8d. to the Publisher of "Wheeling," 152 Fleet st., London, will find the same acknowledged in the "Ans. to Cor." column of that Wednesday weekly; and their books will be mailed as soon as the orders thus printed arrive in N. Y. Purchasers who may prefer to deal directly with the Publisher (whether they reside in foreign countries or in the U. S.) should make all money-orders payable to him at Station D, New York City. Orders on the American Ex. Co. are preferable in the U. S. "Wheeling," the London weekly (36 pp. excl. of adv.), has an annual sub. rate of $1.62 for it. British and $2 for other countries; and I recommend it as containing more matter of interest to Americans than any other English cycling journal. It's special arrangement for mailing the "Wheelmen's Gazette" (the largest and best-printed cycling monthly in the world, whose annual sub. rate is 50 c.) will send both papers for $2 year or $1 a half-year, paid in advance to him. I recommend, also, as the most readable book of cycling travel ever issued, "From San Francisco to Teheran" (547 pp. of 230,000 words; 110 illustrations; cloth bound; $2; pub. May 31, '87, by T. Stevens, 12 E. 17th st., N. Y., by T. Stevens, who will mail autographed copies on receipt of price at Outing office, 140 Nassau st., N. Y. The chief English book on the subject is "Cycling," by Lord Bury and G. L. Hillier (472 pp. of 150,000 words, 70 illus. $1.50).

(H)

NEWSPAPER NOTICES

AND

SUBSCRIBERS' OPINIONS

OF

"TEN THOUSAND MILES ON A BICYCLE"

["A GAZETTEER OF AMERICAN ROADS IN MANY STATES; AN ENCYCLOPÆDIA OF WHEELING PROGRESS IN MANY COUNTRIES" (908 pages, of 675,000 words; 200 contributors of records; 3400 subscribers' names and addresses; photogravure frontispiece but no advertisements), bound in blue muslin, with beveled edges and gilded top; sent by mail or express, boxed and prepaid, on receipt of $2 by the Publisher, KARL KRON, *at the University Building, Washington Square, New York City, D.*]

TOGETHER WITH

SPECIMEN PAGES OF ITS MAIN TEXT,

CONTENTS TABLE, PREFACE AND INDEXES

ALSO THE

INSTRUCTIONS AND ARGUMENTS OF THE PUBLISHER

TO HIS

THREE THOUSAND COPARTNERS

———

Each recipient of this pamphlet will confer a favor by handing it to any acquaintance who is interested in cycling; also by supplying the Publisher with addresses of possible buyers of the book, to whom the pamphlet can be mailed.

(First edition, 5000 copies; 25 Jan., 1888)

PUBLISHER'S PREFACE.

IN compiling this collection of "notices and opinions," the endeavor has been made to render them readable by careful selection and arrangement. Every page is complete in itself and is headed by a different title, and almost every page contains a variety of quotations appropriate to its heading. Many of these are in sharp conflict, or in amusing contrast with each other; for I have reprinted without reserve everything evil which I have been able to find afloat in the press concerning the book and its author (except a few mis-statements of physical facts), in the belief that such censures serve the pur-pose of arousing curiosity about expressions of the opposite sort. As I have failed to hear from a dozen or more journals to which I ordered that copies of the book should be sent for review, it is possible that some of them may have indulged in appetizing sarcasms, ridicule and abuse not found in the present pamphlet. I only assert that I have included in it every bit of such stuff within reach,—aiming in strictly scientific spirit to show my chosen public *all* the evidence,—and that I have included enough to make the pam-phlet rather interesting on its own account. People who like to "watch the workings of the human mind" ought certainly to be amused by these speci-mens which so well illustrate the tricks and manners of "reviewers."

My request that these reviewers should treat of the book "as a unique business enterprise, rather than as a literary curiosity," has been very generally disregarded; and a chief factor in the problem of persuading a large enough contingent of my 3400 subscribers to really serve as "copartners" (in forcing for it a successful sale of 30,000 copies) is the difficulty of making them dis-tinguish clearly between the "personal" and the "business" phases of the case. "My labor and risk as 'publisher' are what I seek pay for,—not my writings as 'author.'" So runs the opening phrase in my argument on page 715; and I wish it were possible for my supporters to look upon me as a "publisher" simply,—just as they might if some one else had prepared the manuscript (containing his own road-reports and those of all other tourists whom he could persuade to contribute any), and had worked upon my cycling enthusiasm enough to induce me to invest the large sum of $12,000 in giving this manuscript to the public.

There is plenty of proof, scattered through the 116 pages of this pam-phlet, that no regard for "the author's feelings" has caused me to suppress any evil words spoken against him, which could serve to awaken curiosity in his work. The distribution of 5000 copies of so elaborate an advertisement is therefore inspired by "business" rather than by vanity; and those recipi-ents who may help secure as wide a reading as possible for each pamphlet, as a means of helping such business to success, will greatly oblige

THE PUBLISHER.

WASHINGTON SQUARE, N. Y., Feb. 29, 1888.

Taking all things into consideration, strong and weak points alike, we believe that the author has most faithfully kept his promise and that "Ten Thousand Miles on a Bicycle" will always hold the undisputed place of the first great work on the subject of cycling, bearing to all wheelmen that relation that Isaac Walton's Complete Angler bears to fishermen, the world over. —*Wheelmen's Record, Indianapolis.*

An *olla podrida* of endless variety.—*Scientific American.* As comprehensive as a file of newspapers.—*Baltimore American.* Most useful to those wishing such information.—*The Times, N. Y.* Invaluable to one contemplating a tour.—*The Bicycle South.* A valuable encyclopædia, well worth the price asked for it.—*L. A. W. Bulletin.* For the public it seeks it will be a handy volume.—*The Nation, N. Y.* Invaluable to all who follow in his footsteps, or wheel-tracks. — *Lippincott's Magazine.* Those who are just beginning the sport will find it a work of absorbing interest.—*New Englander.* Although a veritable cycling encyclopædia, it is really of especial value to all horsemen who drive for pleasure.—*Spirit of the Times, N. Y.* This manual will prove indispensable to the wheelman. It is most valuable to the bicycler who has time for riding long distances.—*Boston Advertiser.*

The chief characteristic is its comprehensiveness.—*Canadian Wheelman.* Unique in literature and unsurpassed in its line.—*McGregor News, Ia.* The largest and most complete work on cycling ever published.—*The Cyclist, Coventry, Eng.* The most thorough book that any recreative sport has ever had published.—*Boonville Advertiser, Mo.* Not alone unique, but prodigious; this monument of cycling must stand.—*Australian Cycling News.* A really wonderful work, the first classic of cycling literature.—*Wheeling, London.* The work will stand as "the Domesday Book of Cycling."—*Sewing Machine & Cycle News, London.* As an insight into American cycling, the volume is very valuable.—*Irish Cyclist & Athlete, Dublin.* Statistical and historical, amusing and pathetic, it has charms for every reader.—*Saturday Night, Birmingham, Eng.* Whatever has been said in way of praise of this book, by the wheel literature of the world, is well merited.—*New Zealand Referee.*

A masterpiece of egotism.—*Pall Mall Gazette, London.* The most ridiculous book of the season.—*Philadelphia Press.* His individuality has asserted itself, and some of his literary excursions are exquisite.—*Hartford Courant.* A monument only to be compared with Webster's Dictionary or the Great Pyramid.—*The Bookmart, Pittsburg.* One of the most worthless volumes ever written; it is the work of an idiot, not of a sane man.—*Boston Herald.* Cyclists of all nations may get from it many useful "wrinkles." To Americans, especially, it will be invaluable and almost indispensable. The author is a genial and kindly philosopher, who makes no false or undue pretensions of any kind.—*The Saturday Review, London.* An autobiography of a singularly self-sufficient mediocrity; a faddist of the worst order; an egotistical nonentity; a gigantic sham; the self-confessed committer of every literary crime.—*Bicycling News, London organ of "the Coventry ring."*

MAGNITUDE.

An enormous volume.—*Louisville Commercial.* Excessively long.—*The Congregationalist, Boston.* A compact cyclopædia of the sport.—*Boston Advertiser.*—A tremendous book for its subject.—*Chicago Times.* An encyclopædic guide for bicycle-riders.—*San Francisco Argonaut.* Its ponderosity shows the extent of the sport.—*St. Louis Post-Dispatch.* An enormous volume, with an enormous amount of information.—*The Evening Telegram, N. Y.* It derives its virtue from its correctness and its mass.—*The Times, N. Y.* This work of years has at last assumed enormous dimensions of closely printed matter.—*Irish Cyclist & Athlete, Dublin.*

The small and exceedingly clear type makes it contain the substance of three or four volumes of respectable size. The amount of matter cannot be estimated by the number of pages.—*Scientific American, N. Y.*

The mass of details has been arranged with skill, backed by enthusiasm and tireless patience.—*The Critic, N. Y.*

For quantity of matter, detail and reference, it is not only unique but prodigious.—*Australian Cycling News, Melbourne.*

It is a monument of patience and energy only to be compared with Webster's Dictionary, or the Great Pyramid.—*The Bookmart, Pittsburg, Pa.*

A veritable cycling encyclopædia, including more, and more diverse, information than was ever before crowded into one book.—*Spirit of the Times.*

The labor which entered into its composition has been something enormous, and we can only hope that the author will be amply rewarded for it.—*New Englander.*

I am simply amazed at the extent and interest of the book,—a monument of the ability and indefatigable industry of its author.—" *The Tyre,*" *in Saturday Night, Birmingham, Eng.*

We have again been dipping into Karl Kron's great book, though the immense size of the monster has as yet prevented us from grappling with the whole.—*Irish Cyclist & Athlete, Dublin.*

If carried with one on a bicycle, it would be impossible to take anything else ; and we, for our part, prefer a change of clothes to a gazetteer, dictionary, cyclopædia and thesaurus.—*Pall Mall Gazette, London.*

Its ponderosity is its chief defect, but we trust that that drawback will not interfere with the industrious editor meeting with a return sufficient to fully reward him for his many years of laborious work.—*Canadian Wheelman.*

Growing as time went on, it has assumed the proportions of over 800 pages of closely printed matter, and, although somewhat tedious in places, will evidently be the largest and most complete work on cycling ever published.—*The Cyclist, Coventry, Eng.*

The mere form of advertisement adopted is evidence, if evidence were needed, of the smallness of mind which has produced this big-little book,—this monument of egotism,—which resembles a Brobdingnagian infant's primer, in quantity stupendous, in quality petty and infantile.—*Bicycling News, London organ of " the Coventry ring," printers to the C. T. C.*

The best two dollars' worth ever offered to cyclists.—*Spirit of the Times.*

Well worth the money asked for it, and should be owned by every wheelman.—*Bicycling World, Boston.*

Wonderfully cheap at $2. There is not a chapter in the book which is not worth, alone, more than the price of the volume.—*Star Advocate.*

So cheap that we are afraid the publisher will die as poor as the poor dog to whose name it was dedicated.—*L. A. W. Pointer, Oshkosh, Wis.*

The book is a good book, well worth the money. There is no Englishman who has had it and not pronounced it really good value.—*Wheeling.*

Vastly beyond my expectations. It is the first time I ever got a $5 book for $1, and I'm glad of a chance to pledge for your next volume.—*W. R., Holyoke, Mass.*

The more one looks into it, the more does its value increase, and I would not part with my copy for considerable many times its price.—*H. P. Merrill, Los Angeles, Cal. (formerly cycling editor of Springfield Union).*

A valuable book, well worth the price asked for it. It is cheap at $2. We should want it in our library, and should have it there, if we had to pay $5 for it.—*L. A. W. Bulletin, official organ League of American Wheelmen.*

I would willingly pay more, too, for maps and illustrations, though I fully appreciate the fact that more value than the price of the book is already given. I consider the great mass of material atones for delay in publication. —*J. J. Bliss, San Francisco.*

Most assuredly, I am well paid for waiting so long for your book. It was a stupendous undertaking, and has been carried through in a manner which convinces me my money has brought a great return. The book is well worth $3.50 or $4, and should be in the possession of every wheelman in America.— *W. V. Gilman, Nashua, N. H., ex-Treasurer L. A. W.*

Having been in the publishing business for a term of fifteen years, more or less, the peculiarity of your advertisements attracted me as a subscriber, though I take little or no interest in cycling. My opinion is that you would sell the book more rapidly if you had put its price up to $3.50 or even $5. People simply will not believe that any $2 book can contain such a vast bulk and variety of information.—*J. W. J., Washington, D. C.*

The volume is in many respects a remarkable one, and certainly a very valuable one to every American bicycler. Simply as a book of reference, it is worth more than the price asked. The minute account of your travels, and the number of personal experiences of other cyclers, omitting no details, serve to render it, I think, more useful and more readable. It is not, in my opinion, too long. In fact, I would like to see it longer, and even more exhaustive in describing the roads of the United States. Altogether, it is a very interesting book, and one that no cycler should be without, showing, as it does, what may be done by a man of ordinary physical ability, but of extraordinary and indomitable pluck and energy.—*L. D. Aylett, Birmingham, Ala. (treasurer of the Georgia Pacific Railroad Company).*

INDEXING.

The book is a regular dictionary of roads, well-indexed.—*N. O. Picayune*.

The many indexes give it a solid character as a book of reference.—*Worcester Spy*.

The indexes are a feature of the work, and the most complete and handy we ever saw with any published book.—*Cape Ann Breeze*.

All this mass of information has been placed within easy reach of the reader by an elaborate system of indexing.—*Lippincott's Magazine*.

The indexing has been most carefully done, and any subject, place, person or book mentioned may be instantly turned up.—*The Epoch, N. Y.*

The indexes, which are a complex system and need "a day off" to be mastered, endeavor to set the reader on the right road.—*St. Louis Post-Dispatch*.

Aside from its defects, the book is valuable, as the work of compilation and indexing appears to have been done conscientiously.—*San Francisco Chronicle*.

It has, what too few books are furnished with, an elaborate system of indexing, and it will undoubtedly be a *vade mecum* to all bicyclers.—*New Haven Palladium*.

It is all so cleverly indexed that the reader in two minutes can find out all about any particular place or thing which has a bicycling interest.—*San Francisco Argonaut*.

The elaborateness of its indexing shows that it is designed less for reading than for reference. The information wanted can be found at once if contained in the book at all.—*World Travel Gazette, N. Y.*

So wide is the scope of the work, we doubt if it be possible for the wheelman to select any cycling subject that he will not find properly indexed, with several references.—*Wheelmen's Record, Indianapolis*.

The admirable indexing of the work renders its information readily accessible,—an important consideration, inasmuch as it is as a book of reference that this volume will find its principal use.—*Boston Advertiser*.

As the book is intended as an encyclopædia of reference for wheelmen, the contents are indexed with especial care. This redeeming feature enables the reader to extract the kernel, which is excellent in its line, and likewise ensures to the author's mental and physical efforts, in connection with the bicycle, a wide-spread appreciation among certain classes.—*Alta California*.

I am perfectly astonished at the enormous amount of material included within its covers ; but more, at the skill, care and ingenuity of the indexing, which has rendered all this material practically available for reference purposes. Such cursory examination as I have found time to give the book has caused me a great deal of pleasure as well as information. If the accuracy and faithfulness shown in describing sections of the country with which I am familiar, are continued throughout the volume, the work will be indispensable to the touring wheelman,—even to one to whom the literary excellence is a minor consideration.—*L. W. Seely, Washington, D. C. (lawyer and tourist)*.

The side remarks and anecdotes will bear reading well for their literary value.—*Worcester Spy.*

It also holds the interest of the non-cycler who chances to come in contact with it.—*Louisville Commercial.*

Written in a very bright and clever style, it is a notable book, outside of its relations to the wheel.—*Buffalo Courier.*

There is a vast deal of this book that is of interest to the general reader as much as to the bicycler.—*Detroit Free Press.*

Will also greatly interest the general reader, touching, as it does, the "Undiscovered Country" in Literature.—*Bangor Commercial, Me.*

Despite these special features, the book contains a large amount of matter in which the general reader could take more or less interest.—*Cleveland Leader.*

Some chapters are very good reading for anybody, whether wheelman or not, although the author expresses a lofty scorn of literary excellence.—*Buffalo Express.*

There are several readable chapters, and the book has literary merit of rare quality, in spots. His individuality has asserted itself, and some of his literary excursions are exquisite.—*Hartford Courant.*

It gives a good deal of information concerning American roads; is crammed with statistics; and people who make long tours with horses will find it an excellent guide.—*Turf, Field & Farm, N. Y.*

The chapter-headings are sufficiently suggestive to awaken curiosity, and (aside from those devoted to record and detail) I venture to say there is not one but will interest even the general reader.—*St. Louis Spectator.*

As an encyclopædia of cycling, it deserves front rank among the books of the decade, while there is enough of general interest in it to attract the attention of a person who has no connection with the wheel.—*The Bicycle South, New Orleans.*

Even that composite person "the general reader," and the man who has never mounted, and never means to mount, the iron horse, may find in these pages information well worth possessing on many matters besides "shop."—*The Saturday Review, London.*

To many readers who might care little for the rest of the book, these two irrelevant chapters ("Curl" and "Castle Solitude"), together with the first ("On the Wheel"),—the only ones which have much literary merit,—would be worth the price of all.—*Boston Advertiser.*

I have not read it continuously, but have browsed over here and there with much interest and delight. There's an enduring literary quality and a certain unique flavor in parts of the book for many who will discover it, and I think the after-sales will stretch through the years. A good-sized volume could be condensed and separated from the encyclopædic parts, sometime, that should be ranked with Erasmus's "Praise of Folly" and Walton's "Complete Angler."—*Charles E. Pratt, author of "The American Bicycler."*

ECCENTRICITY.

An eccentric genius who gives the world his experiences on a wheel.—*Cleveland Leader.*

Those who enjoy thoroughly characteristic books will appreciate this one.—*Scientific American, N. Y.*

A unique book, which loses nothing of interest because it reflects the eccentricities of its author.—*Commercial Advertiser, N. Y.*

It is something of a literary curiosity, for much of the author's peculiar personality crops up in several places.—*The Bicycle South, New Orleans.*

The author is an eccentric genius, and every one of these 800 pages shows traces of his peculiar methods and ideas.—*Spirit of the Times, N. Y.*

The author is eccentricity personified, and his book is full of eccentric notions and ideas, but these raise it above dullness, and make it all the more interesting.—*L. A. W. Bulletin.*

The author is eccentric in more ways than one, and is not only his own publisher, but refuses to allow a publisher to handle his work in the ordinary way of business.—*Land & Water, London.*

Only a wheelman can understand how such a book came to be written ; but it serves a useful purpose, and its eccentric author will harm no one but himself should he publish the second volume, which he promises.—*The Times, N. Y.*

He thinks a great deal of himself and his performance, though not from the literary point of view, which he rather contemns, but from the financial point of view, which he has constantly before him, and against which nothing need be said.—*The Mail & Express, N. Y.*

The manner in which the author states that he does not intend to pay the slightest commission to agents, and endeavors to make his readers honorary canvassers for the sale of the precious volume, is very refreshing. It is about the coolest piece of impudence I have ever read. For cuteness in advertising the Yankees can give us fits.—*Athletic News, London.*

There is also an immense amount of discursive matter which any good editor would have cut out, and thus brought the volume within reasonable bounds. As it is, we have the author's opinions on a great variety of topics that have nothing to do with bicycling, and his opinions, as a rule, are neither profound nor pungent. There is also much clumsy humor of the German type.—*San Francisco Chronicle.*

All of this and more has he borne without flinching or halting in his determination to present to the world a book, not the product of a callow brain, rushed through printers' and binders' hands, just to oblige us scribblers of the press, but a work of such a kind as the world has never seen, and will not soon, if ever, again see duplicated, being, as it is, the result of years of constant thought and labor of a trained and scholarly mind, and written by a pen that is no prentice one. Long after the writer of these notes shall have passed away and been forgotten, the name and book of Karl Kron will remain as a work and author the like of which in their peculiar way do not elsewhere exist.—*" The Owl," in L. A. W. Bulletin, Boston.*

A veritable cycling encyclopædia, including more, and more diverse, information than was ever before crowded into one book. The author is an eccentric genius, and every one of these 800 pages shows traces of his peculiar methods and ideas. It is the best two dollars' worth ever offered to cyclists, and no wheelman can afford to be without a copy. Not the least curious feature of this remarkable book is the fact that, although named " 10,000 Miles on a Bicycle," and apparently appealing only to bicyclists, *it is really of especial value to all horsemen who drive for pleasure.* Its authentic and detailed information concerning the roads of the United States and Canada, is such as cannot be found elsewhere, and renders it a necessity for all who make pleasure tours on wheels or horseback.—*Spirit of the Times.*

It gives a good deal of information concerning American roads; is crammed with statistics; and people who make long tours with horses will find it an excellent guide.—*Turf, Field & Farm, N. Y.*

The author distinctly states that the book is for reference, and he does not expect the general public to read it. To the traveler, however (unless he go by train), the work would be valuable, as it contains records of distances and descriptions of roads and towns, together with much more like information which would be highly prized by any one intending to take an extended journey by wheel or carriage. The countries covered include Australia, America, Austria, France, Germany, India and many other parts of the world.—*New England Homestead, Springfield, Mass.*

The work is infinitely more than a personal narrative. It has over 200 contributors from all parts of the globe, and is a compendium of modern travel and general information.—*McGregor News, Ia.*

A work that no active bicyclists can afford to be without, as it contains an astonishing amount of information concerning roads, etc., applicable to every section of the country.—*Sporting Life, Philadelphia.*

A curious hodge-podge of a volume, but one containing in great profusion the sort of information wheelmen would naturally seek.—*Army & Navy Journal, N. Y.*

It presents minute descriptions of about 6000 miles of American highways, explored by the author in 24 States and Provinces. The mass of information is carefully indexed for ready reference.—*Book Chat, N. Y.*

The author is a cycler who has journeyed far and wide in his own country on the nickel-plated steed, and he has been careful to gather information for other riders. With this end in view his book is elaborately indexed.—*Philadelphia Times.*

Karl Kron is evidently a man who has not only traveled much but has also had his eyes open and his hands out of his pockets; and his book will tend to beget a similar condition in the young men who run across it. While he insists upon calling it a unique business enterprise, we think it is not difficult to detect in it traces of literary merit. It will surely be a valuable book to wheelmen and other travelers.—*University Chronicle, Mich.*

VERDICT OF THE METROPOLIS.

Karl Kron's journeys were made in familiar localities, and over routes most traveled by wheelmen. Any one of them intending similar trips would certainly profit by his experiences and descriptions of the routes and hotels, of the surface of the roads, and of their hills, etc. All such matters are set forth in detail most useful to those wishing such information, but, we grieve to say, most uninteresting to the general reader. Karl Kron gives a chapter to the cryptic building on Washington Square wherein was laid the scene of "Cecil Dreeme"; and no one can grudge the score of pages devoted to the humors and virtues of a companion of his boyhood, to wit, a bull-dog. This is the only portion of the book done with any literary skill. The rest is in excellent guide-book style, and derives its virtue from its correctness and its mass. Only a wheelman, and perhaps not even all that fraternity, can understand how such a book came to be written. But, being in existence, it serves a useful purpose, and its eccentric author will harm no one but himself should he publish the second volume, which he promises.—*The Times, N. Y.*

As regards its literary form, it is a rattling affair, the animal spirits of the writer bubbling well into the pages, with the pronoun of the first person thrust unsparingly forward. Two chapters of the book—one devoted to a biography of Curl, "My Bull Dorg, the very best dog whose presence ever blessed this planet" (to whose memory the book is dedicated), the other called "Castle Solitude in the Metropolis," and giving an account of life in the New York University Building—seem quite irrelevant to the volume's purpose and to be introduced without sufficient reason. For the most part, however, the book is packed with information of interest to wheelmen, collected, it is plain, with great labor and, so far as we can judge, accurate. Of especial interest is a biography of Thomas Stevens, beginning page 473, which all who read "Around the World on a Bicycle" will be glad to see. The chapters throughout are most frank and unconventional, and many a graphic passage occurs to relieve statistical detail. For the public it seeks it will be a handy volume, the shortcomings of which one feels disposed to overlook, since the compiler has been so hard working and good-natured.—*The Evening Post, N. Y.*

The author hardly traveled over more space in the making of his memorable journeys than his pen has traveled in the making of their records. If Karl Kron is an indefatigable traveler he is still more an indefatigable writer. He is a walking, or, one might rather say, a wheeling encyclopædia, and he imparts his information and the results of his observations on any and all subjects and places, with a prodigal impartiality that is superb. Mr. Kron, however, designs his book to serve for one of reference rather than as one for simple amusement. He is a careful observer and note taker, and to a man who desired to journey over the ground Mr. Kron had covered, this book would prove altogether indispensable.—*The Star, N. Y.*

The author has conveyed so much of his very marked and interesting personality into every page,—his reading and notes and views of men and things crop out so profusely,—the interest never flags.—*Scientific American.*

He has collected an immense body of information of interest to wheel-men. An enthusiast on the subject of bicycling, he has produced a work which ought to become a sort of *vade mecum* to all lovers of that exhilarating sport. It is, in reality, a gazetteer, a dictionary, a directory, a cyclopædia, and a statistical guide all in one. Besides what the author has to say about bicycling proper and its varied statistics, he finds space to speak about the politics of the wheel, the literature of the wheel, and the hotel question as it affects wheelmen.—*The Sun, N. Y.*

Doubtless the manual will be greatly sought after, not only by American wheelmen but by all "foreigners" bent on a tour in the States. It is certainly one of the biggest things on wheels ever attempted.—*Sporting Life, London.*

It comes first, last, and all the time under the class of writings which Lamb designated as "books which are not books," and which include direct-ories, dictionaries, reports of societies, and arid but bulky information of all sorts in regard to the mechanical arts and inventions. To criticise such pub-lications from a literary point of view would be absurd. One reason why we have not read the wordy lucubrations of Mr. Kron is that we are not particu-larly interested in the subject, and are not drawn to it by Mr. Kron's Preface, which is rather contemptuous respecting literary readers and literary critics. The defect of his writing is that it is altogether too business-like to be en-joyed by ordinary readers. That nine-tenths of these 800 pages will be let alone, we have no doubt, partly because they are unreadable, they are so dry, dull and prosaic.—*The Mail & Express, N. Y.*

We are convinced that the volume, when completed, will be one of the very most reliable and most readable books of travel that has ever been issued in connection with the sport. We feel confident that the work will justify our encomiums. It promises to be at once unique, useful and interesting.—*Tricycling Journal, London.*

The fact is, there is an enormous amount of information in the book, and we should think very great labor must have gone into its composition. The mere mention of the departments under which different subjects are treated of makes forty-one numbers. Happily it is not made for reading but for refer-ence. Nevertheless, the author does seem to believe, with amusing self-con-fidence, that people are actually going to peruse his enormous volume from beginning to end, if not for information, then for attractiveness of style.—*The Evening Telegram, N. Y.*

The advance sheets convince us that it will be a *sine quâ non* in the wheelman's library, possessing intrinsic interest of no mean order.—*Wheeling.*

Contains information to be highly prized by any one intending to take an extended journey by wheel or carriage. The countries covered include Australia, America, Austria, France, India, and many other parts of the world.—*New England Homestead, Mass.*

It will be many years before another work that even approximates "X. M. M." in value will ever be produced.—*Wheelmen's Record, Indianapolis.*

COMPREHENSIVENESS.

A remarkable encyclopædia. A monument of patience. A unique and curious book, which it is expected no bicyclist can possibly do without. Almost every subject that can possibly relate to the bicycle or its rider is here treated in gay and hilarious style, but with evident desire to be truthful and scientific in the treatment of facts. The effects of wheeling upon mind and body, the multifarious experiences, sensations, observations and studies of the writer on the highways and byways of the United States and elsewhere, the odd characters encountered, the literature of the bicycle, are well written. The mass of details has been arranged with skill, backed by enthusiasm and tireless patience. There may be some things of possible interest to devotees of the wheel omitted from this book; but if so, we have been unable to discover the omission. The number of slips of the pen and printer's mistakes, in this publication of about a million and a half words, is remarkably few. Despite fineness of type, the text is clear and easily read. For ourselves, "Coasting on the Jersey Hills" and "White Flannel and Nickel-Plate," were the chapters enjoyed most in the perusal of this book, which is emphatically one for the times.—*The Critic, N. Y.*

The chief characteristic of the volume is its comprehensiveness. Every step of the road over which the author has ridden is described with almost painful particularity. Nothing seems to have been too minute to escape his observation, or too insignificant to be undeserving of record. To Canadians, the most interesting portion will be the description of his experience in Canada, which he gives at great length. On the whole he speaks flatteringly of our country, and describes our roads as being on the average better than the main roads of the United States. The book is thoroughly practical, is well written, and must be of great value to wheeling tourists.—*Canadian Wheelman.*

Fortunately, there is a brighter side to the picture, which owes its brilliancy to individuals, rather than associations; and we should feel deeply grateful to such pioneers whose experiences on wheels have been brought under notice through the general press, as well as by means of their own publications. For example, both Thomas Stevens and Karl Kron have succeeded in making known the benefits to be derived from touring, and the hidden beauties of nature only within the reach of itinerant cyclists.—*Sewing-Machine & Cycle News, London.*

Decidedly the greatest value of the work lies in its last third part—compendium of routes, riders' journals. It may yet be made completer; but, even as it is, it shows pretty clearly what has been done in the sport. I am happy to be able to recommend the book as of a general interest and value for *that*, even alone.—*Hugh Callan, M. A. of Glasgow University, author of "Wanderings on Wheel and on Foot through Europe."*

Taking all things into consideration, we believe it will always hold the undisputed place of the first great work on the subject of cycling, bearing to all wheelmen that relation that Isaac Walton's Complete Angler bears to fishermen, the world over.—*Wheelmen's Gazette, Indianapolis.*

To American cyclists especially, we can understand that this book may be invaluable. Cyclists of all nations may get from it many useful "wrinkles" as to the choice and management of their velocipedes, the best kind of garment to wear when "in the saddle," the most opportune hours for refreshments, the most judicious selection of foods and drinks, and innumerable other details. As a book of reference as to the most judicious mode of traveling on wheels in America, the distances accomplished by the author and other eminent bicyclists, the best routes to be chosen, and a thousand other kindred matters, "Ten Thousand Miles on a Bicycle" will be found almost indispensable. Even that composite person, "the general reader," and the man who has never mounted and never means to mount the iron horse, may, if their eyesight be sufficiently strong, find in these detestably close-printed pages, information well worth possessing on many matters besides "shop." The author proclaims that he is a Yankee of the Yankees. We think that we should have guessed as much if he had not told us so. Sam Slick himself has no keener eye to business, but he is as honest as he is shrewd. With winning straightforwardness, he plainly tells us the scope of the book, and makes no false or undue pretensions of any kind. It is inexpressibly sad to think that so genial and kindly a philosopher should, by his own weak prejudice, or "by sour physician, be debarred the full fruition" of life which a moderate use of tobacco would give him on his journeys and at his resting places.— *The Saturday Review, London.*

Once again must the notice of cycling matters by a mighty organ of the press be chronicled. *The Saturday Review* of last week actually devoted two columns of its eminently conservative space to a notice of the book by Karl Kron. It even went so far as to quote twenty-four lines of his poetry, which, to say the least of it, was inadvisable, and almost rash. Still, when the mighty come down from their seats in this way, we groundlings must be grateful for small mercies. We progress, my masters.— *The Cyclist, Coventry.*

A close examination of the matter leads to the conviction that the work will stand as "the Domesday Book of Cycling." Karl Kron has not been contented with furnishing most vivid descriptions of cycling in the United States, about the hills, the lakes, the rivers, or cycling in one season only— spring, or summer, or autumn—but gives entrancing accounts of runs in winter; and then ravages the world to index the literature : books, maps, and papers. The history of every news journal is given, and an outline of every leading dispute now agitating the world of wheel riders. In pronouncing judgment upon many questions Karl Kron exhibits a very fine discrimination and an undoubtedly sound judgment; and his conclusions should commend themselves to the consideration of English cyclists. The story of his own adventures is written in admirable taste, and with much picturesqueness ; and the book will rank as a classic on cycling.— *Sewing-Machine & Cycle News.*

To the wheelmen of the world it appeals, its interests being in no way circumscribed by the limits of the American Continent.— *Wheeling, London.*

LAUDATION AT LONDON.

The Greek Kalends and Karl Kron's book were by many assumed to be synonymous, but the hope deferred has at length been fulfilled, and we are in possession of what may truly be called the first classic of cycling literature. Consisting of 900 pages, well and closely printed, the book offers a store of information which we shall not exaggerate by describing as simply marvelous. To the wheelmen of the world it appeals, its interests being in no way circumscribed by the limits of the American Continent.

To review this book is difficult, to find fault with it well-nigh impossible. It is what it purports to be, a description of ten thousand miles traveling by bicycle in the New World; and we venture to say that the reader who conscientiously examines its wonderful collection of facts and fancies will rise from his perusal with a knowledge of America, her roads and scenery, which no other book in existence will afford him.

There is many a noble thought nobly expressed in this book, with its bold originality of style and daring impudence of advertisement and egotism. Karl Kron is well read and entirely free from superficialism, a searcher after truth and a merciless prober of what he considers offenses. He is also possessed of a vein of smart American humor, which illuminates the dry text of his book from beginning to end. In places, such as the inimitable chapter devoted to his bull-dog " Curl," he soars to a pitch which reminds the reader very forcibly of Mark Twain and Max Adeler; and the cyclist who loves his dog will read this chapter over more times than once. To " Curl," whose noble and expressive features act as frontispiece, the book is dedicated, and there is a certain pathos in the selection.

" Ten Thousand Miles on a Bicycle " teems with valuable information, supplied in witty phraseology, and as a work of standard reference and exhaustive interest is likely to remain for many a day unrivaled. In addition to a literary taste, the book is distinctly appetizing from the mingled acridity and simplicity of its style. It is a really wonderful work, which we have no hesitation in saying will be the greatest work on cycling the world has seen. Beside its far-reaching interest, literary style and completeness of detail, the English work to which we have referred above [" Cycling," in the Badminton Library Series] sinks into insignificance; and in recommending our readers to buy the book, we suggest it not only to men who buy cycling literature as a matter of course, but also to the large division which reads no more than it can avoid. This is a good book, written and compiled by a clever man, and we hope it will be blessed with a very large circulation.—*Wheeling, London.*

An American paper (the *Athlete*, of Philadelphia) says that the general English verdict on Karl Kron's book is against it. This is not so. The book is a good book, well worth the money, and its only hostile critics are two men, one of whom has compiled a very onesided English book, while the other, it is rumored, is about to produce another. We believe this latter will be good, but common modesty should have prevented both men from laying themselves loose on poor Karl Kron.—*Wheeling, London.*

Qui s'excuse s'accuse, says a very ancient proverb, and we emphatically deny that an excuse, however fully made, is always an ample palliative for an offense. Mr. Lipski, who was recently executed for murder, would, doubtless, have made many excuses, but that would not have prevented the Home Secretary from permitting the law to take its course; and in exactly the same way we are of opinion that, though Karl Kron has offered apologies for the commission of every literary crime in the volume under notice, he must still be held responsible for them, despite his efforts to "hedge." As regards English cycling, English institutions, and English wheelmen, Karl Kron's remarks are necessarily wholly "hearsay." Had he drawn his information from many various sources, and brought the most ordinary common sense to bear upon the facts so obtained, he might perchance have succeeded in writing something worth reading. As it is, his comments upon English cycling matters are jaundiced and prejudiced caricatures, drawn apparently from one cycling publication, which has almost invariably taken the "wrong side" in every popular movement. With the single exception of the riding records, contributed by Englishmen, there is not one single item having reference to cycling matters on this side of the Atlantic which is not jaundiced and distorted by the medium through which Karl Kron has observed it. He complains that, "out of the half-million wheelmen in England, only two dozen have sent him personal statistics"; and we should say that, had but half that number sent him details,—provided always that the remaining dozen were *the best,*—his tables would be the more valuable. In the chapter devoted to "Long-distance Routes and Riders" we have a fine example of the want of selection, if we may so call it, which distinguishes our author. He has apparently printed at length anything that has been sent to him, and whilst some few of the accounts are of interest, others are not worthy of the space they occupy; in fact, with one or two exceptions, they are of no practical value at all. All Karl Kron's personal handiwork concerning English cycling is absolutely unreliable in any one particular, and prejudiced to the last degree— the work of a rabid partisan, written by one who does not possess the partisan's excuse, who is, in short, simply too careless, or too lazy, to attempt to ascertain the truth upon any one of the subjects upon which he dogmatizes. There are constant impertinencies showered upon "the Iliffes," and libelous attacks upon the C. T. C. Secretary, not to mention the thousand and one gibes and jokes against leading practical English cyclists. Such irretrievable nonsense as is solemnly quoted against the N. C. U., gives a sample of the spirit and style in which Karl Kron treats English institutions. Evidence of his animus as regards the firm of Messrs. Iliffe & Son is to be found in the "Literature of the Wheel" chapter, whose account of the cycling papers in England is utterly incorrect—outside the mere registry of birth, death or amalgamation—and is simply a prejudiced view without any basis of fact, the statement that the *Tricyclist* lost money for its proprietors being absolutely untrue.—*Bicycling News,* pub. by *Iliffe & Son (known as "the Coventry ring").*

COVENTRY RINGING THE CHANGES.

We have no prejudice against the author, no feeling against him individually, and it will be false in every way for a certain section of persons on
the other side of the Atlantic to assert that the opinion expressed in this
lengthy review is unfavorable because K. K. is an American. In conclusion,
after a careful and laborious perusal of the work, our views are these: As
regards practical cycling, it is of little value, the views advocated being the
views of a faddist of the worst order. As regards English cycling and all its
surroundings and concomitants, it is worse than useless, it is utterly misleading. Its driest statistics and most carefully elaborated details are vitiated by
an obvious bias, whilst its "facts" are in the main fictions, not always desti-
tute of malice. As a road book, it would prove of little service, owing to the
redundancy of personal details of the most microscopic interest, any decent
route book being more serviceable, inasmuch as the information would be
more easily obtained. The copious indices are decidedly over-elaborated, and
the lists of wheelmen will be obsolete in a twelvemonth. The book is fairly
well printed in absurdly small type, upon a poor and thin paper, and is as far
as English cyclists are concerned not worth the price. As a "thesaurus of
facts," Phillips's "Things a Cyclist Ought to Know," price one penny, is
infinitely more reliable, whilst in other respects, the work can only be regarded as an autobiography of a singularly self-sufficient mediocrity.—*Bicycling News, London weekly organ of " the Coventry ring," printers to the C. T. C.*

Having secured pledges from 3000 persons to take copies of his work,
he publishes it, and expects the 3000 to find him fresh customers, so as to
enable him to sell 30,000. From what we know of the matter we should say
he has spent much more in postage, printing, time and labor during the last
four years than the best and most enterprising firm of publishers would have
charged him for their services in putting the work in the market, and we feel
sure that if the proverb concerning the man who is his own lawyer be true, it
must equally apply to a man who, under such conditions as these, is his own
publisher. There would, however, have been, without doubt, one serious
drawback in this particular case, for no publisher who understood his business would have permitted his client to waste so much money on paper and
printing, for the work is best described in the words of Macbeth: "It is a
tale told by an idiot, full of sound and fury, signifying nothing."—*Land &
Water, London (article contributed by editor of the Bicycling News).*

I was soft enough not to become a subscriber to Karl Kron's work, and
I now immensely regret it, for I am simply amazed at the extent and interest
of the book. It appears to me to be far and away the best contribution to
wheel literature that the world has yet seen. Statistical and historical,
amusing and pathetic, it has charms for every reader, and is a monument of
the ability and indefatigable industry of its author. Karl Kron's "Ten Thousand Miles on a Bicycle," and his Bull-Dorg, will, I am confident, occupy a
prominent position in the history of the cycle. I would we had an English
Kron.—" *The Tyre," in Saturday Night, Birmingham, Eng.*

BRITISH FAIR-PLAY.

We deem it our duty to check any attempt at unjust criticism, and of this we have a glaring specimen in last week's papers. The article appearing in *Land & Water* is really on all fours with that appearing in the *Bi. News*. Both criticisms were penned by the same hand, and the sum and substance of each article savors more of decided abuse than fair comment, hidden hatred rather than professed friendship. What has the mode of publishing a book to do with its merits? Nothing, of course. The fact that there are already 3000 subscribers to this book, which this critic has attempted to condemn, reflects great credit upon the author's recognized ability and worth; therefore it is but right to assume that Karl Kron has the confidence of his subscribers,—purely owing to the merit of his work, whereby the subsequent demand for it may yet reach the desired number,—namely, 30,000. He has produced a volume entirely without aid, and it has met with success. For this his critic resorts to " Macbeth," in order to call him an idiot. His critic's joint work, in connection with the Badminton Book on Cycling, has had the advantage of hailing from the publishing house of Messrs. Longmans, Green & Co.; yet, with this great start off, we venture to assert that Karl Kron's book has enjoyed, and will continue to enjoy, greater popularity than that with which his critic's name is associated. It is the old story. Two men have fought for literary success. In this case Karl Kron has won, whilst his critic has lost, and that with ill-conceived grace and consequent mortification. Probably he will live to see the day when he will wish he could retract his charge (under cover of " Macbeth ") of idiotcy against Karl Kron's labors.—*Sewing-Machine & Cycle News, London.*

Several correspondents have written us, drawing contemptuous attention to the attacks upon Karl Kron's book made by the editor of a contemporary. We think the critic in question would have consulted his own dignity better by remembering that he was associated with the publication of another somewhat similar volume, especially as he has to descend to the exposition of such *minutiæ* as the printing of the word " Hinchcliffe " with a " k." If the paper the book is printed on is thin, so is the spirit of this critic.— *Wheeling, London.*

Among the many favorable notices of the book, which have reached us, is the following from Mr. R. P. Hampton Roberts: " It is certainly a wonderful storehouse of information, and we have had something worth reading for our long waiting. I hope that Karl Kron will reap some pecuniary advantage in a large sale, in order to repay him for the years of labor he has expended over the work." Mr. H. R. Goodwin, of Manchester, writes us and says: " It is far in advance of what I expected it to be, and very well worth the present price of 8s. 8d." Mr. J. W. Webster, of Dublin, also writes : " Certainly it was well worth waiting the extra time, for, even after a hasty glance at it, one could not help being pleased with it in every respect. Please offer my name again as a subscriber for his ' 2 X. M.' which he purposes publishing. I sincerely hope he will get all the support he deserves."—*Wheeling, London, independent organ of the trade; opposed to " the Coventry ring."*

APPRECIATION AT THE ANTIPODES.

Karl Kron—of whom, I should say, nearly every cyclist this side of the grave has either read or heard about—appears to have more faith in human nature than any dozen people living. He spent upwards of four years of his time—and a good many dollars besides—in writing and compiling a book on cycling, which, for quantity of matter and reference, is not alone unique, but prodigious; and he hopes to sell 30,000 copies of it, a fifth of that number having been already issued. May he succeed! This monument of cycling must stand; and, if succeeding generations are not cyclists, why, it's no fault of their predecessors.—"*The Hub*," *in Australian Cycling News, Melbourne.*

There is no doubt that whatever has been said in way of praise of this book, by the wheel literature of the world, is well merited. I have before occasionally alluded to it, when advance sheets have reached me, and my readers will be well aware by this time of its value not only as a work of reference, but as a means of instruction, amusement and information. In its review of the clubs of the world, reference is made to those in N. Z., and I notice several local names amongst the contributors of wheel statistics. To those who take an interest in cycling, or to the general reader, I recommend "10,000 Miles on a Bi." as a valuable work.—*New Zealand Referee.*

"Ten Thousand Miles on a Bicycle" has at last arrived here in Australia; and, at a cursory glance through its pages, one is repaid for his patience in waiting for its arrival. It is a creditable work, and one which will commend itself to all wheelmen.—*Melbourne cor.* ("*Arabic*"), *in Irish Cyclist & Athlete, Dublin.*

I am astounded at its completeness and its details, and can readily see the four years' work spent therein. There is a great deal in it, you will admit, that will not in any way interest an Australian; but even if all that be passed by, there will still remain more than enough for our money. I may say that the style in which it is written is so interesting and concise (not forgetting the humor as well) that it makes the reading positively distinct from any other cycling literature. It is very different from what I expected to peruse. Several of the pages it did my heart good to read.—*Geo. R. Broadbent, Melbourne, whose six years' riding record, to Oct. 3, '87, was 31,620 miles.*

We have no hesitation in stating that, from a literary point of view, his book is certain to prove both readable and a success.—"*Ollapod,*" *in Melbourne Bulletin.*

The pages bear the impress of a clever pen, and speak volumes for the untiring energy and intellectual capacity of the author.—*Aust. Cycling News.*

The "Australian Cycling News" was revived August 11, 1887, under the editorship of F. J. Llewelyn, and is published in Melbourne every alternate Thursday, at 5 Collins st., West. It is mailed to any part of the world for fifty cents a quarter; and subscriptions at that rate, which may be sent to the Publisher of "Ten Thousand Miles on a Bicycle," will be duly forwarded without charge or commission. The first series of the "News" was published continuously as a fortnightly, from May 11, 1882, to Sept. 25, 1886, and is fully described in the book.

TWO WAYS OF LOOKING AT IT.

Whatever interest this book may have for the 3000 subscribers who have their names printed in the place usually assigned to the index, it will have small interest for the general reader. The author is eminently bumptious; he disregards the ordinary method of bookmaking, and follows a plan of his own. He is a man of one idea, and that idea sticks out in his story to the exclusion of everything else. Though he has ridden 10,000 miles on a bicycle, he has not traveled ten honest miles with his understanding. The bicyclers have queer literary tastes, and possibly they may like this sort of literature, but it is all Dutch to the man who does his traveling on two feet instead of two wheels. Why on earth this self-conceited son of genius has put the story of his senseless wanderings through America into 908 pages, of which the type is so small that you must put on eyeglasses to read it, is beyond one's guess. The text reminds one of the young man who could boast that he had ascended every mountain in the United States, but when you asked him anything about them, he could only say that he climbed this one in so many hours, and that one in so many other hours, but entirely forgot when he was on top to look around, because he was in such a hurry to descend and climb the next one. For absolute stupidity, even to bicyclers, this volume must take the prize as being one of the most worthless volumes ever written. It is the work of an idiot, not of a sane man. The only sign of common sense is shown in the beautiful portrait of Karl Kron's favorite bull-dog, to whose memory the book is aptly dedicated. More rubbish was never more closely compacted into small space.—*Boston Herald.*

Our best recommendation of this work is to say that we find it very hard to convey any idea of its variety to a short notice. The author has conveyed so much of his very marked and interesting personality into every page, his reading and notes and views of men and things crop out so profusely, the interest never flags. Though ostensibly devoted to an account of ten thousand miles made on his 'cycle, "No. 234," it is an *olla podrida* of endless variety. The matter contained cannot be estimated by the number of pages. The small and exceedingly clear type makes it contain the substance of three or four volumes of respectable size. His accidents with his machine, from his first ride of one rod, resulting in a broken elbow and damaged machine, the cost of which ride he puts at $234, to the entanglement with a tow rope on the canal path and the runaway of the mules with the 'cycle, are all graphically told and described at length. Chapters on other long-distance riders, a list of the original 3000 subscribers to the book (copartners he calls them) and a variety of other matter are included. Those who enjoy thoroughly characteristic books will appreciate the one under review. Exhaustive indexes of persons and things are contained also.—*Scientific American, N. Y.*

It gives a good deal of information concerning American roads; is crammed with statistics; and people who make long tours with horses will find it an excellent guide.—*Turf, Field & Farm, N. Y.*

The best two dollars' worth ever offered to cyclists.—*Spirit of the Times.*

OFFICIALLY RECOMMENDED.

The book is not one to be read through from beginning to end. It is an encyclopædia of reference, and as such it is a valuable addition to literature. Karl Kron has given several years of his life and much of his money to the completion of this work, and it credits him to a great degree. The author is eccentricity personified, and his book is full of eccentric notions and ideas, but these raise it above dullness and make it all the more interesting. The collection of his wandering essays between two covers makes a valuable book and one well worth the price asked for it. The book is cheap at $2. We should want it in our library, and should have it there, if we had to pay $5 for it. We hope that every League member will see his way clear to the purchase of the book, and we will guarantee that he will be satisfied with his outlay.—*L. A. W. Bulletin, Boston, weekly official organ of the League of American Wheelmen.*

If we expect a story-book, we shall be disappointed, just as Bill Nye was in Webster's Unabridged Dictionary, "because it was too wordy and lacked plot." But the best way to find a standpoint for judging a book is to read its preface, and see what the author has given us a right to expect. In the present case, he promises portions of a narrative nature and portions intended solely for reference. As a matter of convenience, then, let us arbitrarily divide his book into reading-chapters and reference-chapters. The former are in charming style, and throw a great deal of light upon the inside of cycling subjects. Summing the matter up, we find 244 pages thus devoted to narrative. This in itself is a good-sized book.

It must not be supposed, however, that the rest of the book is unreadable. We only urge that the reference-chapters must be read with an index to be read with interest or profit.

If the reader is interested in any particular subject, he has only to look at the index, find his subject and reference, and proceed to enlighten himself. So wide is the scope of the work, we doubt if it be possible for the wheelman to select any cycling subject that he will not find properly indexed with several references. Thus, by reading according to subjects, the reader who uses his index, will find a great deal to interest and instruct him in the chapters that have been frequently pronounced the most dry and tedious. There is a vast fund of information within some of these closely-printed statistical pages, and no one can expect to get it out by the same methods that he would use in extracting the few sparse ideas from a French novel. "This Book of Mine, and the Next" is a chapter that may be read with interest, as telling how the volume grew from 300 to 900 pages, and what the author plans for the future.

Taking all things into consideration, strong and weak points alike, we believe that the author has most faithfully kept his promise and that "Ten Thousand Miles on a Bicycle" will always hold the undisputed place of the first great work on the subject of cycling, bearing to all wheelmen that relation that Isaac Walton's Complete Angler bears to fishermen, the world over. —*Wheelmen's Record, Indianapolis, official organ Ind. and Ill. Divs. L. A. W.*

EAST, WEST AND SOUTH.

It contains much that is interesting, more that is valuable,—to the tourist,—some that is tedious in its detail, and a great' deal that makes one laugh. Although we as well as many others have chaffed K. K. a good deal, we must admit that his book is well worth the money asked for it, and should be owned by every wheelman.—*Bicycling World, Boston.*

To say that we are highly pleased is only putting it mild. It is a most valuable work of cycling information, and should be found in the library of every wheelman who has interest enough in the sport to want to know about roads and other wheelmen. The cyclist who has the means, and won't afford himself a copy of this gazetteer of American roads, is too small to be called a wheelman. One feature of the book which particularly strikes our attention, is the author's impartiality towards all makes of machines. He favors none and suppresses none. This alone should commend itself to all honest friends of "the wheel." We consider that we were in luck to get so valuable a volume for so small an outlay.—*Star Advocate, East Rochester, N. H.*

A handsomely bound book, which every one should read, for it is worth its weight in gold to every rider. It is the best bicycle-book published, and contains valuable road information, besides many other things interesting to riders of both sexes. Every wheelman should have it. The price ($2) is very small, considering the bulk.—*L. A. W. Pointer, Oshkosh, Wis.*

It is so seldom nowadays that we find manifestations of over-conscientiousness, that we are apt to misconstrue their outward symptoms. But it is developed in a limited few, nevertheless. This commendable fault, as it might be termed, is the one striking characteristic of Karl Kron. He is over-conscientious. If, when he completed his asked-for list of 3000 subscribers, he had rushed a hastily and ill-prepared work on to the market, it would have been taken as a matter of course. He would only have been following the example of nine-tenths of contemporary publishers. As it was, he did nothing by halves. He investigated the most insignificant facts, and went into the minutest details of everything he touched upon (and he touches on about every subject in the past and present history of American bicycling). This he did at an endless expenditure of time and labor, which we know will not be appreciated by one-fourth of those who read the book. But the result is a book that will live and continue to be standard authority on such matter as it treats of, for a long time to come.—*Wheelmen's Record, Indianapolis.*

It is not a book to take up and read through for amusement, but, as an encyclopædia of cycling and history of the wheel, it deserves front rank among the books of the decade. As a directory of roads, men and places, it would be invaluable to one contemplating a tour; while there is enough of general interest to attract the attention of a person who has no connection with the wheel. We fear it will never become a popular book, with the mass of wheelmen, or, at least, that the author will never find enough remuneration in its publication to pay him for the many years of labor and patient attention to detail he has given it.—*The Bicycle South, New Orleans.*

(V)

FUN FOR PENNSYLVANIANS.

Do Pennsylvanians want "something funny"? Then let them buy and read "Ten Thousand Miles on a Bicycle." Why? Because the *Philadelphia Press* calls it "the most ridiculous book of the season, full of rank egotism and nonsense," and says "there is not the faintest reason why any one should buy or read it." Another Philadelphia paper, the *American Athlete* (edited by a man whose "removal for malfeasance" from a high office in the L. A. W. is recorded, in official language, without comment, on p. lxxxiv. of the book) declares that this opinion of the *Press* "just about sizes it up. The general opinion seems to be that the work is a dismal failure. There is no demand for it either from wheelmen or the public. The large portion of it has been standing so long as to be entirely out-of-date and therefore worth-less; there are many glaring inaccuracies in the statistics; and the road-reports made by Karl himself are wofully inaccurate and misleading." The *Philadelphia Times* calls it "an odd and cranky specimen of bookmaking, though useful to wheelmen." The *Bicycling World*, of Boston, says it "contains much that is interesting, and a great deal that makes one laugh." "For absolute stupidity, even to bicyclers" (asserts the *Boston Herald*,—whose use of "even" shows that all bicyclers are to be despised as the stupidest of mortals), "this volume must take the prize, as being one of the most worthless volumes ever written. It is the work of an idiot, not of a sane man."

If these 958 pages really are "idiocy and rank nonsense," they certainly ought to supply at least two dollars' worth of fun to any investigator. They are handsomely bound in blue and gilt, and they will be sent, boxed and prepaid, to any town in Pennsylvania, on receipt of price by the Publisher, KARL KRON, *at the University Building, Washington Square, New York City, D.*

An American paper (the *Athlete*, of Philadelphia) says that the general English verdict on Karl Kron's book is against it. This is not so. The book is a good book, well worth the money, and its only hostile critics are two men, one of whom has compiled a very onesided English book, while the other, it is rumored, is about to produce another. We believe this latter will be good, but common modesty should have prevented both men from laying themselves loose on poor Karl Kron.—*Wheeling, London.*

His short description of Mr. Thomas Stevens's ride is far more readable than the elaborations of "Around the World on a Bicycle."—*Pall Mall Gazette, London.*

With the great American road-rider, the reader wanders at random from Maine to the Mammoth Cave and from New York to the Mississippi, and takes an occasional spin into the provinces or whirls over the coral reefs of Bermuda.—*Louisville Commercial.*

You have made the book so large, and the type so small, that it will be used, it seems to me, only as a matter of reference. If you had made it into about six volumes, with larger print, I should have enjoyed it better; and still better if you had boiled the whole thing down into one volume of coarse print.—*A. A. Pope, Boston, President of the Pope Mfg. Co.*

THE STORY OF STEVENS.

What sort of a man was he who pushed a bicycle round the world? Too modest a man to print any personal details in his book; but all may be found in "Ten Thousand Miles on a Bicycle."

Of especial interest is a biography of Thomas Stevens, beginning p. 473, which all who read "Around the World on a Bicycle" will be glad to see. —*The Nation, N. Y.*

His first volume of that name tells only of the tour from California to Persia. Chapters for the second volume, giving his adventures in Afghanistan, India, China and Japan, appear each month in "Outing"; but a summary of the whole tour may be found in "Ten Thousand Miles on a Bicycle."

The story of Thomas Stevens's wheel around the world is graphically described, and in the words of the renowned tourist himself.—*Cape Ann Breeze.*

His short description of Mr. Thomas Stevens's ride is far more readable than the elaborations of "Around the World on a Bicycle." It is to be regretted there are not many such readable passages in the book which Mr. Karl Kron has not only written, but printed, published and advertised, and undertaken the sales of, with an industry worthy of a better cause.—*Pall Mall Gazette, London.*

The above false praise, from a lying and mean-spirited attack on Stevens's most entertaining book, is here reprinted by the Publisher, as a preface to the remark that said book is recommended in the highest terms by "Ten Thousand Miles on a Bicycle" (see pp. xcvi., 483, 655), as well as by the chief newspapers of the world.

It is a difficult matter to get a book reviewed by the *Times*, but on Oct. 18th this paper devoted a column and a quarter to Thomas Stevens's account of his ride round the world, and a paragraph to Karl Kron's work. The *Times* praises Stevens's book, but is not very complimentary to Karl Kron's. —*Wheeling, London.*

Do you wish to compare Stevens's tour with the greatest ones taken by German, French and Australian wheelmen? Then consult the long-distance chapters in "Ten Thousand Miles on a Bicycle."

It gives brief accounts of Thomas Stevens's great ride, and the trips of many other long-distance wheelmen, and tells of Canadian and foreign roads and riders.—*Hartford Evening Post.*

Interesting statements about Thomas Stevens and other long-distance tourists.—*Wheelmen's Record, Indianapolis.*

I would much rather undertake to ride ten thousand miles on a rail, not to speak of a bicycle, than to write such a book as this, containing 800 pages of upwards of 800 words each. It contains the complete literature of bicycling, and I know not what else besides. It is a monument of patience and energy only to be compared with Webster's Dictionary, or the Great Pyramid. There is a great deal of entertaining as well as instructive and useful reading in it. Of course I have not read a fortieth part of it. Nobody ever will or can. But everybody who owns, or means to own, a bicycle will read some of it, to his undoubted pleasure and profit.—*The Bookmart, Pittsburg, Pa.*

RECOGNITION BY THE L. A. W.

Do the officers of the L. A. W. think the Publisher deserves any reward for investing $12,000 in the circulation of an elaborate electioneering document in their behalf? If so, let each of them put up $2 for "Ten Thousand Miles on a Bicycle," and persuade his friends to do likewise.

We hope that every League member will see his way clear to the purchase of the book, and we will guarantee that he will be satisfied with his outlay. The book is cheap at $2. We should want it in our library, and should have it there, if we had to pay $5 for it.—*L. A. W. Bulletin, Boston, official weekly organ of the League of American Wheelmen.*

Do the officers of the L. A. W. think the Publisher helped their prosperity by helping expose the hollowness of a privately-owned London trading concern, which attempted to usurp their functions? Then let them help advertise and circulate "Ten Thousand Miles on a Bicycle."

The addenda gives a clear and impartial statement of the late difficulties in the League, resulting in the removal of the Secretary-Editor; also particulars of the theft of the L. A. W. badge by the C. T. C.—*Wheelmen's Record.*

To any one who takes an interest in the history of the wheel and the League, the book is invaluable.—*The Bicycle South, New Orleans.*

Do the officers and members of the L. A. W. wish to be informed as to its origin, its struggles and achievements? Do they wish to have at hand, for ready reference, a summary of its several constitutions and modes of government, a statement of its treaties with the railroads, a list of its officers from the outset, and statistics of the growth of membership? Then let each of them add to his library "Ten Thousand Miles on a Bicycle."

The 36th chapter contains a history of the League and of every cycling association of a legislative and protective nature in the world. I used to think I was as well posted as the average cyclist on these questions; but, after reading advance sheets of the foregoing, I find that what I knew would not have filled a dozen pages, while what I did not know Karl Kron uses 38 closely filled ones in telling me.—*"The Owl," in L. A. W. Bulletin.*

Does any one wish to know the ages of League officers, tourists, and other prominent wheelmen? The birthdays of nearly 100 of them are starred in the index of "Ten Thousand Miles on a Bicycle."

It contains a great amount of information about the roads in the Eastern part of the country, dips into League politics, and tells of many other matters of a statistical nature of interest to wheelmen. But if wheelmen or others open the book with the expectation of finding much entertaining reading in the 675,000 words within the binding they will be disappointed. Still, considering the vast amount of work which it plainly has taken to bring the book out, it is well worth the price, $2.—*Hartford Evening Post.*

Taking all things into consideration, we believe it will always hold the undisputed place of the first great work on the subject of cycling, bearing to all wheelmen that relation that Isaac Walton's Complete Angler bears to fishermen, the world over.—*Wheelmen's Gazette, Indianapolis.*

"CO-OPERATIVE TAILORING" AND TOURING.

For complete exposition of the London "C. T. C.," and list of "the council-ors" employed in upholding its owner, who was dismissed from court as a self-con-fessed forger (by Mr. Justice Wills, Nov. 22, 1886), see "Ten Thousand Miles on a Bicycle." Mailed postpaid to any part of Great Britain on receipt of 8s. 8d.

This book on bicycling is the most thorough that any recreative sport has ever had published. It is in reality a gazetteer,—an encyclopædia on wheels, so to speak,—and contains every fact worth knowing. As the first genuine classic for wheelmen, it should be in every bicycler's book-case.— *Boonville Advertiser, Mo.*

Humors of collegiate velocipeding in 1869, condensed from contemporary rec-ords. See "Ten Thousand Miles on a Bicycle." (The chapter called "Bone-Shaker Days," giving careful details of the evolution of the modern bicycle from the véloce of '69 and its predecessor of 1819, will be mailed separately for 25 cents.)

Contains pretty much everything which has been said, or can be said, about wheels and wheelmen.—*Baltimore American.*

For reports from English, Scotch and Irish tourists; for annual mileage records from clergymen, lawyers, and business men in Great Britain and Aus-tralia, as well as Canada and the United States, see "Ten Thousand Miles on a Bicycle."

This is a pretty large contract, but in a great many respects it has been fulfilled. The book has distinct value to bicyclers as giving a mass of in-formation about roads, distances, hotels, etc., etc.—*The Epoch, N. Y.*

For racing-rules in the United States, Canada, England, Ireland, France, Germany, Australia and New Zealand, see "Ten Thousand Miles on a Bicycle."

He has done his work faithfully and written a book which the wheelmen needed. Probably that was all he intended to do. He deserves credit ac-cordingly.—*Buffalo Express.*

For reports from the "Big Four" and "Down East" touring parties of 1883-6, see "Ten Thousand Miles on a Bicycle."

We have read with great pleasure this elegantly bound work, whose author and publisher has done so much to promote cycling in this country.— *Bangor Commercial, Me.*

For history of the English "National Cyclists' Union," and the similar gov-erning bodies of several other countries, see "Ten Thousand Miles on a Bicycle."

It has assumed enormous dimensions, and needs only to be seen to be appreciated. It is a complete encyclopædia of wheeling progress, and no man fond of a bicycle can well afford to be without it.—*East End Signal, Cleveland, O.*

For testimony of local English sufferers, against the "danger-board hotels" of the London "C. T. C.," consult "Ten Thousand Miles on a Bicycle."

We most cordially recommend it as a valuable guide and aid to the tour-ing wheelman, and all others seeking knowledge of routes and distances in the vast extent of territory the volume covers.—*Cape Ann Breeze.*

One of the biggest things on wheels ever attempted.—*Sporting Life.*

A FIVE DOLLAR BOOK FOR TWO DOLLARS.

The enormous risk incurred by the Publisher in putting so low a price as $2 upon a volume which would retail for at least $5, if sold through the ordinary methods of the book-trade, can only be justified by an unprecedented sale. Do wheelmen wish to see "Ten Thousand Miles on a Bicycle" have greater vogue than the representative book of any other sport? Then let each buyer exhibit it to his acquaintances, and help to secure its purchase by the local libraries.

Whatever may be said of Karl Kron's intelligence and personal peculiarities, his business-faculty is abnormally small, as it quite often is with literary men. His book will be a failure unless every wheelman in the land subscribes for it.—*N. Y. cor. of American Wheelman, St. Louis.*

Kron has given us more pork for our $2 than we want. Larger print and less matter would have been more popular with the average reader. But I enjoy the book—parts of it—and I propose to do all I can to help him to a fat pocket, for his labor in the interest of wheeling.—*Little Rock cor. American Wheelman, St. Louis.*

Pretty or ugly, dry or entertaining (the book is all of these), fraternal sympathy should send the hand of every wheelman in the land down into his pocket, for the sake of a hard-working, self-sacrificing historian like Karl Kron.—*"Phœnix," in American Athlete, Philadelphia.*

His perseverance is of the heroic order, and it should certainly meet with ample reward. So we say to every wheelman, Do all you can to help the visionary enthusiast who has lost two good years working out an idea, which was solely based on "love of sport" at the outset, but on the financial success of which now depends a wheelman's future welfare.—*The Wheel, N. Y.*

We have not read the wordy lucubrations of Mr. Kron. The ground over which he wheeled and whirled himself abounds in picturesque and romantic scenery, but it might as well have lain in the midst of a desert for any use that he has made of it in his descriptions. He is lavish, however, in indices. There is a General Index, an Index of Places, an Index of Persons, a *catalogue raisonné* of Literature of the Wheel, a list of his Three Thousand Subscribers, a Dictionary of Wheelmen and a Trade Directory. We have thus a thesaurus of facts, a statistical guide, a cyclopædia, a dictionary and a gazetteer—in a word (or rather in eight hundred pages), a "book which is *not* a book."—*The Mail & Express, N. Y.*

But out it is at last, and, like a dinner made all the more acceptable from a long wait, its contents are eagerly devoured by the cycler. The descriptions of the author's rides are sometimes amusing and thrilling. Often, however, he falls into prolixity. The pages of this book, whose ponderosity shows the extent of the sport, are like the roads written of—some very good, some only passable and some bad. Of the latter there are not many, and to the skilful reader, like the skilful rider, the badness may all disappear before they are finished.—*St. Louis Post-Dispatch.*

A book of American roads for men who travel upon the bicycle. Its ideal is that of a statistical guide, a thesaurus of facts.—*Minneapolis Tribune.*

REWARD WANTED: $60,000.

Do wheelmen think the Publisher deserves any recompense for bringing out what the "Boonville Advertiser" calls "the most thorough book that any recreative sport has ever had published"? Then let them buy "Ten Thousand Miles on a Bicycle," and help him make the phenomenal sale of 30,000 copies requisite for its success. This is the straight tip.

In view of the great quantity of matter here condensed and classified, the picture of the bull-dog which embellishes the first page, would seem to be a fitting emblem of the perseverance with which the author has pushed to completion his three years' task. Starting with a less comprehensive plan, which he thought would occupy him about six months, he constantly found new wants to satisfy and new material to work up, until, tired with laborious writing, his right arm gave out and he was forced to learn to drive his pen with his left! Such devotion should not go unrewarded, and the wheel-loving public, surely, will repay their earnest, thorough and competent chronicler for his pains, by extending to this compact cyclopædia of their sport a hearty welcome.—*Boston Advertiser.*

The Publisher has staked $1,000 on an attempt to prove the falsity of the following expert opinion, written to him by the present Secretary-Editor of the League (Jan. 23, 1884): "Experience will show you that, no matter how much the bicyclers may howl for a thing, they fail to come to time when asked to pay for it." Do wheelmen wish to see this imputation of penuriousness removed most impressively? Then let them pay promptly for 30,000 copies of "Ten Thousand Miles on a Bicycle."

The cyclist who has the means, and won't afford himself a copy of this gazetteer of American roads, is too small to be called a wheelman.—*Star Advocate.* This is a notable book for many reasons, but chiefly, perhaps, in showing what tremendous perseverance and powers of application can reside in one man.—*Yale Literary Magazine.* It is a monument of patience and energy only to be compared to Webster's Dictionary or the Great Pyramid.—*The Bookmart, Pittsburg, Pa.*

An enormous volume, filled with the good things the cycler so delights to read, time and again, with never-failing interest. It should find a ready sale.—*Louisville Commercial.*

If ever any man deserved to reap the reward of perseverance, it is this publisher.—*The Cyclist, Coventry, Eng.* We really consider the wonderful perseverance and tenacity of purpose displayed by the author deserve rewarding.—*Irish Cyclist & Athlete.* He deserves to get on, for he has pertinacity enough for twenty men.—*Wheel Life, London.* His pertinacity is undying.—*C. T. C. Gazette, London.* Men may come and go; championships be won; reputations made and shattered; but still Karl Kron worries on.—*Wheeling, London.* He is now exercising all that perseverance and enterprise so peculiar to Americans.—*New Zealand Referee.* These three years of solid work have been well spent. The pages speak volumes for the untiring energy and intellectual capacity of the author.—*Australian Cycling News.*

SENDING BOOKS "ON APPROVAL."

Any one who holds or has held the office of "consul," or a higher office, in the L. A. W. or C. W. A.; any librarian, clergyman, lawyer, physician, dentist, journalist, merchant, government employee or college graduate; any citizen of legal age whose application shall be recommended by one of my "copartners" or a later buyer of the book, may sign and forward the appended application-form, and the request will be promptly attended to.

If applications reach me from Canada, I shall order duty-paid books to be forwarded by my Montreal agent (A. T. Lane, of 1421 St. Catherine st.), so that no further customs charge can be levied on them. Applications from any colony in Australia may be sent to my agent in Victoria (W. J. Parry, of Wills st., Sandhurst); but such senders should substitute his name for mine, and also "8s. 8d.," "1s.," and "7s. 8d.," in place of $2, 20 cents and $1.80.

To Karl Kron, at the University Building, New York City, D.

Dear Sir :—I wish to buy a copy of "Ten Thousand Miles on a Bicycle," provided a month's examination shall cause me to approve it, as worth the $2 charged. I therefore enclose 20 cents in postage-stamps, to cover the cost of sending me a specimen, and I will immediately acknowledge its arrival by mailing to you a postal-card inscribed as follows : "HAVING THIS DAY RECEIVED THE BOOK, WHOSE DELIVERY CHARGE OF 20 CENTS I PAID YOU FOR IN ADVANCE, I AGREE TO WRITE YOU ANOTHER LETTER, WITHIN A MONTH FROM DATE, AND EITHER ENCLOSE $1.80 IN FULL PAYMENT, OR ELSE NOTIFY YOU THAT I HOLD THE VOLUME (IN AS UNSOILED CONDITION AS WHEN RECEIVED) FOR RESHIPMENT AT YOUR ORDER." [Here sign and date the duplicate form retained.]

As regards the latter alternative, I agree to pack the book in the same pasteboard box or tin corners which enclosed it on its arrival, to re-wrap and label it as directed, and to mail you a report of my disposal of it, in one of the following forms : (1) "I ENCLOSE RECEIPT OF THE EXPRESS COMPANY, SHOWING THAT THE BOOK HAS BEEN PREPAID TO DESTINATION REQUESTED IN YOUR LETTER WHICH SENT ME 15 CENTS FOR THAT PURPOSE ;" *or else :* (2) "I THIS DAY DEPOSITED IN THE POST-OFFICE THE BOOK HELD BY ME AT YOUR ORDER, AFTER ATTACHING THERETO THE PREPAID LABEL WHICH YOU SENT ME WITH 17 CENTS IN POSTAGE STAMPS APPENDED ;" *or else :* (3) "I THIS DAY HANDED THE BOOK TO MR. ――――, AS REQUESTED IN YOUR LETTER, AND TOOK HIS RECEIPT THEREFOR."

I also agree that, in case of removal from town (after giving a "hold-at-disposal" notice, without receiving any "directions for disposal" in return), I will notify you either that I hold the book at my new residence, or else that I have arranged with a friend to obey your directions at the first-named town.

Finally, I declare that I have signed and dated a duplicate of this present application-form, and that, when I send you a postal-card acknowledging the arrival of book, I will write the date of said card upon said duplicate, at the end of its first paragraph, and will file the duplicate in the book, as a reminder of the date when the month's loan thereof expires.

[Name, address, and date to be written below. Prepay by 2-cent stamp.]

Any one who holds or has held the office of "consul," or a higher office, in the L. A. W. or C. W. A.; any librarian, clergyman, lawyer, physician, dentist, journalist, merchant, government employee or college graduate; any citizen of legal age whose application shall be recommended by one of my "copartners" or a later buyer of the book, may sign and forward the appended application-form, and the request will be promptly attended to.

If applications reach me from Canada, I shall order duty-paid books to be forwarded by my Montreal agent (A. T. Lane, of 1421 St. Catherine st.), so that no further customs charge can be levied on them. Applications from any colony in Australia may be sent to my agent in Victoria (W. J. Parry, of Wills st., Sandhurst); but such senders should substitute his name for mine, and also "8s. 8d.," "1s.," and "7s. 8d.," in place of $2, 20 cents and $1.80.

To Karl Kron, at the University Building, New York City, D.

Dear Sir :—I wish to buy a copy of "Ten Thousand Miles on a Bicycle," provided a month's examination shall cause me to approve it, as worth the $2 charged. I therefore enclose 20 cents in postage-stamps, to cover the cost of sending me a specimen, and I will immediately acknowledge its arrival by mailing to you a postal-card inscribed as follows : "HAVING THIS DAY RECEIVED THE BOOK, WHOSE DELIVERY CHARGE OF 20 CENTS I PAID YOU FOR IN ADVANCE, I AGREE TO WRITE YOU ANOTHER LETTER, WITHIN A MONTH FROM DATE, AND EITHER ENCLOSE $1.80 IN FULL PAYMENT, OR ELSE NOTIFY YOU THAT I HOLD THE VOLUME (IN AS UNSOILED CONDITION AS WHEN RECEIVED) FOR RESHIPMENT AT YOUR ORDER." [Here sign and date the duplicate form retained.]

As regards the latter alternative, I agree to pack the book in the same paste-board box or tin corners which enclosed it on its arrival, to re-wrap and label it as directed, and to mail you a report of my disposal of it, in one of the following forms : (1) "I ENCLOSE RECEIPT OF THE EXPRESS COMPANY, SHOWING THAT THE BOOK HAS BEEN PREPAID TO DESTINATION REQUESTED IN YOUR LETTER WHICH SENT ME 15 CENTS FOR THAT PURPOSE ;" *or else :* (2) "I THIS DAY DEPOSITED IN THE POST-OFFICE THE BOOK HELD BY ME AT YOUR ORDER, AFTER ATTACHING THERETO THE PREPAID LABEL WHICH YOU SENT ME WITH 17 CENTS IN POSTAGE STAMPS APPENDED ;" *or else :* (3) "I THIS DAY HANDED THE BOOK TO MR. ———, AS REQUESTED IN YOUR LETTER, AND TOOK HIS RECEIPT THEREFOR."

I also agree that, in case of removal from town (after giving a "hold-at-disposal" notice, without receiving any "directions for disposal" in return), I will notify you either that I hold the book at my new residence, or else that I have arranged with a friend to obey your directions at the first-named town.

Finally, I declare that I have signed and dated a duplicate of this present application-form, and that, when I send you a postal-card acknowledging the arrival of book, I will write the date of said card upon said duplicate, at the end of its first paragraph, and will file the duplicate in the book, as a reminder of the date when the month's loan thereof expires.

[Name, address, and date to be written below. Prepay by 2-cent stamp.]

13

PROSPECTUS OF "MY SECOND TEN THOUSAND."

On the first and last pages of the latest-written chapter in my book (Dec. 31, 1886; pp. 572, 590), I mention the necessity of a supplementary volume (" 2 X. M."), to contain the stock of road-information even then left on my hands, in spite of my having printed nine times the mass of matter promised by my first prospectus. The possibility of such a supplement had occurred to me as early as May, 1885, as shown by allusions on pp. 211, 501 ; and my formal " proposals " for it, on pp. 716, 717, were written in Sept., 1886. Events of the year-and-a-half which has since elapsed have shown that the suggested book cannot be brought out as early as 1890; perhaps not at all.

Hence, in putting out a feeler for evidence as to whether it may be worth my while to risk a second experiment as a publisher, I desire to put no real obligation upon those of my copartners who may vote to encourage that experiment. I do not, as before, ask them to pledge any money, even conditionally ; and, as I do not promise ever to issue the book, I will not consent to accept any money on its account until after it is issued. If any cash be sent me in advance, I shall at once return it ; for I will not again give any one the chance to indulge in the hallucination that, at some remote past time of " subscribing," he sent the price of the book instead of the pledge to pay.

I should be gratified if a third of my original subscribers of 1884-5, would sign the certificate at the foot of this page, in token that they appreciate what I have already done, and that they think it probable, in case I ever venture upon a supplementary book, that they may be willing to buy it at two-thirds the regular rate. My own agreement to allow them this chance, in return for the " moral support " implied in the ability to enroll their names as approving patrons of " X. M. M.," is the only obligation that is assumed about " 2 X. M.," on either side. Unless at least 1000 such names are enrolled, without any other effort than the circulation of this general appeal, I shall not be likely to attempt such a book at all. If printed, I shall include in it a roll of these supporters, arranged in chronological order, according to the dates of their signatures ; and also a summary of the advice which they may have given me about the contents of the book, as requested on pp. 716, 717. I hope each supporter will consent to read those pages anew, as a preliminary to filing with me a signed and dated copy of the following formula :

In order to formally certify my satisfaction with " Ten Thousand Miles on a Bicycle," and to encourage the preparation of a supplementary volume on American roads, I hereby authorize Karl Kron to print my name in the list of supporters of his proposed second book (to be called " My Second Ten Thousand," containing not less than 300 pages of large type, with at least 250 words to the page, and retailing at $1.50) ; and I agree that, if at any future time I receive notice from him that such a book has been published, I will reply within a month, and either enclose a dollar to pay for a copy or else give notice that I resign the privilege (which K. K. insures to me in return for the present pledge) of securing one from him at two-thirds the regular rate.

[Name, address, date and occupation to be plainly written below. Prepay by a 2-cent stamp.]

" No. 3600 " was the final fly-leaf signed by me for the " subscribers' autograph edition " (see pp. xx., 710) ; but, as I expect that no more than five-sixths of these will be claimed by the men whose names are written upon them, I can mail copies to any new buyers who may care enough about the matter to pay a five-cent fee. If preferred, I can write the buyer's own name, on a duplicate of one of these leaves, instead of sending an " original " numbered leaf addressed to a subscriber. In case such a fly-leaf reaches either a new buyer or an old subscriber, independently of the book, I would remind him that it should be pasted in at the front part thereof, just before the dog's head ; and perhaps a little trimming of the margins may first be necessary. When a subscriber wishes to claim his book at some other town than the one where I have deposited his autographed copy, I do not order the identical book reshipped to him, but let him have another (perhaps from a stock already waiting in that second town), and ask him to paste in it the duplicate numbered fly-leaf which I send him. Depositaries are requested, before selling an uncalled for sub. book at the regular $2 rate, to pull out its fly-leaf and return the same to me in next following report. This autographed sheet contains a small cut of the University Building, as noted on p. 434.

As regards my special *edition de luxe* (on heavy paper, tinted and calendered ; only 200 copies printed), I can supply it in sheets at $2, or in the regular blue muslin binding at $2.25 per copy, but I reserve the right to advance the price without notice, as the remnant decreases (present stock : 150).

As I intend hereafter to operate a type-writer and seldom use a pen, I shall attach no autographs to any second book I may publish. The idea has occurred to me, however, that a page of the original manuscript of " X. M. Miles " might be readily bound in at the end of " 2 X. M.," in case I ever issue such a volume, and in case the advance supporters of the same should request me so to do. I also offer them another notion in regard to its make-up,—being led to the offer by remembering certain requests that I " exchange photographs," or insert my portrait in " X. M. M." In explaining on p. 280 why I invariably refuse such requests (though very glad to receive the likeness of any of my correspondents who will thus favor me), I present as a reason my dislike of any personal notoriety. I object to having my appearance known to any save my private acquaintances. I decline to limit my liberty by giving strangers the power to identify me, since " to see me against my will is to rob me." Nevertheless, I feel no objection to letting any one know how I looked as a boy, years ago ; and in case any considerable curiosity exists among my copartners to see my face as it appeared in 1853, '55, '58, '62, '65, '67, and '69 (" bone-shaker days "), I may decide to gratify it by reproducing pictures of those dates in a single photogravure for " 2 X. M." Provided, therefore, that half my proposed roll of 1000 patrons for that proposed book declare themselves as desirous of seeing what sort of a looking creature I was between the ages of 6 and 23 years, I shall have a fair excuse for indulging in a custom which usually seems laughable for its vanity.

L3

CHAPTER PREFERENCES.

Chapters of special interest are: " Kentucky and its Mammoth Cave," " Coasting on the Jersey Hills," " In the Down East Fogs," " Straightaway for Forty Days," " From the Thousand Islands to the Natural Bridge."—*Louisville Commercial.*

Does the tourist wish to know about Manhattan Island?—the best modes of entering or leaving it with a bicycle?—the ferries, car-lines and steamboats by which he may be carried to, through and around it?—its hotels and restaurants? —its guide-books, maps and " sights"? Then let him study the index of " Ten Thousand Miles on a Bicycle," and purchase for pocket use its 37 pages devoted to the region of the metropolis (25 c. postpaid).

" Around New York " is an extremely interesting chapter, full of information to any who may wish to visit this " small world of itself." There is not a chapter in the book which is not worth, alone, more than the price of the volume.—*Star Advocate.* (Each chapter, in sheets, 25 c.)

For ourselves, " Coasting on the Jersey Hills " and " White Flannel and Nickel Plate " were the chapters enjoyed most in the perusal of this book, which is emphatically one for the times.—*The Critic, N. Y.*

For full details of the only hundred mile straightaway race yet wheeled in America; and of many long Canadian tours by parties and individuals, read the Ontario chapter in " Ten Thousand Miles on a Bicycle."

We find more good reading in " Straightaway for Forty Days "; and in " A Fortnight in Ontario " a most interesting account of the original Big Four road race, in which the late Cola Stone and George Webber were the first and second successful contestants. Last of all that may be read with interest is the chapter " This Book of Mine and the Next."—*Wheelmen's Record, Indianapolis.*

We have been highly entertained in reading the Preface, which is quite a volume in itself.—*Star Advocate, East Rochester, N. H.*

One reason why we have not read the wordy lucubrations of Mr. Kron is that we are not particularly interested in the subject, and we are not drawn to it by Mr. Kron's Preface, which is rather contemptuous respecting literary readers and literary critics.—*The Mail & Express, N. Y.*

To the ordinary reader, not especially interested in bicycling, the Preface is the best part of the book. It is humorous, frank and conceited. The body of the book is statistical and contains every species of information which a bicycler can need.—*New Haven Palladium.*

The portions of the book that I most particularly liked were, first of all, the opening chapter, " On the Wheel," which I consider the masterpiece: then the chapters on " Curl," " White Flannel and Nickel Plate," " Castle Solitude," " Bermuda " and " Bone-Shaker Days."—preference given according to the order named. The extraneous chapters are certainly amusing. All lovers of the dog must like to read the chapter on " Curl,"—and who is there that does not love a dog? I think one could find a greater number who do not love their own race.—*J. J. B., San Francisco.*

W₂

HISTORY OF WHEEL LITERATURE.

Do you want information about all that has been printed in regard to cycling? Then consult "Ten Thousand Miles on a Bicycle." Its special chapter on the subject (48 pages of 43,000 words) gives a full history to August, 1886, and is completed by addenda (11 pages of 10,000 words) to May, 1887. The indexes to this immense mass cover six pages of fine type, and give alphabetical references to 200 books and pamphlets, 125 journals, and 300 writers, editors, publishers and printers. (Chapter mailed separately for 25 c.: addenda and indexes for 25 c.)

The chapter on "The Literature of the Wheel" is an exhaustive piece of compilation, and is worth the hundreds of hours the author is particular to state he spent thereon.—*The Epoch, N. Y.*

For works on tricycling, training, touring, racing, wheel-mechanism and numberless other subjects, consult "Ten Thousand Miles on a Bicycle."

His chapter on the "Literature of the Wheel" embraces pretty nearly everything which has ever been printed in connection with cycling in the Old World and the New; and certainly no such compendium of information has ever before appeared.—*Wheeling, London.*

For maps, guides and road-books of the various States and countries, with details as to style, scale, date, price and publisher, consult "Ten Thousand Miles on a Bicycle."

He ravages the world to index the literature: books, maps and papers. The history of every news journal is given, and an outline of every leading dispute now agitating the world of wheel-riders. In pronouncing judgment upon many questions, he exhibits a very fine discrimination; and his conclusions should commend themselves to the consideration of English cyclists.—*Sewing-Machine & Cycle News, London.*

For railroad and steamship pamphlets useful to the cycler; for route-slips, distance-tables, time-cards and calendars, consult "Ten Thousand Miles on a Bicycle." The sheets of "Literature" chapter will be mailed separately for 25 c.

A bulky volume in which the author seeks to do for the bicycle and the literature of that machine what the gorgeous guide-books of summer travel do for the railroads.—*Newark Advertiser, N. J.*

For an account of the cycling journals in all countries and languages, their births and deaths, their successes and failures, consult "Ten Thous. Miles on a Bi."

If Karl Kron ever rewrites the chapters relating to "journalism," in his remarkable and standard work, the remarkable history of the "Exodus from the Coventry Ring" would form interesting reading.—*Sewing-Machine & Cycle News.* The addenda contains the history of cycling journalism up to date of the publication of the book.—*Wheelmen's Record, Indianapolis.*

Decidedly the greatest value of the work lies in its last third part—compendium of routes, riders' journals. It may yet be made completer; but, even as it is, it shows pretty clearly what has been done in the sport. I am happy to be able to recommend the book as of a general interest and value for *that*, even alone.—*Hugh Callan, M. A. of Glasgow University, author of "Wanderings on Wheel and on Foot through Europe."*

(T2)

Do beginners on the wheel want a guide that shall tell them where to look for all existing information? Let them buy "Ten Thousand Miles on a Bicycle."

We feel no hesitation in saying that this is a book which it would be greatly worth the while of all bicyclers to get. Those who are just beginning the sport will find it a work of absorbing interest. More than that, the author's enthusiasm is contagious. The tired cycler who comes in from a long or hilly jaunt and takes up this book will soon lose his sense of weariness and the recollection of steep ascents; his spirits will return, and he will eagerly lay plans for the morrow. Even when the novelty wears off, he will not forget his indebtedness to Karl Kron.—*New Englander.*

For legal opinions and books as to cyclers' rights and liabilities upon the road, see "Ten Thousand Miles on a Bicycle."

It describes, in the clearest language, the various trips in the United States and Canada, which are practicable for bicycles, mentioning points of interest along the route; it tells in amusing fashion some of the author's experiences; it has lists of wheel literature, of the clubs, of the wheelmen in the various cities and towns in each State of the Union; it gives advice about hotel charges, transportation taxes, and general traveling expenses; and it is, in short, an encyclopædic guide for bicycle-riders.—*San Francisco Argonaut.*

Do you wish to study the evidence, before securing a mileage register? Cyclometers of 15 varieties are given nearly 100 bits of testimony, good and bad, in the contributors' records to "Ten Thousand Miles on a Bicycle."

To wheelmen who intend to take long tours through the country, the book will be of great value. It is a manual of minute directions as to roads, routes and other particulars of practical importance.— *Yale Courant.*

For list of books and pamphlets on the construction and repairs of roads, and of bicycles, see "Ten Thousand Miles on a Bicycle."

A treasury of information to wheelmen about routes, hotels, personal experiences, and bicycling matters in general. It might easily have been rendered much more enjoyable and useful, yet it does not lack either spirit or information, and we do not doubt that many of its readers will like it greatly.— *The Congregationalist, Boston.*

The Valley of Virginia,—"the incomparable Shenandoah." For various reports and statistics, see "Ten Thousand Miles on a Bicycle."

It is simply what it claims to be—a book of American roads for men who travel on the bicycle. Wheelmen will find it useful, notwithstanding it is an "odd and cranky" specimen of book-making.—*Philadelphia Times.*

For history of "Canadian Wheelmen's Association" (rules, officers and publications) see "Ten Thousand Miles on a Bicycle."

This volume of 900 pages is not only a complete gazetteer of American roads suitable to the bicycle, but it contains a mass of information in regard to topics of interest to wheelmen. There is also an immense amount of discursive matter.—*San Francisco Chronicle.*

A DIRECTORY OF CLUBS AND CLUBMEN.

Do you want the addresses of the cycling enthusiasts in every State of the Union? Then consult the appendix of "Ten Thousand Miles on a Bicycle."

The names of the 3000 subscribers he captured are printed alphabetically and then printed in geographical order according to residence. This takes sixty-five pages.—*Buffalo Express.*

Do you want the dates when the chief clubs were organized, and official titles of their leading members until the spring of '86? See "Ten Thousand Miles on a Bicycle."

The "Directory of Wheelmen" alone is worth more than double the price of the book to dealers, tourists, and all interested in cycling.—*Star Advocate, East Rochester, N. H.* (Mailed for 25 c.)

Poems and parodies from twenty well-known authors have been reprinted in "Ten Thousand Miles on a Bicycle," and have been highly commended; but some critics assert that even these are less admirable than the monumental roll of corners' signatures.

The names of the 3000 subscribers that Kron "bagged" are printed in full; and these, as literature, are better than the poems or parodies which Kron has thought worthy of preservation.—*The Epoch, N. Y.*

The tourist through any of the 850 towns recorded as supporting "Ten Thousand Miles on a Bicycle" may be profited by knowing the names of those supporters, as the most probable possessors of knowledge about local roads and routes.

The directory of over 3000 subscribing wheelmen is alone worth more than the price of the whole book.—*Cape Ann Breeze, Gloucester, Mass.* (Directory mailed in sheets for 25 c.)

How much does cycling cost? See index to prices and expenditures in "Ten Thousand Miles on a Bicycle."

In spite of the irrelevancy of much that finds a place between the covers, there is no doubt a good deal of information about bicycle clubs, the rules which must be observed by wheelmen who travel in different countries, and the like, that owners and riders of bicycles cannot but find useful.—*Boston Post.*

For most complete account of the first tour ever anywhere taken by a large party of wheelmen (a week's experience of three dozen " in the Down East fogs"; 25 pages, price 25 cents), see "Ten Thousand Miles on a Bicycle."

It gives all the author's experiences, all his opinions, all his observations on all subjects, and all the facts about how to ride, when to ride, where to ride, who riders are in all parts of the country, where they live, and—well, the book is as comprehensive as a file of newspapers.—*Baltimore American.*

"There is too much fine type," it has been said. Let us see about this. Here are 173 pages of indexes, etc., which surely ought to be in fine type, leaving 373 pages in coarse and 362 pages (less than half of the entire reading matter) in fine type. Thus we have more coarse type alone than the publisher promised to give us in all; and it would seem that we might accept the fine print, especially as it is given free gratis.—*Wheelmen's Record, Indianapolis.*

NOT SIMPLY A PERSONAL NARRATIVE.

Two-thirds the text of "Ten Thousand Miles on a Bicycle" (as demonstrated on p. xv.) is devoted to matters entirely distinct from the author's own wheeling experiences. The index of about 200 contributors of records covers nearly a page of fine type (p. lxvi.) and is reprinted elsewhere in this pamphlet.

The queerest book that has come into this office for a long while. The writer is a bicycle rider. He has it worse than any one else on record, and his book is in the main an account of how far he rode, where he took a header, when he dismounted for lunch, what roads are stony, how much distance can be covered in an hour, what he did after 1 h. 13 m., etc.; but there are several readable chapters, and the book has literary merit of rare quality, in spots.—*Hartford Courant.*

For Thomas Stevens's route from San Francisco to Boston, with daily mileage (not given in his book), see "Ten Thousand Miles on a Bicycle."

It is not an account of travels on the wheel, like Stevens's noted book. Each chapter deals with some American bicycle route or gives wheel information. It is a book for every wheelman's possession.—*Worcester Spy.*

For a great variety of contributions from Australians and New Zealanders (11,000 words on long-distance tours, road-races, all-day runs and annual mileage statistics), see "Ten Thousand Miles on a Bicycle."

A cyclopædia of bicycle tours (with advice and descriptions of roads), bicycle literature, index of clubs, and general miscellaneous information on the subject of bicycling.—*Baltimore Sun.*

For 3000-mile route of H. J. High, from Pennsylvania to Nebraska and back, with daily reports of weather and mileage, see "Ten Thousand Miles on a Bicycle."

Containing an immense store of information, it is in fact a perfect encyclopædia of wheeling.—*Buffalo Courier.*

For reports of winter touring, in three States, over the snow and ice, see "Ten Thousand Miles on a Bicycle."

It presents a mass of detail, which must have been accumulated with great labor, and which will doubtless be of use and advantage to the bicycler.—*Washington Post.*

From Detroit to Montreal; down the St. Lawrence to Quebec and beyond. See Canadian tourists' records in "Ten Thousand Miles on a Bicycle."

An invaluable book for the wheelman. In reality, a dictionary for tourists on the bicycle. It contains extended and minute information as to prices, hotels, roads, scenery, literature of the wheel, long-distance rides,—everything that the cyclist could want to know, much of it the result of patient research.—*Buffalo Express.*

For reports of tricycle touring by young ladies in Australia, read "Ten Thous. Miles on a Bicycle." Its "index of women" exhibits more than 100 references.

A volume which all bicyclers should have, and which most of them do have.—*Baltimore American.*

The book is a good book, well worth the money. There is no Englishman who has had it and not pronounced it really good value.—*Wheeling.*

"A FREE ADV" OF CYCLING IN GENERAL.

As explained on pp. 702, 714, the Publisher has excluded all advertisements from the book, in order to make it serve most effectively as a free advertisement of cycling in general. Those of his copartners who appreciate the neat typography thus secured (at a sacrifice of the "trade" feature which all other cycling prints rely upon as a sole pecuniary support), are invited to pay for it by helping push the circulation of "Ten Thousand Miles on a Bicycle" round the world.

There has been no end of sport made of Karl Kron and his wonderful book, but, at heart, every wheelman cannot but feel grateful to the author of a book which will prove of such great value to cycling.—*Boston Globe.*

As an insight into American cycling, and as a guide to a large portion of the great continent, the volume is very valuable. A vast deal of valuable and also of useless statistics are given, and the book is interesting for its own sake.—*Irish Cyclist & Athlete, Dublin.*

How about cyclometers? No previous collection of experiences with them is comparable in extent to that contained in "Ten Thousand Miles on a Bicycle."

Apart from much irrelevancy, the book contains very serviceable information for those interested in bicycle travel. The ten thousand miles extended in various directions, and principally in the United States and Canada. There are valuable details given as to the conditions of roads, obstructions, accommodations, charges and the facilities for ordinary travel when the locality was unfit for further progress on the bicycle.—*Alta California, San Francisco.*

For "Clerical wheelmen's Canadian tour," and riding-reports from individual clergymen, see "Ten Thousand Miles on a Bicycle."

Like the Coast Guide to the yachtsman, this manual will prove indispensable to the wheelman. Within its covers are contained the minutest descriptions of some 6000 miles of highways in the United States, Canada and Bermuda which the author has explored with the definite purpose of publishing his observations; reports upon about 6000 additional miles of road traversed by others; a mass of statistics regarding distances, persons and places, and a multiplicity of other details useful to travelers. It is most valuable to the active bicycler, who has time and taste for riding long distances upon the road.—*Boston Advertiser.*

Winter wheeling in that "ocean paradise," Bermuda. See "Ten Thousand Miles on a Bicycle"; and, if you take the voyage, procure for pocket use the sheets of the Bermuda chapter (postpaid for 25 cents).

As a cyclopædia of places and library book of reference, this volume stands unique in literature and is unsurpassed in its line. It is redolent with the fresh breeze of the prairie and the ocean, of the city pavement smells, and the onion-laden air of the "still vexed" Bermudas.—*McGregor News, Ia.*

For list of "League railroads" carrying passengers' bicycles free as personal baggage, in U. S. and Canada, see "Ten Thousand Miles on a Bicycle."

Well written and thoroughly practical, it must be of great value to all wheeling tourists.—*Canadian Wheelman.*

X2

CUSTOMS DUTIES AND TRANSPORTATION.

For custom-house rules as to duties on cycles, in United States, Canada, Mexico, Bermuda, France, Italy, Switzerland, Belgium, Holland and Germany, see "Ten Thousand Miles on a Bicycle."

Bicyclists will find in this volume worlds of new thought and a familiarity with our great country that will impart to any reader an air of traveled leisure, such as is not often attainable even from personal experience.—*McGregor News, Ia.*

Tourists going abroad, who wish to have their cycles classed as baggage on the ocean passage, and who wish to know the transportation rules and rates of the British and continental railroad and steamboat lines, should consult "Ten Thousand Miles on a Bicycle."

The author, with pardonable pride, calls the book "a gazetteer, a dictionary, a cyclopædia, a statistical guide, a thesaurus of facts." It gives a record of his journeys over the United States, describes the scenery, the condition of the roads, etc., in every locality, and furnishes other details which should make the book invaluable to all who follow in his footsteps, or wheel-tracks. —*Lippincott's Magazine, Philadelphia.*

For autobiographies of the pioneer wheelmen and long-distance tourists of the United States, see "Ten Thousand Miles on a Bicycle."

There may be some things of possible interest to devotees of the wheel omitted from this book; but if so, we have been unable to discover the omission.—*The Critic, N. Y.*

For long-distance tours by Frenchmen and Germans, and by Englishmen in France and Germany as well as Great Britain, see "Ten Thous. Miles on a Bi."

A compendium of information about routes and roads in the Eastern States, Canada and Bermuda, accompanied by wheelmen's scores and various topics of interest to bicyclers. A large amount of money has been spent in its preparation.—*Cincinnati Commercial Gazette.*

For records of ladies' tricycling, in America, England and Australia, read "Ten Thousand Miles on a Bicycle." Of 100 references in its "index of women," fully one-fourth refer to this subject.

A voluminous "thesaurus of facts" which every bicycler will find extremely useful.—*Worcester Spy.*

The main purpose of the book is to present minute descriptions of about 6000 miles of American highways which the author has explored while driving his wheel the distance named in the title, through 24 separate States and Provinces.—*Outing, N. Y.*

For information and advice about securing free transportation of passengers' bicycles, as personal baggage, on American and foreign steamship lines, see "Ten Thousand Miles on a Bicycle."

The modern world, as seen through the eyes of such a Bayard Taylor of the wheel, has, to say the least, a novel interest that cannot be experienced in any other way.—*McGregor News, Ia.*

It should certainly find a large circle of readers.—*St. Louis Spectator.*

NATURAL HISTORY OF "THE HOG."

"Porcus Americanus," or Great American Road-Hog. First designated a such in the introductory essay (1882) of "Ten Thousand Miles on a Bicycle." See index for description of and legal checks upon the Hog.

A book which will appeal to the large and growing class interested in bicycling. It represents an enormous amount of careful work, for no one but an enthusiast would spend four years, even of his leisure time, in the gathering of materials and the writing of such a work as this.—*San Francisco Chronicle.*

A veritable cycling encyclopædia, including more, and more diverse, information than was ever before crowded into one book. The author is an eccentric genius, and every one of these 800 pages shows traces of his peculiar methods and ideas. It is the best two dollars' worth ever offered to cyclists, and no wheelman can afford to be without a copy. Not the least curious feature of this remarkable book is the fact that, although named "10,000 Miles on a Bicycle," and apparently appealing only to bicyclists, *it i really of especial value to all horsemen who drive for pleasure.* Its authentic and detailed information concerning the roads of the United States and Canada, is such as cannot be found elsewhere, and renders it a necessity for all who make pleasure tours on wheels or horseback.—*Spirit of the Times.*

For Yosemite Valley tour and other notable explorations by riders in California, see "Ten Thousand Miles on a Bicycle."

The lesson of the book is that, even in this land of bad roads, the bicycle is a practical means of long-distance locomotion.—*Commercial Advertiser, N.Y.*

Canal paths and railroads as touring tracks for the cycler. See adventures and accidents in "Ten Thousand Miles on a Bicycle."

The book is a regular dictionary of roads, well indexed, and admirers of outdoor sports will take kindly to it.—*New Orleans Picayune.*

"Land's End to John o' Groat's,"—the long-distance route from the south-west to the north-east corner of Great Britain. For complete list of tours, '73 to '80, read "Ten Thousand Miles on a Bicycle."

It is certainly worth reading by any wheelman who cares to inform himself as to the early days of the great and growing pastime, as well as to refresh his memory concerning events of more recent occurrence.—*St. Louis Spectator.*

For official definitions of "amateurism" by L. A. W., A. C. U., C. T. C. and N. C. U., see "Ten Thousand Miles on a Bicycle."

Well written and thoroughly practical, it must be of great value to all wheeling tourists.—*Canadian Wheelman.*

The much-neglected preface and index of a book are of more use to the reader than is generally supposed. Some of our great geniuses are expert in the art of index-reading. We venerate the inventor of the index. We often learn the character of a work through these sources. Read both preface and index, as the light thus obtained will help regulate your course as to the amount of time to be devoted to the book.—*Magazine of American History.*

Kron has done a vast amount of good for the cause of cycling, as anybody can see by glancing through his volume. Its bright thoughts, witty anecdotes, valuable statistics, biographical sketches, and historical data insure his book the appreciation it deserves from all who buy and read it. How many will buy and read it? is now the question. If the desired 30,000 purchasers could be brought to a proper knowledge of what they were going to get for their money, they would surely respond far quicker than he could turn out the books. That Kron's great enterprise has cost him a vast amount of work is conspicuously apparent; that the proposed sale of 30,000 copies will involve a great deal more, he readily comprehends. Will he succeed? Yes, beyond a doubt.—*Thomas Stevens, in The Wheel.*

Karl Kron's book is floating around here, and it is curious to hear the different expressions of opinion respecting it. Some people express unqualified satisfaction with it, others extreme disgust at receiving what they consider a conglomeration of facts of little interest to them, or, as they think, to any one else. A verdict pitched middle way between the two extremes would convey perhaps about a fair estimate of the value of the work : it cannot be altogether praised, nor can it be wholly condemned.—*Philadelphia cor. ("Chris") of Wheelmen's Gazette.*

The book is an ornament to any man's library and I shall always esteem it a valuable acquisition to mine. Those who have been jeering at poor old Karl, for the last couple of years, now wish they had sent on their names, and had them printed with the 3000.—*Kentucky cor. (" Norb ") of The Wheel.*

The *American Athlete* is pretty hard on the inspired Kron, whose book is worth the two beans asked for it to any wheelman,—if only to show the amount of gall (which is, to quote the *Athlete,* " prodigious ") that Kron displays so freely.—*Chicago cor. (" Geis ") of Wheelmen's Record.*

Karl Kron has been a great traveler on the bicycle, and his book is full of that kind of information sought for by the wheelman: It has had such an extensive sale among wheelmen in advance, that those who contemplate using it as a gift book should inquire first whether the intended recipient has a copy.—*Philadelphia Ledger.*

We republish below, in full, as a representative English estimate, *Wheeling's* critical review of Karl Kron's work. We find ourselves in hearty accord with every assertion in this most polished critique, and we hope its perusal may place the work in a new light, to those who have regarded it as an intangible curiosity, a mere trash basket of accepted and long discovered bicycular facts and fancies.—*The Wheel, N. Y.*

The chapter of " Statistics from the Veterans " is really very interesting, and we can only regret that it is not more complete : but that is not K. K.'s fault.—*Bicycling World, Boston.* Such writing for the " Veterans " seems over-ripe. Since the inception of the volume and its completion a new generation, as it were, of cyclists has sprung up, for whom these ' tales of a grandfather " have but little interest.—*Philadelphia cor. of American Athlete.*

We have here a ponderous volume of 800 closely-printed pages, dedicated to the memory of a bull-dog, and containing a biography of the dog, done in the style of a sincere mourner with Boswellian proclivities, and detailing the observations of the author and mourner as he was whirled along the highways and by-ways of half a continent, astride of a bicycle, until he had completed a mile for every supposititious Greek in the flying band led by the immortal Xenophon. The work, as briefly described by the author, is "A Gazetteer of American Roads in Many States," and "An Encyclopædia of Wheeling Progress in Many Countries," with twenty personal and general indexes; and although the picture of the dog, as he looks with canine benignity toward the title page, inclined us to accept the chapter of biography *cum grano*, yet the author assures in his dedicatory lines that "Curl" was "the very best dog whose presence ever blessed this planet." We commend this volume as a curiosity, and trust the ingenious author may have at least one reader for every mile he traveled on his wheel, and for every tear he shed for his dog.—*Public Opinion, Washington.*

My wife asked me why in the world I bought a book dedicated to a bull-dog? I could not tell her why, but it is a big affair and well worth the $2. The 6th and 7th chapters (pp. 35-63) are of particular interest to me.—*J. J., Salt Lake City, Utah.*

I think it is a book which every wheelman, who wants to be informed about what has been done, should read. As I am of a statistical turn of mind, perhaps I appreciated it more than the average man. Anyway, I found a great deal of good reading in it, and I like the book. I didn't see just what a bull-dog's story had to do in a wheeling book, but nevertheless I read it and liked it much for the fun it contained. I have no doubt that had "Curl" lived to see you on a wheel, he would have made you wish you had an iron boot.— *G. C. McN., Akron, O.*

We are all putting in our spare time here in reading Karl Kron's book. Some like it, and some don't. With my canine taste, the chapter on the bull-dog "Curl" goes right to the spot. As a piece of literary work it is very far superior to anything else in the book, and I will take off my hat to the man who wrote it should I ever meet him.—*Phila. cor. ("Cal Wallace") Am. Athlete.*

I think it very valuable,—in fact, a wonderful book in many respects. I was much interested in the story of Curl's life, among other things.—*W. H. E., Winona, Minn.*

The book is as it should be now, and you could not have improved it by any omissions or additions. No true lover of the dog can read "Curl's" story and its finale with dry eyes. In the name of the cyclists of the East, let me thank you for your noble work.—*G. O. H., Bangor, Me.*

Wonderfully cheap at $2. There is not a chapter in the book which is not worth, alone, more than the price of the volume.—*Star Advocate.*

So cheap that we are afraid the publisher will die as poor as the poor dog to whose name it was dedicated.—*L. A. W. Pointer, Oshkosh, Wis.*

FROM A FEMININE POINT OF VIEW.

From a feminine point of view, there is little interest in Mr. Karl Kron's book. I say this without regard to the other interests, for I am inclined to believe that he has covered everything else with painful detail, but the little army of lady riders has been passed over without so much as an acknowledgment of its existence. He can write scores of pages on a savage bull-dog, and more upon the history of a lodging-house in New York, but he has no word whatever to say regarding the lady riders who have come forward as devotees of the sport and made themselves an important factor in it. In such a mass of matter, there was no room for us. It was to be expected. Karl Kron is a bachelor.—*Boston cor.* ("*Daisie*") *of L. A. W. Bulletin.*

Ah, "Daisie"! how *could* you be so careless? If you will but turn to the final page of my seventy-five page index, you will find I have there devoted more than a solid column of fine type to a special alphabet of "women,"—a catalogue of nearly one hundred references where my monster volume makes mention of your own sweet sex. The "lady tricyclers" alone claim a dozen references, and the "wives of wheelmen" about as many more. After the great painstaking given to this special index, to have you declare that my book "has no word whatever to say regarding the lady riders," does seem, indeed, the "most unkindest cut of all!" Must I suggest, also, that you are cruelly inaccurate in saying I have written "scores of pages on a savage bull-dog"? Nineteen pages are not "scores," and Curl was never savage. Indeed, the sole literary object of the volume is to justify his memory in history as the most tender-hearted specimen of his race, as having always "roared you as gently as a sucking dove." So, please don't condemn Curl until you have formed his acquaintance, and don't assume that his character may not be voted charming, even "from a feminine point of view." Let me confess, too, that it was a woman's praise (given long ago, in the days when we both were young) of my verbal reminiscences about Curl, which finally led me to conceive the notion of writing his biography, and so led to the production of the monumental tome which his portrait adorns. Since lively modern girls of sixteen and eighteen and twenty have all, more recently, laughed their approval to me of the actual biography, I may surely be pardoned for hoping that "the little army of tricyclers" contains many who will also be able to find some fun in it. My own personal chance for favor among them may have everlastingly gone by, but I want to have Curl be given a fair show for becoming "a pet of the ladies." As for my sketch of "Castle Solitude," I am certain that, among an equal number of men and women, who might have the patience to peruse it, more of the latter would be interested than the former. Curiosity in studying the secret and forbidden phases of life is not the exclusive attribute of either sex; but, as regards the peculiarities of the queerest lodging-house that ever existed on this planet, there can be no doubt of their making the stronger appeal to the imagination of that half of humanity whose interests are chiefly domestic, because taken "from a feminine point of view."—KARL KRON, *in L. A. W. Bulletin.*

A "nasty horrid girl" is cruel enough to suggest that "Daisie" grumbled at Karl Kron's "slight" to the ladies in his book, because the principal and almost only feats of lady riders recorded therein were credited to Jersey women. I, of course, would not venture to uphold her in her spiteful jealousy.—*New Jersey cor. ("Jer. C.") of L. A. W. Bulletin.*

The *Boston Herald, Pall Mall Gazette,* and many leading papers condemn Karl Kron's book in most emphatic terms. "Daisie" also thinks there is little in it to interest any one. She is level-headed this time sure.—*The Bicycle, West Rutland, Vt. (pub. by a Chief Consul of L. A. W., at 12 cents a year.)*

A Yankee of the Yankees,....he makes no false or undue pretensions of any kind,....but is ...a genial and kindly philosopher,....as honest as he is shrewd.—*The Saturday Review, London.*

He has prepared a book which is not only interesting and entertaining, but which is invaluable both to the wheelman and the general traveler.—*Carroll Democrat, Westminster, Md.*

It is certainly a complete thing, and should be in the library of every wheelman. I send you the full price ($2), instead of the $1.20 which you request of me as a subscriber; for the work is worth double the regular price. The more I read, the better I like it, and I shall be glad to be of some service to you in return.—*T. M. B., South Pittsburg, Tenn.*

I read your book on my journey from Kansas to California, and can very truthfully say that it is more than I expected could be written on wheeling, although I had my expectations sufficiently exalted.—*L. J. B., Emporia, Kan.*

It is a marvel; and the subscriber who is dissatisfied should be published. My little experience in the making of bicycle road-books only enables me to appreciate better the splendid success you have achieved.—*H. B. Donly, Secretary of Canadian Wheelmen's Association, Simcoe, Ont.*

While much of your book is not to my liking, in point of personal interest, it is certainly a most marvelous monument of your perseverance.—*J. S. Dean, Boston.* I read it "in snatches" and, while there may have been objections, was highly pleased with it. The style is charming, and the knowledge you display of human nature and certain accepted facts (that is, what I think they call introspective philosophy) secured at once my admiration.—*F. P. Prial, editor of The Wheel, New York.*

I think it has been got up in excellent shape, and there's lots of good stuff in it. What a pile of work you have put in that book! I hope you'll get your money back, and much more, too; but you've got a big task before you, sure. The quality is unquestionably caviare to the multitude. Still, as you argue, having done so well with the 3000, the capture of ten times as many may not prove impossible.—*H. P. Fellows, author of "Boating Trips on New England Rivers" (Boston: Cupples, Upham & Co., 1884).*

The more I read, the better I like it. It is a most valuable book. Put my name down for "2 X. M."—*E. H. Corson, author of the "Star Rider's Manual" and editor of the Star Advocate, East Rochester, N. H.*

THE PERSONAL EQUATION.

It ought to have been called " Ten Thousand I's and My's." In spite of your editorial, last week, I am one cycler who can find very little that is useful or entertaining in it, and that little is so completely buried in literary rubbish and fine print, that it is not worth while to try and find it. Stevens's " Around the World on a Bicycle " is worth a dozen of it.—*Cleveland cor.* (" *Holy Joe* ") *of Wheelmen's Record.*

I have read a number of criticisms both pro and con on Karl Kron's book, and I feel inclined to congratulate him on their tenor. The adverse ones are marked for the most part with an unmistakable dent of maliciousness, and the claims made are either gross misrepresentations or near enough so to be what Chicago people call rank lies. It is true that the identity of the author is apparent all through the work, and equally true that many of the greatest literary efforts of our time have been written from a personal standpoint. It is true, too, that the author is eccentric to a degree, as is shown by the careful manner in which he guards his real name. And one might (should he choose, and know the gentleman) say a great many other things there is no particular occasion to cite. But that the book is just what it is represented to be as a gazetteer, cannot be denied by anybody who takes the trouble to carefully glance over it ; and it is, I think, in the opinion of the majority of these, the most important work exclusively cycling hitherto published.—*Chicago cor.* (" *Verax* ") *of Wheelmen's Gazette.*

It has become the affected fashion, I know, to give vent to chestnut sarcasm at the expense of my friend Karl Kron's " X. M." book, on the ground of its antiquity. All I have to say is, Let those read, who laugh. I picked up the book on my return home, the other evening, and began glancing over its encyclopædic contents. I found them anything but dry reading, and soon became deeply absorbed, as I went along, skipping from page to page, in every one of which I found something that caught my eye and well repaid me for my trouble in reading. As an evidence of my sincerity, let me say that I found so much to engage my attention that it was long after midnight before I thought of the lateness of the hour and laid it down. Now for the past three years I guess I have kept myself as far " up " in cycling literature as the next fellow, yet I must own that at no time was the realization forced on me that I was wandering in a chestnut orchard. I found plenty of Karl Kron, to be sure, and why not ? Does he pretend to create a work with any other foundation than his own experiences ? And then again I must own that I have never found anything about Karl Kron personally or in his writings that was disagreeable or a bore. I anticipate passing many pleasant half hours in the perusal of " X. M.," and the valuable statistics that it contains will make it a volume of frequent reference by me. I shall be most happy to enroll myself as a subscriber to " X. M., No. 2," and consider myself running in rare luck to be able to get so much value for my money.—*Elizabeth cor.* (" *Jonah* ") *of The Wheel.*

A beautiful portrait of his bull-dog forms the frontispiece.—*N. Y. World.*

My admiration for the book is unbounded, and I wish you the greatest of success.—*L. L. P., Salem, Oregon.* Your big book is a veritable bonanza to wheelmen.—*G. J. T., Salt Lake City, Utah.* I am extremely pleased with it.—*W. T. W., Yantic, Ct.* A valuable addition to my library.—*E. J. K., Birmingham, Ct.* A thoroughly good hand-book of the sport.—*W. S. R., Madison, Wis.* I think it worth $10 to any man riding a wheel.—*O. C. N., Walnut, Ill.* I am satisfied in every respect.—*F. M. W., Sibley, Ill.* It is ever so much more interesting than I had thought it could be.—*Rev. F. S. D., Allentown, Pa.* We are all greatly pleased, and hope you will sell the 30,000. —*C. W. S., Walden, N. Y.*

I cannot but admire the extreme diligence exhibited in preparing such an exhaustive index.—*F. L. G., Bermuda.* I consider it the best book on cycling that has ever been published.—*L. P., Stanford Rivers, Eng.* It is certainly a capital book and does you great credit.—*A. J. L., Birmingham, Eng.* I am amply repaid for the long wait. The chapter on "Curl" is splendid.—*H. J. J., London, Eng.* A masterpiece of compilation, a gem of perseverance and a most useful fund of reference.—*A. M. B., London, Eng.* Your painstaking is beyond all praise. You read as if you were Argus-eyed, and pronounce a judgment worthy of Solon. All hail to your Pen, dear K. K.! Long may you live! May your books ever grow bigger and bigger : better they cannot be.—*J. B. M , London, Eng.*

The circulation already given to the book in the Brooklyn Library, shows that it is and will be popular.—*W. A. B., Acting Librarian.*

It is indeed a wonderful book, far exceeding my expectations, and I cannot help thinking it must be highly typical of its author. I do not believe another Karl Kron exists, and therefore the book must ever be unique in the literature of cycling.—*Dr. J. H. M., Westerly, R. I.*

The reading of your accounts of tours at once arouses in me an ambition to go and do likewise. Though your type is necessarily fine, my eyes have not suffered.—*L. B. G , Minneapolis.*

I have examined it sufficiently to be assured that it is a treasure,—not only full of information, but full of entertainment,—a book that can be read every day with no loss of interest.—*T. B. S., Millville, N. J.*

I am very well pleased indeed with it, though just a little bit disappointed that you did n't say anything about our splendid ocean beach. But of course you could n't get everything in, or you never would have finished.—*W. J. F., Fernandina, Fla.*

I am not able to write it up, as I feel like doing, but I am awfully pleased with it. It is the cheapest book I ever bought. It reads more like a person talking to you than anything I ever read.—*B. L., Lafayette, Ind.*

I hope that every subscriber will succeed in selling every extra copy sent him, in order that you may be *partly* rewarded for your long and arduous work in preparing so good and exhaustive a book. Enclosed please find $4 for the two which you asked me to sell.—*Rev. E. P. J., Woodlawn Park, Ill.*

A FIRM HOLD ON THE FUTURE.

I don't want to "give you taffy," but, really, it is a splendid work, and one which will grow. It's a little too deep for first reading, perhaps, but it will continue to be looked into, years from now. The print is all right. Of course it is fine, but the book is not a novel, but a work of reference, a staple guide. If people criticise the print, let them remember that the touring and bicycling majority is composed of fellows whose eyesight is unimpaired. Tell such complainants to go to!—*B. B. Ayers, Chicago, First Tourmaster, L. A. W.*

I have no doubt that all your subscribers will be glad they have waited for the complete book, instead of receiving a half-way affair. The non-cycling chapters are a pleasant relief, and should "wire on" a good many outsiders. I should say that "Castle Solitude" was one of your best chapters. Your plan of confiding personal matters to your "copartners" can hardly fail to enlist their sympathy.—I even hope to the extent of winning your fabulous number of 30,000. Personally, that book just suits me, and you may put down my pledge for "2 X. M."—*J. A. M., Ohio.*

As a work of reference it is invaluable, and if its price were five times as great, I would not like to be without it. I do not doubt that it will be more appreciated fifty years hence than it is to-day; but I hardly believe it can ever be made a financial success. I have heard many wheelmen speak of you as a "crank," and I must say you must be either very wealthy or very eccentric, to waste so many years on a labor which I fear will never be fully appreciated, and which certainly can never bring either the honor or emoluments which would have been derived if such labor had been applied in some other directions.—*S. M. P., New Orleans, La.*

Of the three extraneous chapters (27, 28, 29), I think I like "Castle Solitude" the best, especially the first part. This matter, which has as little to do with cycling as the average "cycling romance," is very interesting to me; both by reason of what I hope you will excuse me for calling the audacity of your egotism, and by reason of the original way you have—not of looking at things, perhaps, but of telling us honestly just how you do look at them. What you show here of your personality makes me think you'll not mind the inevitable penalty: that the very quaintness which is the charm will be the reason why all the "every day young men" will dub you a "crank."—*E. J. S., New York Bicycle Club.*

I consider it an indispensable cycling gazetteer, showing a marvelous exhibition of patience and attention to detail. I do not mean that the book is perfection. Perhaps at first glance it may prove disappointing,—may seem too bulky and not practical enough. But the more one looks into it, the more does its value increase, and I would not part with my copy for considerably many times its price. I think those who have to deal with cycling topics will bear me out in this statement. In fact, the book occupies a unique position, as being the first, and a highly creditable attempt, at a cycling cyclopædia.—*H. P. Merrill, Los Angeles, Cal., formerly editor of the cycling and literary columns of Springfield Union.*

No velocipedist worthy of the name can fail to make himself familiar with this guide for the perfect bicycler.— *Journal de St. Pétersbourg.*

We have read this elegant book, and pronounce it worth $10 instead of $2. It is the greatest authority ever published on cycling, and gives a description of every ridable road in the United States.— *Oregon Siftings.*

Karl Kron's greatest need is an editor armed with a rackful of the biggest blue pencils.— *The Epoch, N. Y.*

It is, without a doubt, the most comprehensive work yet issued in the cycling world; and, considering the information contained therein, the price charged is only nominal.— *Australian Cycling News.*

It contains a mass of information likely to be useful to cyclists in America, and one or two general essays which are interesting, and its ample indexes give it value as a book of reference.— *The Times, London.*

The printing is characterised by the excellence and clearness of type which distinguishes the best American productions; the indices are marvels of completeness, and the literary merit is considerable. Indeed, the production is in striking contrast to the majority of English literature of a similar class, most of which is contemptible, and designed solely as pegs whereon to hang advertisements. The chapter on "British and Colonial Records" deals with road riding and touring, and we find here many interesting accounts of English bicyclists who have covered enormous distances in their time. The author appears to revel in statistics of bicycling in this country, and does not shirk the labor their compilation demands.— *The Field, London.*

I think your book will "live." I enjoy it more and more.— *H. C., Glasgow, Scotland.* I have read your book over and over again, and its pages always seem to gleam forth full of interest.— *R. E. B., York, Eng.* I enjoy the reading of it immensely.— *C. H. S., Harrisburg, Pa.*

As regards your long and wonderful book, I have as yet done little more than roam about it, like a butterfly in a flower-garden, but I have found that I want "Curl" separately, for a friend who is a lover of bull-dogs, and so I enclose the price of that chapter.— *A. H., London, Eng.*

Mr. Kron, who graduated at Yale in 1869, where he was the author of that lively work known as "Four Years at Yale," is not named "Kron" at all. Everybody knows what his name is, but he says he hates and despises those who will review his books, and he asks them as a favor to let his real name alone. Thus courteously approached, what else can we do but comply with his request? His "Ten Thousand Miles on a Bicycle" is the queerest book that has come into this office for a long while.— *Hartford Courant.*

Connaissez-vous M. Kron? M. Kron de New York? Karl Kron, l'auteur de "Quatre ans à Yale?" Vous ne répondez pas; avouez que vous avez honte de confesser votre ignorance.— *Paris reviewer ("M. R.")* in *Journal de St. Pétersbourg, Feb. 24–March 7, 1888.*

THE HUMORS OF COVENTRY.

The next picture was thrown upon the screen, exciting universal amusement, not unmixed with derision. It represented a small man clad in a very dirty and oily corduroy coat, and a still dirtier pair of white flannel pants, heavily-darned stockings, and badly-patched shoes, all the items of his costume being labeled in the most peculiar manner. Thus, his stockings were labeled "My Go-its stockings," with details as to price, date of purchase, and number of miles that the diminutive man had ridden in them, whilst each darn or patch in his other garments was similarly labeled with date and cost. The lecturer said, in introducing this picture : This, ladies and gentlemen, is a Transatlantic study. The portrait thrown upon the sheet is that of a great author—in his own estimation. He produced that matchless work, in nine volumes, of 500 pages each, entitled " XVII. Miles on a Bicycle," and is now at work upon another monumental labor, the outcome of a visit to England, called " From Ditton to Ripley on a Cycle." In dealing with this novel subject the author under notice has followed out the wonderfully clear, concise, and unencumbered style which distinguished all his previous works. As, however, he is present, I will ask Mr. Edwin George Oliver Tist to speak for himself. A little man, the counterpart of the illustration, hastily scrambled on the platform and pushed the lecturer aside, leaving several conspicuous dabs of oil on the latter's dress-suit, and humming under his breath:

" Whatever I try, sir, I fail in, and why, sir? I'm diffident, modest, and shy,"

with a dim recollection of the air from " Ruddigore," he addressed the audience as follows: Ehem ! wall! You must regard me as an average man—a representative average man, of course—rather in front of the rest, you know, but—ehem ! My name is—wall ?—*Introduction to heavy British funny business in " The Lantern," illustrated Christmas annual of " the Coventry ring."*

The author's motto, " My motives pure ; my satire free from gall," is too delicious when compared with the text. A far more appropriate motto would be, " My motives mercenary, my gall free from satire"; for on the very page that faces the motto I find it distinctly stated that " praise is not sought for, but money," and " I do it to make money." The only paragraphs containing what the author is pleased to call satire are the allusions to our C. T. C.; and any unprejudiced reader will agree that the gall supersedes the satire. Truly, if this book can " make money," no author need have fears concerning his income.—*Anonymous cor.* (" 1432 ") *of C. T. C. Gazette, whose editor confessed in the witness box of a London law court (before Mr. Justice Wills, Nov. 22, 1886; see page xci) that he had used it as a medium for forgery ; and who was thereupon dismissed by the indignant judge, with a scathing reprimand for having " indulged in the lowest and vulgarest abuse of the worst form of journalism."*

There is many a noble thought nobly expressed in this book, with its bold originality of style, and daring impudence of advertisement and egotism. To the wheelmen of the world it appeals, its interests being in no way circumscribed by the limits of the American Continent.—*Wheeling, London.*

LONDON ECHOES AT MELBOURNE.

Karl Kron's opening essay, " On the Wheel," is written in a happy vein, and will not fail to claim the attention of all practical riders; the accounts of his own tours prove him to be a by no means unobservant traveler; while the memoir of his favorite bull dog, although in no way connected with his subject, affords such interesting reading that few will be found to regret its interpolation. It is refreshing thus to come across a book on bicycling in which the author exhibits both the ability to write sense and an evident ambition to give the world something of value; for few, if any, of our books in England dealing with the subject can claim an equal literary merit.—*The Field, London.*

Having ourselves devoted considerable space and attention from time to time to Karl Kron's American road-book,—without doubt the most gigantic publication that has ever been placed upon the wheel-world book market,—we are glad to find that so important a paper as the *Field* deals favorably with it; and we now have pleasure in reproducing for our readers the review contained in this leading organ of sport.—*Sewing Machine and Cycle News, London.*

Of all the many evidences of the kindly feeling of cyclists for one another, or, in other words, " the brotherhood of the wheel," we think the successful publication of Karl Kron's book ranks highest. It brings before us, more forcibly than anything else we can record, the existence of a sentiment, unknown in almost any other branch of sport, that binds the hearts of wheelmen together, the world over. Is this not proved by the publication of a book, after four years' hard work of its enterprising author, with over 3200 subscribers, solicited free? Giving as it does statistics and personal references to wheelmen in almost every part of our habitable globe, we recommend it to all as a veritable " encyclopædia of wheeling progress in many countries." No commission is paid a single person for selling it.—*Australian Cycling News, Melbourne.*

Australia and New Zealand get full prominence, for the author has expended an enormous amount of time and money in making a thorough compilation of Australiasian matter. He has an aptness for expressing himself in such neat and concise language, that there is no necessity for re-reading a sentence to grasp its meaning. So little has escaped his observation, that the chief characteristic of his work is its comprehensiveness; but in expression it is positively different from our ordinary cycling literature,—the constant tautology with which most writers nowadays are afflicted being conspicuous by its absence. The book, in its way, is a marvel, eclipsing in every particular all other publications on the same subject.—*Geo. R. Broadbent, in A. C. News.*

I can endorse what Mr. Broadbent says of it, and feel sure that my fellow cyclists, who may have ample reading time during the coming winter evenings, will be well repaid for their outlay by the unique character of the fare provided for the $2.—" *The Hub," in A. C. N.*

Sandhurst, Australia's "golden city," is situated about 100 miles inland from Melbourne, the sea-port capital of the colony of Victoria, and boasts about a tenth as many inhabitants (350,000), though as late as 1853 it was a mere camp of calico-tents in the wild bush, and was then called Bendigo by the gold-miners who dwelt in them. No American city of 35,000 population has given so many subscribers to my scheme (37); and, in recording this fact, on p. 793. as the most curious one of my round-the-world canvass, I remark that it was due to the energy of one of the earliest enthusiasts and organizers of cycling in that city, W. J. PARRY, who has lived there since 1875, and whose residence and address is "Kenfig Villa, Wills st."

He now offers still further to show his good-will for "the cause" by superintending the distribution and sale of my book throughout the "Island Continent." On receipt of 8s. 8d., he will mail a copy to any address in any colony of Australia; he will hand or send specimen pages and circulars gratis to any applicant; and he will forward the book for a month's examination to any signer of the "approval blank," elsewhere printed in this pamphlet, who may be suitably recommended to him. In addition to subscribers' copies, I sent to Mr. Parry, at Sandhurst, 42 books; and I sent 96 others to depositaries elsewhere, subject to his orders, thus: 35 to Melbourne (G. S. Geddes, 11 Latrobe st., East), 33 to Warrnambool (F. W. Briggs), 5 to Hamilton (W. G. Farroll), 4 to Ballarat (R. A. Thompson), 19 to Hobart, Tasmania (T. F. Hallam, at Glenorchy, or R. O. Bishop, at 58 Elizabeth st.), and 30 to Sydney, New South Wales (James Copland, Sydney Bicycle Club, 85 Market st.).

Books may be bought at 8s. 8d. on personal application to either of these agents, and I presume the last-named would mail a copy to any one who might send him the price from any town of New South Wales or Queensland, though I have not yet received his consent thus to act for me (see p. 564). The money collected by each of them will be sent to Mr. Parry, to be remitted to me; and he will supply them with stamped labels for mailing the books to later purchasers, whenever an agent notifies him that local sales cannot be made. Assuming that buyers are finally found for the 138 books which I have deposited in these 8 towns, as an offset to my losses on the 100 subscribers' copies dispatched thither at the same time, I do not intend to send out additional ones to be put on sale there, but rather to mail them directly from New York, on receipt of order for 8s. 8d., or of notice from Mr. Parry that he has received such sum on my account, or of paragraph in the Australian Cycling News promising that such sum will be sent me on reception of book by the applicant who thus secures the editor's endorsement of his good-faith. I do not expect to ask this help of the News before the end of 1889, for I suppose the stock of 138 copies in Mr. Parry's control will hardly be exhausted until then. If the editor be good enough to print the names of those who may apply to him for this present pamphlet of 132 pages. I will mail copies freely whenever I see such names in the News. It is published in Melbourne, on alternate Thursdays, at 5 Collins st., West. Price per quarter, 1s. 9d.

My representative among the New Zealanders is the ex-Captain of the Pioneer B. C., Wm. H. Langdown, of Christchurch—a city of about the size of Sandhurst, though the entire population of the colony is rated at 500,000. His wheeling biography is given on p. 569; and, in a farewell talk had with me, Oct. 11, '87 [he sailed next day for England, after more than a year's experience of American life ; and he intended to sail homeward from England, in March, '88], the belief was expressed that a goodly number of buyers might be found for the book, among the 300 wheelmen of his native town,—to say nothing of the chances in the lesser cycling-centers of the double-island. I sent 33 books for sale there in advance of him, besides 22 subscribers' copies, and I may forward a later supply if the demand warrants. He will mail the book to any part of the colony, on receipt of 8s. 8d. (or, if the supply be exhausted, will send me monthly orders for mailing them from New York, and for mailing special chapters for which 1s. each may have been paid him) : and it may also be bought on personal application to W. M. Service, at Auckland, and H. Snow, at Oamaru, who will send to Mr. Langdown, for transmission to me, the money received thus and from local subscribers. Residents of Dunedin and Wellington, who may wish to take a look at the book before ordering it, should apply to E. H. Burn and D. W. M. Burn, to whom I also send copies of this pamphlet for distribution. [I assume the present goodwill of my agents at the three latter towns, without having lately heard from them.]

These same 132 pages, which I thus offer to mail gratuitously, are also given as an appendix to each of two larger pamphlets, containing reprints of separate chapters : "Curl, the Best of Bull Dogs" (28 pages, with photogravure) and "Castle Solitude in the Metropolis" (56 pages, with wood-cut). I will mail either of these, or the unbound sheets of any other chapter, at sight of a paragraph in *A. C. News*, saying that the person designated has paid the editor thereof a shilling for the same, in my behalf. Similar payments may also be made to me through my agents at Sandhurst, Vict., and Christchurch, N. Z., but the pamphlets will be mailed by myself in New York, on orders from them. Any Australasian correspondent, who may prefer to purchase a copy more promptly, can enclose a shilling's worth of penny postage-stamps directly to myself, and receive the pamphlet by return steamer. Names designed for enrollment as supporters of "My Second Ten Thousand"—whose terms are explained elsewhere in this pamphlet and on p. 716 of the book—may be sent to me at Sandhurst and Christchurch.

In correction of the statement on p. 570, I may add that the *Australasian*, under the editorship of Charles E. Bevington, now has "*and South American*" for a sub-title, and is issued every fourth week by the Australasian Publishing Co., of N. Y., at 22 State st. (The Battery), with an annual subscription rate of $3. It is a large and apparently prosperous trade-journal (92 pp., 11 by 16 in.), containing information of value to people who have commercial or personal interests in these countries. [Melbourne : 30 Collins st.; Sydney : 120 King st.]

Canada's "tax on knowledge," in the shape of a 15 per cent. duty, has discouraged me from attempting any extensive sales there,—my sole depository being at 1421 St. Catherine st., Montreal, where I have put 40 books in the hands of A. T. Lane, for sale at $2 each. If a Canadian send $2 to myself, I shall order his book mailed from Montreal ; so no second duty need be levied. Mr. Lane not only undertakes to work for me without charge or commission,—the same as all my other agents,—but he appends to the full-page adv. of his own business as a bicycle dealer, in the *Canadian Wheelman*, a notice that he will mail the book to any address in the Dominion on receipt of the price. His example reminds me to hereby recommend every such dealer in America who advertises extensively in the cycling press, to insert at the foot of his own announcements a brief "free adv.," giving at least the name, price and publisher's address of "Ten Thousand Miles on a Bicycle."

No books will be put on sale by me in England, for the cost of mailing them thither is no greater than between towns in the United States, and a British buyer may usually count on receiving a copy within three weeks from the day when he mails me a post-office order for 8s. 8d. If he prefers to send such order to the Publisher of *Wheeling*, 152 Fleet st., London, its arrival will be acknowledged in the "Answers to Correspondents" of that Wednesday weekly, and, at sight of such acknowledgment, I will mail the book from New York. As regards the *edition de luxe* (200 copies only, on heavy paper, tinted), I will mail the unbound sheets for 8s. 8d., or the complete book for 10s., in regulation binding of blue and gold. On receipt of 25 half-penny stamps, either by myself or the Publisher of *Wheeling*, I will mail the unbound sheets of "British and Colonial Records " (42 pages of 37,000 words), or of any other single chapter : or either one of the two following reprints, each of which is bound in an olive-green cover and contains as an appendix the 132 pages of the present pamphlet : "Curl, the Best of Bull-Dogs " (28 pages, with photogravure), and "Castle Solitude in the Metropolis " (56 pages, with wood-cut).

In case of delay in arrival of any book or pamphlet, the buyer should address his complaint to me (not to *Wheeling*, even though he may have sent the money to its Publisher originally), and I will agree to satisfy him. The present pamphlet will be mailed gratis to any applicant by penny post-card, or to one whose request may reach me through the "Ans. to Cor." column of *Wheeling*. Names designed for insertion in the roll of supporters of "My Second Ten Thousand " (thus securing the privilege of buying it for two-thirds its regular price, if published, though incurring no obligation to buy it,—as explained elsewhere in this pamphlet, and on p. 716 of book) may also be sent to me through *Wheeling*. In naming "England" as the residence of those who may allowably deal with me by use of this medium, I do not design to employ the word restrictively. Dwellers in Continental Europe, or in any other part of the world, who may find it convenient to address me through *Wheeling*, are assured that their requests will be duly regarded.

REMITTANCES AND ACKNOWLEDGMENTS.

Acknowledgment is promptly made for every letter which brings me money or its equivalent. A sender who fails to receive such response within a week from the time when it ought naturally to reach him, should write again,—giving exact details as to the nature of his remittance, the presence or absence of a "return request" on its envelope, and the time and place of posting. If this second letter brings no reply, a duplicate of it should be addressed to me in some manner which makes it unrecognizable by the person who presumably stopped the others: *e. g.*, it may be enclosed in a double envelope,—the outer one directed to a friend in some other town, or to the editor of one of the cycling journals, who will remail to me the inner one.

Postal-notes are objectionable, because costing the sender a fee and trouble without giving him any security against loss. A thief can use them with no more question than if they were money. U. S. or Canadian postage-stamps of 1 c. and 2 c. values are acceptable to me for any sum less than $1; half-penny English or Australian stamps for any sum less than 4s. In sending such stamps, and in enclosing greenbacks of $1 or $2 values, care should be taken to have the paper and envelope opaque enough not to reveal the fact of such enclosure, even when exposed to the strongest light. For any sum greater than $2, a post-office order or an express money-order should be bought. Its cost may be deducted from the amount due me. The American, United States, Pacific and other expresses issue such orders at a fee of 5 c. up to $5, 8 c. up to $10, and 10 c. up to $20; and they are bankable, the same as drafts. The sender must put his name at the indicated place on the back of each express order, after assuring himself that the inscription at the top makes it "*payable to Karl Kron, at the University Building, New York City, D.*"

The American, United States, Baltimore & Ohio, National, Erie and some other expresses offer a "special mail-rate" for prepaid packages of printed matter,—namely 15 c. for 2¼ lbs., without regard to distance carried,—provided the place addressed is an office on one of these connecting expresses recognizing said special rate. If an attempt is ever made to levy an extra charge on a book thus prepaid, the person addressed should resist it, and should report the circumstances to the Publisher, giving date and name of town from which the package is billed.

As the book itself weighs only two pounds, its wrappers may weigh four ounces without raising the total beyond the 15 c. express-rate. It should either be enclosed in a pasteboard box, or else be packed with guards of pasteboard or stout paper, so that the covers need not be marred by the string used in tying the outside wrapper. In preparing the book for the mail, two ounces may be added by its wrappers, without raising the postage-rate above 17 c. A set of protective tins for the four corners weigh less than an ounce, and the special pasteboard case which I sometimes use instead of them weighs less than two ounces. In applying the tins, their flat sides should be put *out*-side; the book should then be wrapped in stout paper and securely tied, but without any pasting or sealing.

SUGGESTIONS AND CORRECTIONS.

"New York" is a direction which will suffice to bring a letter to me, ultimately, in case nothing more definite can be remembered; but, on the other hand, the inscription of my address in full is recommended as needed to ensure prompt delivery. Washington Square chances to be divided between three postal districts, and delivery of mail-matter at the University Building is therefore facilitated by mentioning that its district is "D." As the full address is somewhat long, I suggest that correspondents may be saved the trouble of writing it, by cutting it from my envelopes and pasting it on the envelopes which bring their replies. Replies themselves may also often be conveniently made, in informal fashion, by writing on the margins or between the lines of my letters (which are done by type-writer), and remailing those same to me, so that I can file the original questions with their answers.

Personal calls can be attended to only between 4 and 6 P. M., except by special appointment; and an interview even at those hours may be more certainly ensured by sending notice in advance. (All this is explained on p. 730, which prospective visitors are requested to read.) Whenever I leave town for more than a day or two, that fact may be learned at the janitor's office (No. 9, on ground floor); and in such cases, my mail-matter is duly forwarded.

Misprints of book's price ("$1.50" for "$2") occur on pages 707, 711, 732, 734, 799, which were cast before the great increase in size made a change necessary; but they are of course not to be considered as contradicting the true record of the title-page. No attention should be paid, either, to the remark on page 799, that books will be mailed directly by the manufacturers, the Springfield Printing Co. The same remark also appears on 15,000 of my posters, labels and envelopes, which were printed when book was first published; but a limitation should have been made to the year 1887. That preliminary arrangement has now ceased, and all money-orders of $2, from any town in the U. S., should hereafter be addressed directly to the publisher, KARL KRON, at the University Building, Washington Square, N. Y. City, D.

The only region excepted from the foregoing request is the Pacific Slope. In order to ensure prompt delivery there, I have deposited 100 books with J. J. Bliss, at 228 Phelan Building, San Francisco, and he has consented to mail copies to any town west of the Rocky Mountains, in response to all money-orders of $2 which may reach him before the close of 1888. Residents of the city may buy the book of him during business-hours, or may apply for a fortnight's examination of it, "on approval," under prescribed conditions. He offers to take all this trouble as a mere matter of good-will, the same as my other agents, who simply hold copies for me on sale.

The much-neglected preface and index of a book are of more use to the reader than is generally supposed. Some of our great geniuses are expert in the art of index-reading. We venerate the inventor of the index. We often learn the character of a work through these sources. Read both preface and index, as the light thus obtained will help regulate your course as to the amount of time to be devoted to the book.—*Magazine of American History.*

The Publisher desires to file the name and address of every buyer of the book,—"not necessarily for publication, but as a guaranty of good faith." Each buyer will therefore confer a favor by sending me this information, giving time and place of purchase; and he is also invited to heed the requests on pp. 714-17, as to offering an opinion of such "points" as chance to impress him, either for good or for evil, and as to offering his name in support of "2 X. M." Each depositary, when he sends me the price of a book, is also urged to send buyer's name and address. One reason for filing these names is that I want to avoid wasting any literary ammunition on those who have already been captured; another reason is that I want documentary evidence to prove, after I *have* captured the 30,000, that my proclamation of the fact rests upon a somewhat firmer basis than "the ordinary book-agent's lie."

In asking for "opinions," on p. 715, "I specially urge that faults be called to my attention: not only printers' blunders, misstatements of fact and defects of execution, but everything which to the mind of a subscriber seems an error of judgment,—as regards omission as well as commission; for a general agreement of critics concerning objectionable points will give me a valuable warning as to what to avoid hereafter." On the other hand, if points which some object to are approved of by others, I shall receive agreeable evidence of having succeeded in my plan of appealing to a multitude of diverse and conflicting tastes. My theory as publisher of such an encyclopædia is,—not that any single buyer will approve the whole of it, or even read the whole of it, but rather that its mass and variety of matter are so great as to convince any buyer of having "got his money's worth," even if pleased with only a fractional part of it, and indifferent or hostile to all the rest. A book should be supported,—just as a man is, in his private or public life,—not for the absence of faults, but for the presence of merits.

The aim of this pamphlet is to spread the evidence, already given in the newspapers, that this book, despite its manifest faults, is well worth the very low price charged for it. Additions to such evidence, in the form of testimony from appreciative subscribers, would make an interesting supplementary pamphlet,—and this might be even more effective in attracting new buyers, because the opinions of practical wheelmen who had paid for their books might well seem more genuine and significant than mere "newspaper notices." Thus, those of my copartners who are prevented by isolation or other cause from verbally helping win the new patrons needed for the scheme's success, may indirectly help by contributing to the supply and variety of literary bait which it is necessary for me to employ in fishing for them. Aside from this practical consideration, I am glad to have any subscriber assure me, however briefly, that he has received the book, and is satisfied with it; and I wish each new buyer, to whom I send it by mail or express, would promptly acknowledge to me its arrival in good condition. Should any copy be found defective, I will arrange to have it returned to the manufacturers and replaced by a perfect one, without expense.

Q3

SUBSCRIBERS AS AGENTS.

Such as yet hold free copies of Preface and Contents Table (whereof I print 5000 ahead of 10,000, as an aid of the SSK) are invited to distribute the same among their cycling acquaintances and other possible purchasers. I shall account it a great favor if they will show the book itself to local librarians and bookkeepers, and will supply me with the addresses of wheelmen who are **likely to** *be interested in my circulars and specimen pages.*

Ten Thousand Miles on a Bicycle.—By Karl **Kron,** author of "Four Years at Yale, By a Graduate of '69." Cloth bound, gilt top, photogravure frontispiece, 41 chapters, 608 pages, 100 cue-words, elaborate indexes (10,947 titles and 22,880 references), no advertisements. **Mailed** on receipt of money-order for $2, by the publisher, Karl Kron, *at the University Building, Washington Square,* New York City, P. Analytical contents-table, descriptive circulars and specimen pages sent free to any applicant by postal-card. Publication was made May 25, 1887.)

I am perfectly aware that the average hard-headed business-man, whether engaged in the book-trade or in any other, will class me as a crank and a visionary, when I say that my main reliance for success is the simple sentiment of good-will towards myself which I assume that the book will create in the minds of the 3000 strangers whom I call "my co-partners," and to whom I supply it at half-price. If each one of these shall be enough pleased with it to promptly persuade even one friend to buy a copy, I shall get back the money which I have risked; and, if each one shall be enough pleased to sell ten copies for me, within three or four years, I shall win a fair reward for my long labors. I have paid no one anything for soliciting subscribers, and I shall pay no one anything for selling the book. Whoever buys a copy from one of my depositaries may rest assured that the entire profit thereon will reach me as certainly as if mailed direct.

Massachusetts subscribers east of Framingham will call for their books at the Boston office of the Pope Mfg. Co., 79 Franklin st., and copies will be kept on sale also by W. W. Stall, 509 Tremont st.; W. Read & Sons, 107 Washington st. As regards New York City, the 80 club-members of the League B. C. will get their books at the clubhouse and pay the club treasurer; members of the N. Y. Ixion and Harlem clubs, and all residents above 41st st., and in Westchester county, will call at C. R. Boswell's, 313 W. 58th st.; while all the non-club subscribers also live below 42d st., and all the Brooklyn men (except K. C. W., who will be attended to by Mr. Loucks, at the clubhouse), will find their copies at the Pope Mfg. Co.'s, 12 Warren st. I shall also deposit at that agency all Long Island, Staten Island and New Jersey books (except those for Bordentown, Camden, Morristown, Newark, Orange and Trenton). In Brooklyn, the volume may be bought of Schwalbach, Prospect Park Plaza. Chicago subscribers will call at the Pope Mfg. Co.'s, 291 Wabash av.; and three other leading firms there will serve me freely as selling-agents: the Gormully & Jeffery Mfg. Co., 222 N. Franklin st.; the J. Wilkinson Co., 77 State st.; A. G. Spalding & Bro., 108 Madison st. My other most important depositaries are these: Baltimore, S. T. Clark & Co., 2 & 4 Hanover st.; Buffalo, E. N. Bowen, 184 Main st.; Cincinnati, A. A. Bennett, 4th st.; Cleveland, —————; Hartford, Weed S. M. Co.; Newark, H. A. Smith & Co., Oraton Hall; St. Louis, —————; San Francisco, —————; Washington, E. T. Eitterroth, 1713 N. Y. av.

An electrotype of some such as present page, giving names and prices of all American cycling papers now in the market (May 4, '89), will be freely supplied by me to any publisher who is willing to reprint from it. A proof will be mailed on application. I will also freely send proofs of any pages which any one may wish to reprint, without cutting into his own book for the copy."

Pub. at $2 by Karl **Kron,** *at the University Building, Washington* Sq., N. Y. City, P.

On March 31, 1888, when my pamphlet of "Newspaper Notices" was almost ready for issue, the works of the Springfield Printing Company were closed by order of the Insolvency Court, and all my material there was thus hopelessly locked up for two months. The unsecured creditors having at last accepted a compromise of 20 per cent. on aggregate debts of $52,000, the concern re-organized, May 30, as "The Springfield Printing & Binding Co.," with a capital of $100,000, and began moving the plant and material into a new building, for the resumption of business. Unaccountable delays, however, prevented the delivery to me of my property, even in an unfinished condition, until the middle of July, when the final 48 pages were printed in New York, by D. C. Crocker, of No. 1 Winthrop Place, close to the University Building, who also set the type for the half-dozen latest plates used in such printing. Thus, for no fault of mine, the pamphlet is published four months after the time promised, or on the very day named as latest allowable time for delivering to the binder those 96 of its pages which I venture to reproduce in the "Publisher's Trade-List Annual," July 31, 1888.

In addition to and correction of the facts about "Cycling Books in the American Market, March 1, 1888 (p. 66)," the following are offered:

A. J. Wilson, of Powerscroft House, Clapton, London (see pp. xcix., 534 "X. M. Miles"), offers to mail either of his books, "The Pleasures of Cycling" and "Two Trips to the Emerald Isle," profusely illustrated by G. Moore, on receipt of a half-dollar money-order. He has deposited sixteen of the latter book with me, for mailing on the same terms; and if anyone sends me fifty cents for "The Pleasures," I will instruct Mr. W. to mail it from London. I make no charge for this service, which is simply in the line of my theory that all wheelmen should freely help the sale of cycling literature. "Pedal and Path" is now mailed for 25c. (one-third the original price), by *Bi. World* Co., 12 Pearl street, Boston. It has 244 pp., besides 16 inset picture-pages, and its 27 chapters comprise 80,000 words (not "about 140,000," as noted on pp. X3, xcvii.). Of the American cycling papers listed on p. 64, the *Wheelmens*, of St. Louis and San Francisco, seem to have died before July, 1888; but the *L. A. W. Pointer* now flourishes as a semi-monthly at Oshkosh, Wis.

"Forty Years Out of Yale," by a Graduate of '69 (to be published in 1909, by Karl Kron, if alive then), will contain at least one chapter describing the effectiveness of this present collection of "Newspaper Notices" in attracting the 30,000 buyers.

"Ten Thousand Miles on a Bicycle" is very complete indeed; packed full of information.—*F. G. S., Carpenter, Pa.*

A marvel of cheapness at $2. I am so well pleased with it that I shall try and send you two or three more orders soon.—*O. H. C., Santa Fe, N. M.* The book has thus cost me double the sum subscribed, but I would not be without it if its price were $5.—*J. D. D., Philadelphia.*

The unique frontispiece of "Ten Thousand Miles on a Bicycle,"—a clipped-eared bull-dog, done by the new process called photogravure,—is something of a surprise in a book on such a subject, and the question as to its meaning is not answered by reference to some 20 pages of the dog's biography to which attention is called. The volume is inscribed to the memory of "the very best dog whose presence ever blessed this planet." Well, he certainly does not look it, but the account of his life—and death—is the very best thing, from a literary point of view, in a volume of 900 pages. It is capital in itself, but its excellence must be the chief reason for its appearance in the midst of a tedious record of roads and journeys with which it has no sort of connection. That the dog thus immortalized was a great favorite of the author's in his youth, and that the author himself is popular with wheelmen and now avowedly wishes to make money upon his popularity, are facts hardly sufficient to justify the insertion of such a sketch in the body of a work so different in style and purpose. It is a piece of egotism that by no means stands alone. Yet, in view of the great quantity of matter here condensed and classified, the picture of the bull-dog which embellishes the first page, would seem to be a fitting emblem of the perseverance with which the author has pushed to completion his three years' task.—*Boston Advertiser.*

The extraordinary author dedicates his work to "The Memory of My Bull-Dog."—*Boston Post.*

The dedication of the book to the author's bull-dog may have merit as a sentimental freak, but it is a literary execration.—*McGregor News, Ia.*

The author is possessed of a vein of smart American humor, which illuminates the dry text of his book from beginning to end. In places, such as the inimitable chapter devoted to his bull-dog "Curl," he soars to a pitch which reminds the reader very forcibly of Mark Twain and Max Adeler; and the cyclist who loves his dog will read this chapter over more than once. To "Curl," whose noble and expressive features act as frontispiece, the book is dedicated, and there is a certain pathos in the selection.— *Wheeling, London*

Admirers of dogs, and of out-door sports, will take kindly to the book.— *New Orleans Picayune.*

"Curl" and "Castle Solitude in the Metropolis" are well worth reading, but of doubtful appropriateness in "a book of American roads."— *Wheelmen's Gazette, Indianapolis.*

A frontispiece, representing the head of a particularly ill-favored bull-dog, to whose memory the book is lovingly dedicated, forewarns the reader that the intellectual rambles of a bicycler did not necessarily share in the directness and regularity of his routes. The claim of this pet dog to public notice is not clearly established; but his interesting physiognomy, confronting the reader, in some measure compels a perusal of the chapter devoted to the uneventful career of the animal; and the theme apparently draws out the author's best literary powers.—*Alta California, San Francisco.*

The invitation that I contribute my catalogue to the sixteenth yearly "Publishers' Trade-List Annual" (to be issued September 1, 1888, by R. R. Bowker, 330 Pearl street, N. Y.), was received after almost all my pages had been electrotyped. Though not planned for any such ultimate usage, reflection upon the offer convinced me that the experiment of inserting them there might be worth trying. The collected catalogues of '87 made a monster volume of about 3000 pages (seven by ten inches in size, four and a half inches thick, and weighing nine pounds); and the '88 collection promises to be as large,—the edition being fixed at 1750 copies. Many curious contrasts are always shown in the topography and "styles" of the lists contributed; but I think that no previous list has ever occupied anything like as many as 48 pages of the "Annual" in advertising a single book. My decision to use 96 of these electrotypes for such a purpose will therefore give one novel feature to the '88 edition; and it will compel publishers and booksellers to at least recognize the fact that "cycling" is enough of a phenomenon to have caused the investment of an extraordinary amount of capital in this scheme for circulating its literature. They may not believe that the gratitude of my 3400 advance subscribers, for receiving such a book at half price, will be an important factor in securing the needed 30,000 buyers; but the mere mass of evidence, that I am in good-faith trying to work so elaborate a scheme on so unusual a basis, may perhaps make some of my arguments seem worth reading by men " in the trade." If the other contributions to the "Annual" average as in '87, my own pages (placed under " K " in the alphabetical arrangement) will stand almost exactly in the center of the volume.

In modification of the remark upon other pages, that I will not pay postage or expressage upon book except at $2, even to a bookseller, but only offer him the discount of 25 c. on condition of his personally purchasing at one of my depositories (e. g., in New York, at 12 Warren st., near City Hall), I may say that I will deliver it for $1.75 to any forwarding-agent within a half-mile of Washington Square, — which is close beside Astor Place, the center of the publishing district. The Blakeman & Taylor Co., 740 Broadway; Scribner's Sons, 743 Broadway, and James Kelly, 25 Bond st., are agents within the limits named, and through them my orders from out-of-town dealers have thus far been filled. I think the book may be bought in London of S. Low & Co., Fetter Lane. Fleet st.; but, as they pay me $1.75 for it in New York, their price must needs be more than the 8s. 8d., for which I mail it directly to any address in England.

The printer of my contribution to the " Annual" is D. C. Crocker, near the University Building, who supplies 7 of the 96 plates thus used (X4 to T4), and who also prints pp. 33 to 80 of the pamphlet, the other pages having come from the press of the Springfield Printing Company.

BOOKS AND PAPERS RECOMMENDED.

On pp. xcvi, 181, 233 of my book, and also on all its labels and show-bills (13,000 printed to date), I have recommended, as the most readable collection of cycling travels ever issued, Thomas Stevens's "Around the World on a Bicycle." The first volume tells the story of his strange adventures from California to Persia (550 pp. of 230,000 words, 110 illustrations; cloth-bound; $4; pub. May 31, '87, by C. Scribner's Sons, N. Y.), and the second one will enclose the even more remarkable ones in Afghanistan, India, China and Japan, including much material not included in the *Outing* series which terminates in May, '88. That month is named as probable time of appearance of the volume, under the same publishers and presumably of similar size and price as the first. Autographed copies of either will be mailed by Mr. Stevens personally to any one who sends him the retail price; and it any one chooses to send it to him through myself, it will reach him promptly, as we are in frequent communication.

Advertisement has freely been given by me, on 13,000 posters, labels and envelopes, that the chief English book on the subject is "Cycling," by Lord Bury and G. L. Hillier (152 pp. of 134,000 words; 59 illustrations; $1.50; pub. in March, '87, by Longmans, Green & Co., London), in the Badminton Library of Sports; and I devoted nearly a page (xcvi) of the addenda to reprinting all the favorable press-notices I could find of it, and also the adv. of its American importers, Little, Brown & Co., of Boston. The sort of "free notice" accorded me ... may be found by perusing the "Condensation from Coventry," on the 13th and 15th pages of this pamphlet. Longmans, Green & Co. also pub. in Feb., '88, "Our Sentimental Journey Through France and Italy," by Joseph and Elizabeth Robins Pennell (a tricycle tour, with 170 and 122 illustrations; $1.75); and they adv. to mail the same from 15 E. 16th st., N. Y.

A touring book which I can recommend as well-printed and readable is "Wanderings on Wheel and on Foot through Europe," by Hugh Callan, M. A. of Glasgow University (216 pp. and 50 styles; by S. Low & Co., London, at 1s. 6d.). It is fully described by me on pp. xcix, xxx, and the author has agreed to mail it to any address in the U. S. whenever I notify him by mail that 50 cents have been deposited with me and accredited to his account.

Death has overtaken half the 16 American cycling papers catalogued ten months ago, when the list on page cii of my book's addenda was electrotyped, and there has been one birth during the interval. Seven of these 16 were born during the preceding nine months, and death nearly wiped out 5 of the 19 in existence Aug. 1, 1886, as listed on p. 621. As 5 had died before that date, the 8 which are named below as now surviving (March 1, 1888) are the remnant of 25, and are more than doubly outnumbered by those at rest in the journalistic grave-yard. Named in the order of their age, the two oldest are weeklies, the youngest is a semi-monthly, the others are monthlies:—*Bicycling World*, 12 Pearl st., Boston, Mass.; *Wheel*, 23 Park Row, N. Y.; *Wheelmen's Gazette*, 25 Sentinel Building, Indianapolis, Ind.; *Canadian Wheelman*, London, Ontario; *Star Advocate*, East Rochester, N. H.; *American Wheelman*, 208 N. Fourth st., St. Louis, Mo.; *Bicycle*, West Randolph, Vt.; *Pacific Coast Wheelmen and Athlete*, San Francisco, Cal. The annual subscription is $2.00 for the weeklies and 50 c. for the others, except that the *Bicycle* costs only 12 c., and the *Canadian Wheelman* is sent free to each member of the Canadian Wheelmen's Association (price $1 to outsiders).

English cycling journalism is now reduced to the two weekly organs of "the Coventry ring," *Cyclist* (Wednesday) and *Bicycling News* (Saturday), and two opposition weeklies, *Wheeling* (Tuesday), edited by C. W. Nairn, at 152 Fleet st., and the *Sewing-Machine & Cycle News* (Saturday), edited by H. H. Griffin, at 9 Wine-Office ct., Fleet st.—both of which men were until recently in the employ of "the ring." Each paper is sold at a penny a copy, or mailed at 6s. 6d. a year. The *Bi. News* is the only one of the four that gives much attention to touring, or that usually contains cartoons. It is advertised as "the oldest cycling paper in the world," and as "printed for the proprietors by Iliffe & Son," who also advertise that they print the *Cyclist* "for the proprietors, W. I. Iliffe and H. Sturmey." In my book, I use the phrases "Coventry ring" and "the Iliffes," indifferently, as referring to these three men; for the practical relationship to the public is that of a single firm of printers and publishers aiming to control a monopoly of the cycling trade literature in Great Britain, no matter what may be their exact legal status individually, as sharers in the profits of the two firms which they see fit to conduct.

W3

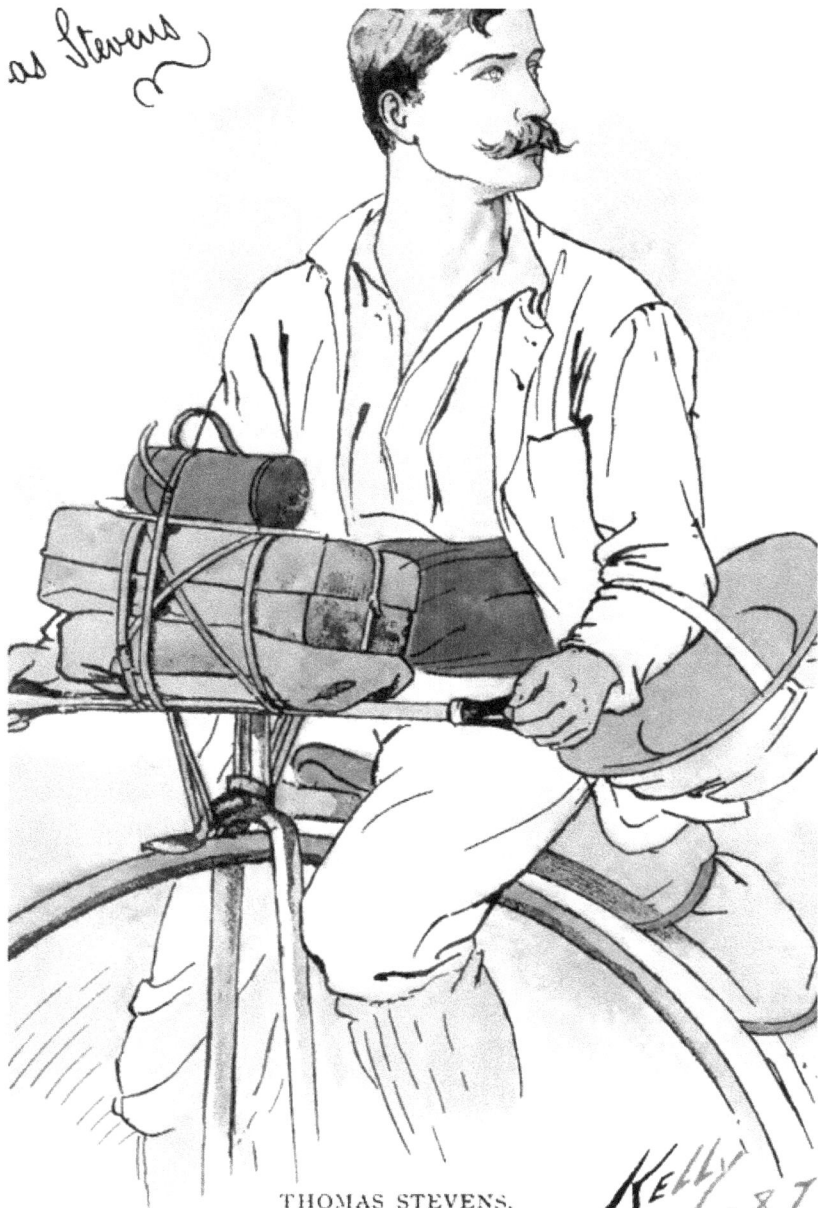

THOMAS STEVENS.

(FROM VOL. I. OF HIS FAMOUS WORK "AROUND THE WORLD ON A BICYCLE," BY PERMISSION OF
CHARLES SCRIBNER'S SONS.)

A BLAST FROM "THE THUNDERER."

Difficult as it is to praise Mr. Karl Kron's book, we can say honestly that it contains a mass of information, chiefly of the Baedeker kind, likely to be useful to cyclists in America. The author seems to have wheeled into most corners of the Eastern States, and has collected a mass of facts and figures. He is evidently an enthusiast on the wheel, and one or two of his general essays upon the amusement are interesting. But the book is, on the whole, dry, and so badly arranged that it can hardly be said to boast of any order. Its ample indexes, however, give it value as a book of reference, in which light we suppose it is to be regarded, rather than as the interesting narrative for which the title prepares us.— *The Times.*

Eight dollars may be well and wisely spent in purchasing the two large illustrated volumes in which Thomas Stevens tells of his marvelous exploits " Around the World on a Bicycle." I have improved every occasion to recommend the same as the most readable collection of cycling travels ever issued, or ever likely to be issued; and my opinion is followed by so cold-blooded and dispassionate an authority as the reviewer of the world's chief daily newspaper, the " London Times," who praises him unreservedly for more than a column. He also adopts my theory, that the literary excellence of the work (considered as the first attempt of a man whose " schooling ended at fourteen ") is almost as much of a phenomenon as the " globe girdling " which it describes, and which another London daily, the " Pall Mall Gazette," calls " the most splendid piece of personal adventure of this century,—and it will pretty certainly remain unequaled in our time." BUT, if any one wishes to have this strange story without the expenditure of $8, he should pay a quarter of that sum for " Ten Thousand Miles on a Bicycle," which contains a complete abstract of it, and also many personal facts not included in the original.

Such is the remarkable epitome of Mr. Stevens's travels. The most sensational of them—those subsequent to leaving Teheran—are not included in this first volume; and we are indebted to Mr. Karl Kron for our facts concerning his journey from Teheran to Yokohama. . . . He tells us little about himself, his outfit, or his history; and it is Mr. Karl Kron again, who informs us that Mr. Stevens never learnt to ride till 1883, at the age of thirty—the year before he started.—*The Times.*

" From Teheran to Yokohama," the second and concluding volume of Thomas Stevens's entertaining narrative, is to be issued in September at $4 (N. Y. : Scribners; London : Sampson Low). Mr. Stevens having presented me with a quantity of the lithographic portraits similar to those forming the frontispiece of his first volume, they will be inserted opposite the present page in 3000 of my pamphlets. This portrait and 105 other illustrations are reproduced in the German edition, translated by Dr. F. M. Schröter, in August, 1887, and published at Leipzig, in 1888, by F. Hirt & Son (" Um die Erde auf dem Zweirad ;" pp. 510; price. 8 m., 50 p.), who will presumably treat the second volume in the same way. The English edition can be bought at Melbourne of S. Mullen.

N₄

The new issue (3d ed., March, '88, price 15 c.; see pp. 111, 677) of "Atkins's Road Book of Boston and Vicinity" deserves mention here because its publisher, C. A. Underwood, of 386 Tremont st., has been liberal-minded enough to volunteer the insertion of a free adv. of mine; though my argument that he ought also to make room for the following free list of all the other cycling books in the American market did not have power to convert him.

"Pedal and Path," by G. B. Thayer (32 chapters, 244 pp., about 140,000 words, illust., see p. xcvii), a record of cross-continent touring; pub. in '87, at Hartford, Ct., by the *Evening Post* Association. "Hints to Prospective Cycling Tourists in England and Wales" "Care and Repair of Wheels" (10 c.), written and pub. in '87 by Stimson, Stamford, Ct. "A Canterbury Pilgrimage," by Joseph and Elizabeth Robins Pennell (N. Y. : Scribners, Aug., '85 : 50 c.). "Two Pilgrims' Progress, or Italy from a Tricycle," by the same (Boston : Roberts Bros., Oct., '86). "In and Around Cape Ann," wheelman's guide, by J. S. Webber, jr. (Gloucester, Mass., Aug., '85 : 100 pp. of about 30,000 words : 11 illust. : cloth bound), mailed by author for 75 c. "Lyra Bicyclica : Sixty Poets on the Wheel" (2d ed., Mar., '85, 160 pp., cloth), mailed for 75 c. by the author, J. G. Dalton, 36 St. James av., Boston. "Rhymes of the Road and the River," by Chris. Wheeler (Nov., '85, 154 pp., elegantly printed and bound, $2), pub. by E. Stanley Hart & Co., 321 Chestnut st., Philadelphia. "Wheel Songs," poems by S. Conant Foster (July, '84, 80 pp., $1.75), pub. by White, Stokes & Allen, N. Y. "Wheels and Whims," a cycling novel by Mrs. F. T. McCray and Miss E. L. Smith (2d ed., May, '86, 288 pp., paper covers 50 c.), pub. by J. S. Browning, 91 Oliver st., Boston. "Star Rider's Manual" (2d ed., Mar., '86, 117 pp., 75 c.), pub. by E. H. Corson, editor of the *Star Advocate*, East Rochester, N. H. "A B C of Bicycling" (April, '80 : 36 pp., 10 c.), pub. by H. B. Hart, 811 Arch st., Philadelphia. "Wheelmen's Handbook of Essex County" (3d ed., Aug., '86, 74 pp., 20 c.), pub. by Geo. Chinn, Beverly, Mass. "Road Book of Long Island" (Apr., '86, 60 pp. with maps, cloth bound, $1), pub. by A. B. Barkman, 608 Fourth av., Brooklyn, N. Y. "Wheelmen's Reference Book" (May, '86, 101 pp., 49 lith. portraits, 50 c.), pub. by Ducker & Goodman, Hartford, Ct. "Canadian Wheelmen's Association's Guide," touring routes. (2d ed., Mar., '87, 124 pp. ; see p. 636), mailed for 50 c. by H. B. Donly, Simcoe, Ont.

Similar to the last named, and more important than many of the other works on the list, are the "road books" (tabulated touring routes with maps) issued by the leading State Divisions of the L. A. W., gratuitously to each member. If sold to outsiders, the price is usually $1, but in many cases their sale is forbidden to all except League members of other States. Books for the following States have issued : Massachusetts, Connecticut, New York, New Jersey, Pennsylvania, Maryland, Kentucky, Ohio, Michigan, Indiana, Illinois, Mo. and Cal.

Trade catalogues are annually issued by the various American makers of bicycles, and may be had by addressing postal-cards as follows : Pope Mfg. Co., 79 Franklin st., Boston ; 12 Warren st., N. Y. ; 291 Wabash av., Chicago. Gormully & Jeffery Mfg. Co., 222-228 N. Franklin st., Chicago. Overman Wheel Co., 182-188 Columbus av., Boston. H. B. Smith Machine Co., Smithville, N. J. King Wheel Co., 51 Barclay st., N. Y. Springfield Bicycle Mfg. Co., 9 Cornhill, Boston. Smith National Cycle Mfg. Co., Water st., Washington, D. C.

Annual catalogues or revised price-lists are also published by many importers and dealers, including the following chief advertisers of the cycling press : A. G. Spalding & Brother, 108 Madison st., Chicago ; 241 Broadway, N. Y. Hart Cycle Co., 811 Arch st., Philadelphia. Clark Cycle Co., 2 & 4 Hanover st., Baltimore. H. A. Smith & Co., Newark, N. J. G. R. Bidwell, 313 W. 58th st., N. Y. W. Read & Son, 107 Washington st., Boston. L. H. Johnson, Orange, N. J. A. T. Lane, 1421 St. Catherine st., Montreal. C. Robinson & Co., 22 Church st., Toronto. E. N. Bowen, 585 Main st., Buffalo. A. A. Bennett, 6 E. Fourth st., Cincinnati. St. Louis Wheel Co., 310 N. Eleventh st., St. Louis. John Wilkinson Co., 77 State st., Chicago. Western Toy Co., Chicago. A. W. Gump Co., Dayton, O. G. W. Rouse & Son, Peoria, Ill. Huber & Allison, Louisville, Ky. W. W. Stall, 509 Tremont st., Boston. C. Schwalbach, Prospect Park Plaza, Brooklyn. Manhattan Wheel Exchange, 49 Cortlandt st., N. Y. E. H. Corson, East Rochester, N. H. "Ten Thousand Miles on a Bicycle" may be consulted at all the above places, and can be bought at most of them.

"*No books are to be returned to me at New York.*" That is a truth which I wish to impress upon every person who may chance to hold any belonging to me and may wish to rid himself of the same. My desire is that all reshipments should be to new purchasers rather than to myself; and I will send labels and directions for that purpose whenever notice reaches me that such action is desirable. If a depositary, or the holder of a book "on approval," changes his residence in such a way as renders inconvenient the transfer of book or books, let him notify me that he has deposited the same in the hands of some local acquaintance, who will reship them at my request.

CURL, THE BEST OF BULL-DOGS: *a Study in Animal Life.* Twenty-eight pages of 14,000 words, with photogravure frontispiece; appendix of 132 pages giving specimens of the text and newspaper notices of "Ten Thousand Miles on a Bicycle." Sent postpaid to any country in the world, on receipt of 25 cents' worth of the lowest denomination of postage-stamps locally current. KARL KRON, *Publisher, at the University Building, N. Y. City.*

CASTLE SOLITUDE IN THE METROPOLIS: *a Study in Social Science.* Fifty-six pages of 34,000 words, with small picture of the Castle; appendix of 132 pages, the same as the above. Sent to any address for 25 c.

Buyers of either the above pamphlets in the United States or Canada should enclose to the Publisher 25 one-cent stamps; in Great Britain, Australasia, or other British colonies, 25 half-penny stamps. Residents of Great Britain who send 25 half-penny stamps with an order for the pamphlet (or for the unbound sheets of any chapter in the book) to the Publisher of *Wheeling,* 152 Fleet st., London, E. C., will find the same acknowledged in the "Answers to Correspondents" of that Wednesday weekly; and, at sight of such notice, I will mail from New York the print thus paid for. Similarly, if any one in Australia sends 25 half-penny stamps to my agent there (W. J. Parry, Wills st., Sandhurst, Vict.), he will notify me, in next monthly letter, to mail the desired print from New York. If any subscriber to the *Australian Cycling News* sends the stamps to that paper, with request that the editor thereof hold them for me and print an order that I forward a pamphlet, I presume he will do so,—though his formal consent to such plan has not yet reached me. I also assume his willingness still further to follow the friendly example of *Wheeling,* by freely printing the name and address of any applicant who wishes me to send him the present pamphlet of 132 pages, gratis.

Either of the two "studies" may be ordered at 25 cents, through any bookstore in the United States or Canada. In such case, the dealer himself will remit 15 cents to me for it,—or 18 cents, if he wishes it sent by mail.

Of blank volumes, ruled for the preservation of riding-records (see p. 676), the three most elaborate are F. W. Weston's " My Cycling Log Book " (Boston : C. H. Whiting, 168 Devonshire st.; $1.25); Richwine Brothers' " Wheelmen's Record Book " (Philadelphia : E. Stanley Har: & Co., 321 Chestnut st.; 70 c.), and C. D. Batchelder's " Record Book " (Lancaster, N. H.; 50 c.). The two latter are for pocket use. All are cased in leather; but a cloth-bound edition of the last-named is also issued at 30 cents.

In the first place, the Darrow Brothers, of Indianapolis, Ind., publish there, at 25 Sentinel Building, the *Wheelmen's Gazette*, an illustrated monthly magazine, at 50 cents a year. Originated at Springfield, Mass., by H. E. Ducker, in April, '83, the change of location and proprietorship was made in July, '87; and the new owners discontinued their weekly *Wheelmen's Record*, which was published acceptably during the whole of '87 (see p cii.), and trans-ferred its good-will to the *Gazette* in January. As this paper has always promptly printed everything I have ever written for it about the book, besides freely helping the sale of the same in other ways, I am specially glad to assist in getting subscribers for it. Its price to Great Britain and the British Colo-nies is doubled, on account of the postage rate. Any one writing to me from those countries, may enclose 4s. (p. o. o.) for a year's subscription or 2s. (in half-penny stamps) for a half-year's, and the *Gazette* will be duly forwarded. If any American correspondent asks me for a specimen copy, I will also send his request to Darrow Brothers. They arrange to have the English weekly, *Wheeling*, mailed from London to any one in the U. S. who will send them its regular price ($2 a year, or $1 a half-year), and they give the *Gazette* as a premium. They offer liberal combination rates with several other cycling papers and with the popular journals.

The chief exponent of the more progressive and liberal-minded section of British wheelmen, and leading independent organ of the trade, in opposi-tion to "the Coventry ring," is *Wheeling*, dated every Wednesday at 152 Fleet st., London, E. C. Its annual rate to home subscribers is 6s. 6d.; to those in the United States, $2; but Americans who subscribe through Dar-row Brothers, Indianapolis, will also receive the latter's *Wheelmen's Gazette* as a monthly premium. A change in the proprietorship of *Wheeling* was effected Nov. 2, '87. Since then, the post of editor-in-chief has been held by C. W. Nairn (a writer on the London cycling press from its earliest days, and for several years in the employ of "the Coventry ring"), with W. Mc-Candlish as his chief assistant.

The new proprietors of *Wheeling* continue towards me the liberal policy of its originator. If any one chooses to send them 8s. 8d. for my book, the amount is acknowledged in "Answers to Correspondents," and at sight of same I mail from New York the book to the indicated address. If any one sends 25 half-penny stamps for the special pamphlets " Carl " (28 pp. and photogravure) or " Castle Solitude " (56 pp. and wood cut), or for the sheets of any other chapter in the book, acknowledgment and dispatch follow in the same way. Names of supporters for " 2 N. M." may be enrolled in simi-lar fashion; and the present pamphlet of 130 pages will be mailed without charge to any one who asks me for it through the columns of *Wheeling*. These same pages are also bound in as an appendix to the two special pam-phlets, which are printed on heavy paper, tinted and calendered, and enclosed in olive-green covers. My *edition de luxe* of book (on same heavy paper, 200 only printed) may be had by sending 10s. to *Wheeling*, 152 Fleet st., London.

In the preface to his forthcoming pamphlet of newspaper notices (which, as an example of purely personal say-so, I feel sure will be worth reading), K. K. endeavors to impress on the minds of its readers that he desires his book to be judged solely as a business venture, not as a literary work; but he quite forgets that his reviewers, as a class, know even less of business than they know of literature or of cycling. He does not seem to bear in mind the fact that a large proportion of his critics know absolutely nothing of the subject, and write criticisms at so much a column, just as they would chop wood at so much a cord, quite careless of the size or shape of their chips, so they get paid for the work.—*St. Louis Spectator.*

The Emerald Isle still boasts its two rival weeklies at Dublin: The *Irish Cyclist & Athlete,* edited and published by R. J. & A. Mecredy, at 49 Middle Abbey st., with a very large advertising patronage, and the *Irish Athletic & Cycling News,* whose editor and proprietor is R. J. Dunbar. I have never yet been favored with a copy of the latter paper, but I believe its price is the same as that of the older one, which is the same as the price of the English weeklies. If any American wishes to examine the *I. C. & A.,* I will mail him a copy freely, provided he so requests by postal-card, and agrees to send it back to me within a fortnight. The first issue of the *Scotch Cyclist* is announced for March 7, 1888, by Hay, Nisbit & Co., of Stockwell st., Glasgow, under the editorship of "Æolus" and "Steersman," who have for a long time past contributed the cycling department of the *Scottish Umpire,* published by the same firm. Each paper is a weekly, price one penny.

The *Australian Cycling News* (founded May 11, 1882) is under the editorship of F. J. Llewelyn,—having been revived Aug. 11, '87,—and is issued every alternate Thursday in Melbourne, at 5 Collins st., West. Its subscription rate per quarter is 1s. 9d. for Victoria; 2s. for any other part of the world. I will send a specimen copy for the inspection of any American who may make the request by postal-card and will agree to remail the paper to me within a month (and I offer to mail specimens of *Wheeling,* on the same terms). If any one sends me a half-dollar for three months' subscription, I will forward the same to Australia without charge. In return for this offer, I assume the Editor will consent to account to me for any money his subscribers may wish accredited to me, through the *News,* just as *Wheeling* does.

For 3000-mile route of H. J. High, from Pennsylvania to Nebraska and back: for Thomas Stevens's route from San Francisco to Boston, with daily mileage (not given in his book), see "Ten Thousand Miles on a Bicycle."

Mailed to any province of **Canada,** for $2, by **A. T. Lane,** of 1421 St. Catherine st., **Montreal;** and. to any colony of Australia, for **8s. 8d.,** by **W. J. Parry,** of Wills st., **Sandhurst, Vict.** Residents of Great Britain who send 8s. 8d. to the **Publisher of " Wheeling,"** 152 **Fleet st., London,** will find the same acknowledged in the " Ans. to Cor." column of that Wednesday weekly; and their books will be mailed as soon as the orders thus printed arrive in N. Y. Purchasers who may prefer to deal directly with the Publisher (whether they reside in foreign countries or in the U. S.) should make all money-orders payable to him, " KARL KRON, AT THE UNIVERSITY BUILDING, WASHINGTON SQUARE, NEW YORK CITY, D."

The Publisher believes that whenever the chief of any public library in America can be persuaded to consider the evidence offered in this pamphlet, he will feel under strong compulsion to purchase the book which it advertises, as a standard work of reference in an interesting field entirely its own.

I shall therefore be pleased to have any recipient of the pamphlet exhibit it to such local librarians as are known to him (on the chance of my not having mailed copies to them directly), and at the same time show the book itself,—if he be the owner of a copy,—and recommend such points in it as seem to him to make it worthy of purchase for public use. In particular, I ask each "copartner," with whom I have ventured to deposit any extra copies for possible sale, that he should take one to every library within easy reach, and (unless payment be made at sight) should persuade the librarian to sign an " approval " receipt, agreeing to examine the book and accompanying pamphlet within a month, and then, when the agent calls for his decision, to either pay him $2 or hand back the book.

I wish to assure all librarians that every such representative of mine acts entirely without pay or commission,—taking all his trouble for no other motive than to help the spread of cycling, or to help reward me for my personal sacrifices in behalf of it. Except for winning the good-will of these unpaid assistants, and thus dispensing with the discounts and allowances needed for making sales through the book-stores, it would not be possible for me to offer the volume at less than half the rate naturally put upon so costly a one by ordinary conditions of the book trade.   .

Even after eliminating this great factor of expense caused by the commissions and advertisements of middlemen, there still remains to me no possibility of profit on the investment of $12,000 until after the first 6000 copies shall have been sold. Elsewhere in this pamphlet, the page entitled " Costs of Book-Making " shows that, at best, I shall have worked steadily for at least five years before I so much as begin to reap any reward on sales at the $2 rate. I have not delivered, and I shall not hereafter deliver, any copy to any bookseller for less than that; and, though I allow the rate of $1.75 to a bookseller who personally buys a copy at one of my agencies, the concession only covers his expense of delivering to a customer, and is too small to admit of underselling.

Each librarian who acknowledges the receipt of this pamphlet by sending me $2 for the book, may attach to such act the privilege of recalling the bargain at any time within a month. In other words, I agree to return the money, and a stamped label for mailing the book to a later purchaser, if the librarian notifies me that he is dissatisfied, and that he will thus remail the book in unsoiled condition. On the other hand, if preference be expressed for delaying payment until after acceptance of the book, I will deliver it "on approval " to any librarian who signs for me the application-form elsewhere printed in this pamphlet, after having erased the allusions to advance payment of 20 cents, and substituted $2 for $1.80 as the amount of final payment.

There are about 4000 public libraries in the United States, and the book may be sold to at least half of them, if their managers can be made to see its true character, as a standard book of reference. Following is a list of 50 which already own the book, more than half of them being advance subscribers. When the name of the library differs from that of the town, it is appended in parenthesis. The star (*) is used in twenty-two cases to show where sales have been made by my agents, since publication day: *Alameda, Cal.; *Altoona, Pa. (Mechanics); Ann Arbor, Mich. (Psi Upsilon); Baltimore, Md. (Pratt); Bangor, Me.; Bar Harbor, Me.; *Belfast, Me.; Boston, Ms. (Athenæum), (State); Bridgeport, Ct.; Bristol, Pa.; Brooklyn, N. Y.; Brunswick, Me. (Bowdoin College); *Buffalo, N. Y.; Cambridge, Ms. (Harvard College); *Canandaigua, N. Y.; Christchurch, New Zealand; Detroit, Mich.; *Dover, Del.; Easthampton, Ms. (Adelphi); *Elyria, O.; *Emporia, Kan.; *Fall River, Ms.; Fort Leavenworth, Kan. (Post); Gambier, O. (Kenyon College); *Gettysburg, Pa. (Pennsylvania College); Hanover, N. H. (Dartmouth College); *Harrisburg, Pa. (State); Irvington, Ind. (Butler University); London, Eng. (British Museum); *Macon, Ga.; Nashville, Tenn. (Y. M. C. A.); *Newburyport, Ms.; New Haven, Ct. (Yale College), (Linonian); *New York (Mercantile); Norwalk, O. (Young Men's); *Omaha, Neb.; Peoria, Ill.; *Providence, R. I.; *Sandhurst, Vict., Australia (Mechanics' Institute); *San Francisco, Cal. (Mercantile), (Mechanics'); *South Bethlehem, Pa. (Lehigh University); Springfield, Ms.; *Templeton, Ms.; Warrnambool, Vict., Australia (Mechanics' Institute); Washington, D. C. (Congress); West Springfield, Ms.; Worcester, Ms.

I repeat the request made upon another page, that any one who has any of my books deposited with him for sale, should show a specimen to the librarians of his locality, and should call their attention to the "points" of the present pamphlet, especially to this list of purchasing libraries, representing twenty-two states. If the librarian will not buy a copy outright, let him be at least persuaded to sign an "approval" blank (page 32) and give a month's examination.

If it be granted that the perusal of such a book will tend to win converts to cycling, every helper of mine must see that he will do "the cause" more good by ensuring the public circulation of a copy than by finding a private purchaser for it. As the libraries are plainly assured that every such helper acts without hope of personal profit, they will be bound to treat him more graciously than if he were a mere hired book agent, trying to earn his own salary.

A librarian in Australia (of the Mechanics' Institute and Free Library, Stawell), writes: "I am greatly pleased at having bought 'Ten Thousand Miles on a Bicycle,' for it shows a thoroughness in its matter that is highly refreshing in these days of hurry and 'shamming'."

As regards my special *edition de luxe* (on heavy paper, tinted and calendered; only 200 copies printed). I can supply it in sheets at $2, or in the regular blue muslin binding at $2.25 per copy, but I reserve the right to advance the price without notice, as the remnant decreases (present stock : 150). Buyers of this edition who request the insertion of an autographed fly-leaf, like that given to original subscribers, will be supplied without charge.

Librarians who may have procured the volume before receiving the present appeal will confer a favor by giving notice of that fact, as I desire to print a list of all public institutions where it may be consulted. To college librarians, in particular, I commend the remark of the *Boston Advertiser*, alluding to the long historical and discursive "study in social science" (addressed chiefly to college-bred men), that it and the other extraneous chapter " would be worth the price of all," even to readers little interested in bicycling.

I also quote this undergraduate opinion from Princeton College : " Published in very attractive form, the usefulness of the work is greatly increased by the presence of a wonderfully complete index, by means of which the reader may obtain information on any subject connected with cycling, without the slightest inconvenience. The book abounds in pleasing anecdotes and important facts ; and, although not written strictly for the general public, many parts of it will surely prove interesting."— *The Princetonian, N. J.*

The Publisher has received so many proofs that the volume is acceptable to those whom it was issued for, that he believes very few mature wheelmen, who have curiosity enough to give it a careful examination, will decline to contribute $2 towards the $60,000 needed for its success. Hence the offer is made to any prospective purchaser, in the United States or Canada, who can furnish suitable evidence of good-faith, to lend the volume a month for a tenth of its price, with privilege of paying the other nine-tenths then, or of returning it at a trivial cost which will make the whole outlay, for four weeks' reading, only a quarter of a dollar. [See application-forms on other pages.]

Publishers of catalogues and pricelists in the cycling trade, as well as publishers of all books and pamphlets in regard to cycling, are invited to insert therein the following free ads,—on the theory that they will help their own business by helping the sale of such a volume :—

TEN THOUSAND MILES ON A BICYCLE : "*A Gazetteer of American Roads in Many States ; an Encyclopedia of Wheeling Progress in Many Countries.*" Forty-one chapters ; 908 pages ; 675,000 words ; bound in blue muslin, with gilded top. Mailed for $2 by Karl Kron, Washington Sq., N. Y.

The main text of book comprises 800 pp. of 585,000 words, and the indexes cover 75 pp. of fine type,—the chief local-index giving 8418 references to 3482 towns, and the chief personal-index giving 3126 references to 1476 individuals. The frontispiece is a photogravure, and the appendix contains the names and addresses of 3400 subscribing " copartners," but no advertisements. Publication was made May 25, 1887, after four years' continuous labor and a cash outlay of $6200. The mailing-price for Great Britain and Australia is 8s. 8d., and money-orders from those countries may either be sent direct to New York, or to "the Publisher of *Wheeling*, 152 Fleet st., London, Eng.," and " W. J. Parry, Wills st., Sandhurst, Vict."

"FOUR YEARS AT YALE."

"FOUR YEARS AT YALE, *by a Graduate of '69*" (*Karl Kron*). This is a hand-book of the student life and customs prevailing, twenty years ago, at the college named, and an encyclopædic history of its undergraduates' societies and other "institutions," up to that date. It contains 728 pages of about 220,000 words (long-primer type and tinted paper), has analytical catch-lines at the head of each chapter, is well indexed and neatly bound in cloth, and is mailed for $2.50 by the publishers, Henry Holt & Co., 29 East 23d st., N. Y. Originally published at New Haven in 1871, the edition of 1700 was exhausted in the course of a few years, except about 100 sets of sheets which, by error of printer, lacked 72 pages. In 1881 these missing pages were put in type again by the present publishers, and the copies thus completed have all been sold but four (March 1, 1888), though I myself hold eight other sets of unbound sheets, lacking only the dozen pages devoted to preface and contents-table. I offer these at $2.25 each, or I will supply them bound (blue muslin and gilded top) at $2.50 each. One set of the eight, which is printed on one side of the paper only, is held at $3, as being unique in the entire edition of 1700. I have also a few broken sets and odd chapters which I can supply at proportionate rates to any collegiate antiquarians who may wish for them. As the book was type-printed, it will never be reissued; and to avoid the trouble of writing answers to occasional inquirers I here publish this final statement concerning it.

Humors of collegiate velocipeding in 1869, condensed from contemporary records. See "Ten Thousand Miles on a Bicycle." (The chapter called "Bone-Shaker Days," giving careful details of the evolution of the modern bicycle from the véloce of '69 and its predecessor of 1819, will be mailed separately for 25 cents.)

The descriptions of the author's rides are sometimes amusing and thrilling.—*St. Louis Post-Dispatch*. There is a great deal of entertaining as well as instructive and useful reading in it.—*The Bookmart, Pittsburg, Pa.* The author's adventures are graphically told.—*Scientific American*.

Many bright thoughts catch the eye even in a hasty perusal.—*Wheelmen's Record, Indianapolis*. It contains very serviceable information for those interested in bicycle travel.—*Alta California*. It ought to become a sort of *vade mecum* to all lovers of bicycling.—*The Sun, N. Y.*

People who take long tours with horses will find it an excellent guide.—*Turf, Field & Farm*. Altogether indispensable to a man who desired to journey over the ground covered.—*The Star, N. Y.*

This is a notable book for many reasons, but chiefly, perhaps, in showing what tremendous perseverance and powers of application can reside in one man. As a dictionary of American roads, intended for reference and instruction rather than amusement, all attempts at a literary style have been abandoned,—the simplest statements of facts being imperatively necessary to crowd such an enormous mass of matter into the required 800 pages. It is, without doubt, the most important cycling work ever written, and can hardly fail of being useful to thousands of bicyclists.—*Yale Literary Magazine*.

THE COSTS OF BOOK-MAKING.

I desire to emphasize the fact that no publisher, relying upon ordinary business conditions, could have been persuaded to invest the large sum requisite for bringing out so massive a work on such a subject. My original prospectus promised a much smaller and cheaper affair (one-third the number of pages, and one-ninth the number of words), whose estimated cost of manufacture was only a quarter-dollar per copy; yet the man of widest experience in such matters offered this prediction about its chances: " I have been selling bicycling literature for nearly three years, and I know a little about the market. Let me say, then, frankly, that you cannot sell 1000 copies of a bicycling work at $1 each, no matter how good it is, nor how much it commends itself. The market will not absorb that quantity of books. I place the outside limit of your sales at 300 copies, and I can't believe you will sell that number. No matter how much the bicyclers may howl for a thing, they fail to come to time when asked to pay for it."

These words were written by the present Secretary-Editor of the League, at sight of an advance copy of my prospectus (Jan. 23, 1884: see p. 704), and, however absurd they may seem in the light of facts actually accomplished, they fairly reflected an intelligent business-view of the probabilities.

Assuming, however, in the face of this most discouraging opinion of an expert, that a publisher might nevertheless have been found sanguine enough to issue a book more than four times as costly and to hope the " outside limit of sales " would even then reach to nearly four times the specified 300 copies,— what would have been his best chances of financial reward? I answer this by saying that the cost of publishing my own book, if the edition had been limited to 1000 copies, would have been $3300 (or $3.30 per copy); if limited to 3000 copies, the cost would have been $4500 (or $1.50 per copy) ; and that, even by taking the risk of so large a number as 6200 copies for the actual edition, I could bring the average cost down no lower than $1 per copy. But, as a publisher commonly rates the retail price of a book at almost four times the cost of manufacture,—in order to cover expenses of distribution, advertising, booksellers' commission, author's royalty, and his own profit on the investment,—the prices per book would have been respectively $13 or $6 or $4, according as the assumed "sanguine publisher" based his calculation on editions of 1000 or 3000 or 6000 copies.

My investment of more than $6000 in actual cash, and of four years' labor which, at a modest estimate, might have earned a similar sum, is a greater investment than any one else has ever risked in a book on any other sport ; and my hope is that those who feel any pride and pleasure in the result will work to help remove from me the implication of financial folly in taking so great a risk. Remembering that, as its actual writer and compiler, I am debarred from saying a word in praise of the literary quality of the volume on which, as publisher, my money is' staked, those who approve its quality should be the more ready to proclaim their opinions, and give me the chance to circulate the same at second hand.

These figures show how impossible it would have been for me to have found any such publisher for any such bulky book. When an experienced dealer had declared " he could not believe 300 copies could be sold of a $1 bicycling book, no matter how good it is," no reasonably prudent publisher would dream of selling 1000 copies of a $13 book,—nor yet of selling the enormously greater number needed to justify offering it at a much lower rate. The figures show, too, that, even if (at the end of 1887, after four full years devoted exclusively to the work) I had received the regular $2 price for every book of the first 6000, I should still have reaped much less profit, despite all my risk of capital, than might have been had without risk, from much easier employment, at $1500 a year. But the real fact is much less favorable than this, for nearly half the 6000 books will be distributed among my subscribers at the promised half-rate, while at least the whole year 1888 will be required for finding $2 buyers of the remainder; and the costs of distribution and advertising will be considerable. Assuming thus that this great number of books are all disposed of on these terms, within five years after the "prospectus of Dec. 3, 1883," I shall still be considerably out-of-pocket on the adventure. By as much as the time of selling may be prolonged beyond that, by so much will my losses be increased. Assuming, as many did, that the payment of five-sixths of my 3600 subscriptions at $1 each would mark the outside limits of my receipts (leaving 3000 unsalable books on my hands as a dead loss), each "copartner's" copy would have cost me more than four times what he paid for it!

Future editions of the book, however, can be made at a cost of about 60 cents per copy; and a sale of 24,000 of them, even at the low rate of $2, would offset the losses on the first edition, and yield a fair profit on the whole investment; but so enormous a circulation can only be secured by the hearty co-operation of all those enthusiasts who favor it as a help to the spread of cycling. Having shown why a prudent publisher would not dare to issue so massive a work, and why even an imprudently sanguine publisher would not dare to put a less price than $5 upon it, I hope my own motive in risking a popular rate like $2, may be popularly appreciated. Those who wish to see the risk justified by a phenomenal result, giving greater vogue to the book than to the representative volume of any other sport, should persuade their friends to send its price to the publisher, KARL KRON, *at the University Building, Washington Square, New York City, D.*

He is a man whom we all know, and ought to honor and help for the good work he has done for us. His book is a wonderful production. It is only occasionally that you find a man who has perseverance mingled with the milk of human kindness in generous enough measure to enable him to devote years of patient labor to such an undertaking. Remember that Karl has worked hard for us, boys, and do something for him.—"*Gentleman John,*" *in Bicycling World, Boston.*

G3

" The people like to be deceived; therefore let them be deceived:" that is the rule which politicians who court personal popularity rely upon to-day as generally as in the old Roman days; and that is the rule whose observance has built up numerous fortunes for publishers and other business men.

There is, then, a certain intellectual interest attaching to this present experiment of attracting a vast multitude of buyers by a rigid adherence to the opposite policy,—by assuming their capacity to recognize and appreciate thoroughly honest work, and their disposition to reward it fairly. The great bulk of testimony collected in the preceding pages is to the effect that the work has been well and squarely done,—that every promise concerning it has been fully and faithfully kept; but the opinion is expressed or implied by many of these witnesses, and by many other correspondents in private, that no adequate reward is likely to result, because the people for whom the work has been done are too few in number, or too ignorant and dull-witted, or too poor and penurious, to readily pay for it. In other words, the belief prevails that, however much they may be pleased by the magnitude and expensiveness of the show, they will not contribute the gate-money needed for its success, but will preferably scale the fence, or crawl under the canvas guards at the bottom, or peep through holes furtively cut in the boards.

CURL, THE BEST OF BULL-DOGS: *a Study in Animal Life.* Twenty-eight pages of 14,000 words, with photogravure frontispiece; appendix of 152 pages giving specimens of the text and newspaper notices of "Ten Thousand Miles on a Bicycle." Sent postpaid to any country in the world, on receipt of 25 cents' worth of the lowest denomination of postage-stamps locally current. KARL KRON, *Publisher, at the University Building, N. Y. City.*

CASTLE SOLITUDE IN THE METROPOLIS: *a Study in Social Science.* Fifty-six pages of 34,000 words, with small picture of the Castle; appendix of 152 pages, the same as the above. Sent to any address for 25 c., in postage stamps.

I repeat below, from the page which contains the full prospectus of " My Second Ten Thousand," the application-form, which will ensure to a bookseller—the same as to any one else—the chance of buying the volume " at the usual 33 per cent. off," in case it is ever published. The act of signing does not bind a person to buy the book at any price; it merely binds the Publisher to give a month's option of buying it at two-thirds the retail rate:

I hereby authorize Karl Kron to print my name in the list of supporters of his proposed second book (to be called " My Second Ten Thousand," containing not less than 300 pages of large type, with at least 250 words to the page, and retailing at $1.50); and I agree that, if at any future time I receive notice from him that such a book has been published, I will reply within a month, and either enclose a dollar to pay for a copy, or else give notice that I resign the privilege (which K. K. assures to me in return for the present pledge) of securing one from him at two-thirds the regular rate.

[Name, address, date and occupation to be plainly written below. Prepay by a 2-cent stamp.]

THE THEORY OF RECIPROCATION.

As my book is a more extensive and expensive " free adv." of the whole cycling trade than any one else has ever produced, I urge that the chief firms in that trade, who advertise largely in the trade-journals, ought to follow the liberal example set them by the leading bicycle importer of Montreal, A. T. Lane, in the *Canadian Wheelman*. I mean that, as a part of every such full-page adv. of their own, they ought to insert a recommendation of " Ten Thous. Miles on a Bi." A short notice of this sort, in fine type, would detract not at all from the force of their own "displayed" remarks, and would add nothing to the cost of the page ; while, if it helped the circulation of the book, it would to that extent enlarge the number of customers who support the cycling trade. I do not anticipate that many of the chief advertisers in the trade-papers will be sagacious and liberal-minded enough to thus exhibit an appreciation of the four years' labor and $6000 of hard cash which I have expended for the sake of putting money in their pockets: but I nevertheless now place on record this appeal to their " intelligent selfishness," as plainly showing how easily they might repay some slight portion of their great indebtedness to me,—not only without spending a cent of money, but with a chance of positive profit to themselves.

Elsewhere in this pamphlet a page is devoted to the free advertisement of the American cycling press, and to urging that every publisher of a trade catalogue ought to freely insert therein the names, prices and publishers' addresses not only of these papers but of all cycling books and pamphlets in the market. I myself devote still other pages to the latter, in addition to the liberal space given them in my book ; and I hope this policy of reciprocation and "enlightened selfishness "—based upon the belief that " the sale of every such book helps rather than hinders the sale of all the others " (see pp. 652, 718)—may finally have general vogue.

I agree to forward, without charge or commission, any money which a patron of mine may find it convenient to address to any one of them through me ; but there are several whom I specify by name, because, as they agree to freely account to me for money received for my books, I can have cash orders credited by them without any actual transfer of the cash.

If I thus seem to show special favors to some, it is only as an incident in my general policy of giving as much help as possible to *all* publishers of cycling books and papers. The system may be called " free," in that it involves no payments of money and no making of contracts ; but it is in fact a system of informal exchanges, and is just as legitimate as a hard-and-fast agreement.

Quite aside from the practical consideration of their possible value to me as aids to advertising, I wish to say that all subscribers' testimonials of their appreciation of the book's "points," and of their friendly interest in helping its financial success, are acceptable to me as aids towards keeping up my spirits during the long years of solitary labor which must be endured in winning such success. I put every letter on file, no matter how short it may be ; and I read every one with care and interest, no matter how long.

U 3

THE SIGNIFICANCE OF "TALKING MONEY."

I wish to clearly remind my subscribers that, of the 60 millions of people in this country, 55 millions do not yet know of the existence of the bicycle; and that, of these 5 millions who do in some measure comprehend that this new sort of vehicle has been added to previously-known instruments of locomotion, there are not a half-million who have any genuine appreciation of it, or believe that it has "come to stay." These truths are seldom thought of by bicyclers, who, though their numbers in America are now probably well beyond 60,000, are apt to forget that their fewness, in comparison to 60,000,000, makes them seem socially insignificant, if not contemptible.

The same strong sympathy in the sport, which causes them to talk and write so much to each other, and to print so many things about each other, blinds them to the truth that the great mass of the population are unconscious of their existence, and that almost all the rest either regard them with a mild sort of derision or with entire indifference. Hence it happens that my own act in risking such a sum as $12,000, on an appeal to the liberality and intelligence of such a trivial and inconsequential set of people (as commonly regarded), exposes me to ridicule. "It is the work of an idiot, not of a sane man," says the reviewer of the *Boston Herald ;* and others, whose words are more civil, evidently think my talk about " selling 30,000 books " is too absurd for serious treatment. I am ignorant of the origin of the commonly accepted statement that a great majority of all the books published never reach a sale of 1000 copies; but I presume it is correct, for I know that the sale of an even smaller number often suffices for a volume whose literary success is recognized. I therefore appreciate how hard it is for "literary men," familiar with these cold facts, to believe I am in earnest in attempting to find " 30,000 buyers" among a very obscure and restricted *clientèle.* I recall the prediction of a most experienced dealer, that I "could not sell 300 copies of a bicycling book at $1, no matter how good it might be"; and I place alongside it the sarcasm of a learned friend of mine, Professor of English Literature in a well known university, that I was wasting my best energies on a necessarily vain appeal to "the distinctively illiterate classes."

Now, as an offset to the weariness of contemplating all these adverse opinions, I like to receive wheelmen's assurances that I made no mistake in rating their character and influence more highly than the general run of people rate them, and in testifying to that belief by "talking money" for their advancement. More than enough sales for the "literary" justification of the book were assured in advance; but the number needed to justify it financially must be monumental. An army of 30,000 buyers, enlisted directly by the Publisher and his copartners, without any help from the ordinary machinery of the book trade, would form too impressive a phenomenon "to be sneezed at." No sophistry could belittle its significance, as testifying to a "certain something " that characterizes no other sport than cycling. Each subscriber's expressed belief in the sport, and in my scheme for proclaiming it, helps strengthen my own belief in the scheme's final success.

As it is well known to book-sellers that "the average man," when he happens to be interested in a particular book, will resort to almost any trick or subterfuge for getting the benefit of its contents without actually *buy-ing* a copy, they necessarily look with derision upon any attempt at persuading bicyclers to proclaim themselves "better than the average" by putting up a testimonial of $60,000 in honor of the book which distinctively represents them before the outside world. No such large sum of money could possibly be collected in behalf of the literary exponent of any other sport; and therefore my belief, that so monumental a pile can be raised by an appeal to the exceptional enthusiasm which characterizes bicycling, appears unreasonable to all who are not themselves enthusiasts.

Large as the pile seems, however, when looked at in a lump, the proportion of profit accruing to me must be small at best. Five years will have been spent before I really begin my chase for buyers, and at least ten more will be needed for capturing them; probably twenty years, possibly thirty. The collection of $60,000 through any such long period, on sales of a book at less than half its natural price, clearly offers but slight reward; yet no other compensation can come to me, for those vanities which are usually classed among the "rewards of authorship" are sedulously shunned by myself. I indulge in none of the things which are supposed to cheer the existence of people who are known as "cycling celebrities." Though advertising with tireless persistency the personal trade-mark under which I must needs push the scheme along, my own name and face are studiously concealed. From the day when my book's prospectus was issued, I have never once shown myself at any wheelmen's meet or parade or banquet or celebration of any sort. I have competed not at all for the pleasures of notoriety and leadership enjoyed on such occasions by other men, but have maintained to the utmost my personal modesty and reserve; and I shall adhere to this policy of non-interference so long as any of the 30,000 books remain unsold.

I assume that the act of selling them will have a certain interest on its own account, throughout the cycling world, as a mere test of physique. The analogy which I ventured to draw (two years ago, when writing page 483) between my own simple struggle to "push a book around the world," and Stevens's marvelous exploit in thus pushing a bicycle, seems somewhat less fanciful now than then. The fact of his conquering the perils which were then ahead of him, and were clearly recognized as desperate ones, is acceptable as an omen for my also "getting through" the obstacles which are now ahead of me, and are generally looked upon as insuperable. There is something significant, too, in the circumstance that he is the only man who has publicly professed confidence in my ability to "get through" (*i. e.*, to sell the 30,000 books); for, though he understands the difficulties of the book-business quite as well as do those doubters who laugh at my assurance he has proved in his own person the power of Sam Patch's inspiring motto: "Some things can be done as well as others."

A STRAIGHT COURSE TO THE END.

"All things are possible to the man who can afford to wait,"—that is, the man who has vitality enough to "hang on" until the end,—and all people like to watch him while undergoing this test as to whether there is enough of this stuff in him or not. Every man's final act, when recognized as such, arouses some degree of sympathetic curiosity merely because it *is* his last.

Chapter 38 may be consulted by any one who wishes to be convinced that the web of circumstances behind me has been woven too skillfully, by a perverse Fate, to allow any loop-hole for my escape except by going ahead. On pages 724-725, in particular, the truth is clearly shown that, having become thus involved, against my wishes, in a scheme far beyond my ambition if not beyond my strength, the stress of inevitable necessity will push me on to expend the last atom of my strength in "getting through." Though my advance may seem to be "without haste," it is bound to be "without rest." However long I may live, it is not possible that I should turn back, or should attempt any other career. I must either finish this or it will finish me. There is no third choice.

The issue of the present pamphlet signalizes the definite beginning of my voyage as a bookseller; and, whether it be short or long, prosperous or disastrous, successful or fatal, it can end in only one way. My prow points clear around the world, and it will never get home again unless it gets around! When thus I make the start, almost exactly five years will have elapsed from the day when I conceived the idea of the book (April 19, 1883; see p. 702); and during more than four of these years I have worked assiduously at "getting ready." It took almost ten months to formulate and proclaim the prospectus; it took seventeen months to attract the "impossible" 3000 copartners from every quarter of the globe; it took two years to compile, print and publish the actual book, and it has taken ten months more to distribute the same among my copartners and erect the present machine for attracting the 30,000 buyers.

That this advertising pamphlet should itself contain more print than the "300 pages of 75,000 words" first promised for the book, is an impressive proof of how the latter's scope increased from a pocket-guide, whose sale would be made and forgotten in a summer, to a bulky encyclopædia, whose sale seems prospectively a life-long task. Yet the ever-growing expense and anxiety caused, through all these wearisome years, by this unforeseen expansion, did not have power to make me swerve at all from the plain path I had undertaken to pursue as a publisher; and so now, when I finally begin my voyage as a bookseller, my copartners may rest assured that, whether they help me much or little, I shall at least steer a straight course to the end. Adopting the famous speech of Seneca's pilot (made newly classic by Mr. Lowell's famous application of it at the celebration of Harvard's quarter-millennial), I simply say: "O, Neptune, save me if you will, or sink me if you will; but, whatever you do, I will keep my rudder true."

WASHINGTON SQUARE, N. Y., March 29, 1888.

CURL,

THE BEST OF BULL-DOGS

A STUDY IN ANIMAL LIFE

By KARL KRON

AUTHOR OF "FOUR YEARS AT YALE, BY A GRADUATE OF '69"

— — ———

PRICE, TWENTY-FIVE CENTS, POSTPAID

——— ———

——————

PUBLISHED BY KARL KRON
THE UNIVERSITY BUILDING, WASHINGTON SQUARE
NEW YORK

1888

(E)

TO THE

MEMORY

OF

My Bull=Dorg

(THE VERY BEST DOG WHOSE PRESENCE EVER BLESSED THIS PLANET)

THESE RECORDS OF TRAVELS

WHICH WOULD HAVE BROKEN HIS HEART

HAD HE EVER LIVED TO

READ ABOUT

THEM

ARE LOVINGLY INSCRIBED

ADVERTISEMENT.

ARTEMUS WARD'S aphorism, " It is n't a bad idea for a comic paper to print a joke, once in a while," seems unfamiliar to the men who, since his day, have grown to the dignity of writing literary reviews for the newspaper press. At all events, several of them who have awarded the highest praise to my bull-dog's biography, as the most readable and best written chapter in an elaborate gazetteer of American roads, censure me for printing it there. One objects to the act as " a piece of egotism"; another says "its entire freedom from the all-pervading *ego* makes the egotism and nonsense of the other chapters all the more inexcusable and exasperating "; but both these opposite-minded critics agree with each other, and with many others, in disapproval of the act, as incongruous and out of place, while they at the same time call the chapter " capital in itself " and " in every way perfect."

The Preface of "Ten Thousand Miles on a Bicycle " in defending the precise, personal style of narrative as best suited for the special purpose in hand, asserts that this "egotism " has not been dragged in for the sake of display or vaunting, but is simply a business necessity for the successful carrying out of a unique scheme of publication and sale. "There is, indeed, no boastfulness in this book, and precious little vanity," says the Preface ; and the most censorious of its many reviewers have not attempted to disprove this quite comprehensive assertion.

The one vanity of the book was the author's decision to insert, as its chief " literary" feature, a biography of the best-remembered companion of his boyhood, in order thereby to make a most impressive appeal from the judgment of the select circle of magazine-editors who had condemned it, to the judgment of the mass of mankind, as represented by his thirty-four hundred "copartners," enrolled in every section of the globe. For an utterly unknown writer to thus have won in advance the attention of a vaster and more widely-scattered audience than many of the most famous of contemporary authors can lay claim to, was a unique opportunity, whose temptation I felt powerless to resist. Evidently, in trying my luck at so phenomenal a chance, I had much to gain from success, and little to lose from failure. If my " study in animal life " proved pleasing to the multitude of patrons whose sympathy with my enthusiasm for bicycling had led them to pledge their dollars for the building of a monumental book upon that subject, they would like the book all the better on "Curl's " account, and would give his memory also a monumental degree of celebrity. On the other hand, if his biography proved powerless to interest them, they would pardon the insertion of it, as a harmless freak, in consideration of its covering but nineteen of nine hundred pages in a book whose bulk had been promised them as three hundred pages only.

The "Compliments for 'Curl,'" elsewhere reprinted, seem numerous and diversified enough to prove that my own advance-judgment, attributing more literary merit to the sketch than to anything else in the volume, was, though "necessarily partial," by no means erroneous in fact. I disagree with the man who said, in writing the biography of a departed friend and fellow-poet, "the eye of affection, if it be not critical, is at least clear-sighted"; for there are abundant examples to the contrary; but I think the remark has been proved a truthful one as regards my own connection with this biography of "Curl."

It was a work of entire affection,—a sort of duty which I had felt for years I was somehow bound to do;—and, when I had finished it, the work seemed to me not only the best that my pen had ever produced, but the best it was capable of ever producing. To my own consciousness, it was a superlative achievement,—a bright, consummate flower of verbal expression,—such as I might not expect to duplicate, and such as I could always take pleasure in, because of its power to vividly remind me of happy days gone by. Whether a sketch so personal to myself would also have power to amuse outsiders, by reason of its intrinsic excellence, was an entirely different matter; and the unanimous rejection of it by a dozen magazine-editors might naturally appear to anticipate a popular verdict to the contrary, in case I appealed from those editors to the public. As my audacity in courting a popular verdict, under such adverse circumstances, was a genuine piece of vanity, so the success which has followed and justified it is a genuine gratification. There is something specially pleasant about this evidence that the element of affection did not impair my clear-sightedness,—that the "personal equation" did not sway my judgment,—that what seemed to me my most attractive piece of verbal workmanship has been commended by the severest judges as in fact my best.

I do not presume to say that "my best" should be classed as "good," according to any absolute standard of excellence, or that the public verdict already given in favor of this brief biography proves that it contains anything of that permanent quality which should entitle it to rank as literature. I only record the fact that I have accomplished exactly what I set out to do, four years ago, by making my bull-dog's memory cherished in every country of the globe where the English language is spoken. With this aim in view, I gave seventeen months to the attraction of three thousand subscribers to my bicycling book, from every State and Territory of the Union, every province of Canada, every colony of Australia; from England, Scotland and Ireland; from Mexico, Bermuda and New Zealand; from a dozen countries of Continental Europe; from Asiatic Turkey, Persia and Japan. Having thus laboriously secured my audience, I was not to be deterred from my purpose of winning their approval for "Curl" because none of the magazine-editors took kindly to him; and, having won that approval, I can now confidently introduce him to the general public as the most distinguished dog of his day.

ADVERTISEMENT OF "CURL."

I say "confidently" because, whatever may be thought of his merits as a dog, or my own as a dog's biographer and general advertising-agent, no one can accuse me of absurdity as a business-man in now assuming that a certain number of people will be glad to buy this pamphlet containing the story of his life and times. To have issued it as an independent work, after proof that all the magazines thought it worthless, would have been a silly act of vanity; to publish it now and circulate it as a help to the capture of the needed 30,000 buyers of "Ten Thousand Miles on a Bicycle" is simply a matter of business. As the capture of these 30,000 seems destined to be the chief and final business-act of my life, it is not inappropriate that my best and final literary-act should be kept prominently identified with it.

Despite the plainest proclamations of its Preface, reviewers of my book have almost unanimously ignored this "business" side of it, and many have spoken as if its ideal were a confessedly "literary" one, like that of a novel or poem. Almost none have seemed to accept as serious my expressed intention of securing 30,000 buyers for the book by an appeal to the good-will and friendliness of my 3000 subscribers; for, if the theory be once granted that I can count on their sympathy as fellow-bicyclers, no one can allege that there is any absurdity in attempting to increase that sympathy by revealing to them the amusing traits of my bull-dog, and the queer characteristics of the house which I live in. Furthermore, it is fair to presume that their readiness to recognize and reward me as their representative spokesman, will be all the greater because of my proving to the public that I *can* write intelligently on subjects of more general interest than bicycling. Since my endeavor to produce a standard work in this special field has necessarily led to the "patient treating of small things as if they were large,"—in accordance with the Emersonian doctrine that "no man can do any work well who does not regard it, for the time being, as the center of the universe,"—it is surely right for me to show that my vision for "small things" is not really distorted.

When I undertook the preparation of that massive encyclopædia, I did not anticipate that I was dooming myself to "four years' solitary confinement at hard labor"; but I did foresee that, no matter how loudly I might proclaim the special and restricted ideal of the book, some reviewers would accredit it with a general "literary" ideal and would condemn it accordingly. Hence, though my statistical guide to roads and riding might not be judged quite as dismal reading as the professedly comic papers of a quarter-century ago, when Artemus Ward was editor of *Vanity Fair*, it seemed "not a bad idea to insert a readable chapter, once in a while." The most readable one was the life of "Curl," and it puzzles me to imagine why critics who praised it thus should still think its insertion a bad idea. Among people who like dogs (and no respect need be paid to the literary standards of such human animals as hate them), a good dog story, like the motion to adjourn, is "always in order."   THE PUBLISHER.

COMPLIMENTS FOR "CURL."

The queerest book that has come into this office for a long while is "Ten Thousand Miles on a Bicycle." It would be as dull, prosaic and borous as the author has aimed to make it, if he had been able to live up to his ideal. Luckily, he could n't. His individuality has asserted itself. He himself has crowded in (among the three-cornered stones, the up-grades, and the pauses to oil the machine), and some of his literary excursions are exquisite. "Curl," the dog to whom the book is dedicated, is the title of a sketch of the animal that is simply delicious. A cleverer, more delicately humorous, or more thoroughly intelligent study of a brute has seldom been written. If we fail to like the animal, it is because we see his true character; but, be the dog good or bad, no one can fail to enjoy reading of his experiences and noting how he revealed his character in his life and walks—as we all do. There are other readable chapters, and the book has literary merit of rare quality, in spots. It seems incredible that the author should have had "Curl" rejected by every prominent magazine, but that is what he says.—*Hartford Courant.*

We have read the biography of "Curl," the bull-dog, with a great deal of interest, though we do not wonder that a dozen magazine editors refused to print it.—*L. A. W. Bulletin, Boston.*

There is a vast deal of this book that is of interest to the general reader as much as to the bicycler. The chapter on "Curl" is especially interesting for the picture it presents of a remarkably intelligent and affectionate animal. A brief extract will show what kind of a dog he was, and at the same time give an idea of the author's admirable style.—*Detroit Free Press.*

One of the most interesting chapters is that on the life of the author's pet bull-dog; and a good photogravure of "Curl" forms the frontispiece.—*Worcester Spy.*

Whether the dedication of such a work to a favorite bull-dog, "not lost but gone before," may be thought congruous, we leave to be settled by debaters on "good form"; but, judging by "the best of bull-dogs'" eighteen-page biography, as genially related by the author, we should say "Curl" is entitled to affectionate remembrance.—*The Evening Telegram, N. Y.*

Some chapters are very good reading for anybody. His bull-dog receives a long one, the most interesting in the book. This animal was almost the intellectual equal of the famous "Calvin."—*Buffalo Express.*

The frontispiece illustration is not that of the author, as a hasty inspection of the book might possibly suggest, but is a likeness of the author's companion. "Curl" was a bull-dog who lived not quite thirteen years. His biography is written in Chapter 28 of this remarkable encyclopædia. The dedication is inscribed to this friendly fellow animal.—*The Critic, N. Y.*

The general opinion of Karl Kron's book seems to be that when it comes to dogs he can write very intelligently and sympathetically, but outside of that one chapter the work is a dismal failure.—*American Athlete, Philadelphia.*

The work is dedicated "To the Memory of My Bull-Dorg," and the portrait of "Curl" is really a work of art.—*New Zealand Referee.*

The frontispiece is the picture of a dog,—not a soft-eyed lap-pet that runs off into the brush at the sight of a wheel, but a big-jawed, fierce-looking bull-dog, that has got the pedal-motion down so fine that he can time the descending feet to a dot, and nip out a piece of $3 hose at every revolution. There used to be two such dogs, out on the Manchester road, several years ago.—*St. Louis Post-Dispatch.*

The one good chapter is that in which he commemorates a deceased bull-dog named "Curl," who after playing the part of Cerberus on the ancestral farm where his master was born and bred, for ten or a dozen years, dropped his last bone eighteen winters ago, and joined the great majority of faithful dogs in the Canine Paradise, where (let us hope) they snarl not, and bite not, and are never more hungry. That he was a determined creature may be gathered from the sketch of his life, and that he was not ill-looking, from the bull-dog standpoint, may be seen by his portrait, which stands by way of frontispiece to "Ten Thousand Miles on a Bicycle."—*Mail and Express, N.Y.*

For absolute stupidity, even to bicyclers, this volume must take the prize as being one of the most worthless volumes ever written. It is the work of an idiot, not of a sane man. The only sign of common sense is shown in the beautiful portrait of Karl Kron's favorite bull-dog, to whose memory the book is aptly dedicated.—*Boston Herald.*

His Bull-Dorg will, I am confident, occupy a prominent position in the history of the cycle. I would we had an English Kron.—*"The Tyre," in Saturday Night, Birmingham, Eng.*

What makes this egotism all the more inexcusable is that the author can write well, and can on occasion drop the all-pervading *ego*, as, for example, in the biography of his bull-dog, which, though sadly out of place in "a gazetteer, a dictionary and a thesaurus of facts," is the one green spot in the desert of flat, uninteresting, and very personal detail. The chapter on "Curl" is, in our view, at once the triumph and the condemnation of this book. That a man who can write such a biography as this—in every way perfect—can then coolly and deliberately bury it in the indigestible mass of verbiage, egotism and nonsense in which we find it, is simply exasperating, and at the same time extraordinary. What this gem has to do with cycling it is difficult to discover, but those condemned for their sins to peruse this work will welcome the restful pause which it affords. "Castle Solitude" belongs to the same category as "Curl's" biography, though of less merit, as being more labored and artificial. These two chapters are like the much-quoted flies in amber, with a modification:—

——"neither rich nor rare,
One only wonders 'how the devil they got there.'"
—*Bicycling News, London organ of "the Coventry ring."*

(K)

INDEX TO THE LIFE OF "CURL."

TABLE OF CONTENTS.

Oct., 65—2013; Nov., 82—2095; Dec., 177—2272; Jan., 112—2384; Feb., 113—2497; Mar., 149—2646; Apr., 139—2787; May, 101—2888; June, 87—2975; July, 128—3103; Aug., 46—3149; Sept., 43—3192; Oct., 37—3229; Nov., 35—3264; Dec., 51—3318; Jan., 39—3357; Feb., 25—3382; Mar., 36—3418; Apr., 108—3526. From May 1 to Dec. 31, '86, there were 50 accessions, at $1.50, raising the total of the "autograph edition" to 3576. (Electro. in Feb., '86; about 19,000 words. See pp. 731-6, for supplementary list of 200 names.)

XL. DIRECTORY OF WHEELMEN, 765-799: Names of 3200 subscribers, grouped according to residence-towns, which are alphabetized by States, in the following geographical order: Me., 15 towns, 45 subscribers, 765; N. H., 11 t., 50 s., 766; Vt., 14 t., 47 s., 766; Mass., 89 t., 311 s., 766; R. I., 5 t., 20 s., 769; Ct., 32 t., 171 s., 769; N. Y., 106 t., 671 s., 770; N. J., 55 t., 257 s., 776; Pa., 96 t., 382 s., 778; Del., 2 t., 4 s., 781; Md., 8 t., 81 s., 781; Dist. of Col., 2 t., 37 s., 782; W. Va., 4 t., 6 s., 782; Va., 10 t., 17 s., 782; N. C., 2 t., 6 s., 782; S. C., 2 t., 4 s., 782; Ga., 4 t., 11 s., 782; Fla., 2 t., 2 s., 783; Ala., 4 t., 12 s., 783; Miss., 3 t., 4 s., 783; La., 1 t., 5 s., 783; Tex., 6 t., 9 s., 783; Ark., 2 t., 7 s., 783; Tenn., 3 t., 26 s., 783; Ky., 15 t., 53 s., 783; O., 48 t., 154 s., 784; Mich., 21 t., 66 s., 785; Ind., 21 t., 60 s., 785; Ill., 25 t., 116 s., 786-7; Mo., 8 t., 25 s., 787; Ia., 14 t., 20 s., 787; Wis., 11 t., 16 s., 787; Minn., 13 t., 22 s., 787; Dak., 3 t., 5 s., 788; Neb., 2 t., 2 s., 788; Kan., 14 t., 21 s., 788; (Ind. Ter., 0); N. Mex., 1 t., 1 s., 788; Col., 4 t., 9 s., 788; Wy., 3 t., 9 s., 788; Mon., 3 t., 6 s., 788; Id., 2 t., 14 s., 788; Wash., 3 t., 3 s., 788; Or., 8 t., 28 s., 788; Utah, 2 t., 7 s., 788; (Nev., 0 t., 0 s., 789); Ariz., 1 t., 1 s., 789; Cal., 9 t., 22 s., 789; Ontario, 21 t., 79 s., 789; Manitoba, 1 t., 1 s., 790; Quebec, 1 t., 5 s., 790; New Brunswick, 2 t., 6 s., 790; Nova Scotia, 9 t., 37 s., 790; Bermuda, 3 t., 5 s., 790; Mexico, 1 t., 1 s., 790; England, 61 t., 138 s., 790; Scotland, 6 t., 12 s., 792; Ireland, 5 t., 7 s., 792; Continental Europe, 9 t., 9 s., 792; Asia, 4 t., 4 s., 792; Australia, 12 t., 86 s., 793; New Zealand, 5 t., 24 s., 794. *Supplementary List of Subscribers* (Feb. to Nov., '86), 795-6. *Trade Directory:* Alphabetical list of 122 subscribers in whose offices this book may be consulted, 796-7. Geographical list of the same, 798-9. (Electro. March to May, '86, except last six pages in Nov.; 22,000 words.)

XLI. THE LAST WORD, 800: Pinaforic chant at the League's first annual banquet, Newport, May 31, '80. (Electro. in Nov., '86; 100 words.)

A summing-up of the estimates for the 41 chapters shows a total of 585,400 words, whereof 362,400 are in fine type ("nonpareil") and 223,000 in larger type ("brevier"). I have estimated the latter at 600 words to the page (44 lines of 14 words each), and the nonpareil at 900 words to the page (53 lines of 17 words each), except that the 66 pages devoted to subscribers' names have been credited with 18,100 words *less* than the latter estimate would give them. The half-dozen blank lines at the top of each chapter, and the short blanks at ends of paragraphs, are fully offset by the repetitions of chapter-titles at the tops of pages. Owing to the great number of abbreviations in last ten chapters, I think their number of nonpareil words exceeds the estimate,—for my actual count of p. 407 revealed 1088 words. On the other hand, the brevier words may fall a trifle short of the estimate,—for actual count of p. 358 revealed only 573. My printers have charged me with 372 brevier pages; and a multiplication of that number by 600 shows 223,200 words, or almost exactly the result gained by adding the chapter estimates. Of the 311,600 words in first 29 chapters (472 pp.), all but 92,600 are in brevier; while, of the 273,800 words in last 12 chapters (328 pp.), which may be classed as an appendix, only 4000 are in brevier. My own road-reports and wheeling experiences are almost all included in the 181,000 brevier words of the first 26 chapters (390 pp.), which also contain 77,000 nonpareil words, mostly given to others' reports and general information. In Chaps. 30-33 (pp. 473-590) are 104,850 words, almost wholly given to others' personal statistics; and Chaps. 34-37 (pp. 591-699) contain 97,550 words of general information. Of the 273,800 words in last 12 chapters, the 29,100 in Chap. 38 are the only ones personal to myself. Adding these to the 6800 brevier words of Chap. 27, and the 181,000 before specified, gives a total of 217,200 words which refer in some way to my own wheeling. Even if the 11,000 words about "Curl," and the 20,000 brevier words about "the Castle," be charged to me as "personal," my entire share in the book rises to only 248,200 words, which is much less than half its text (585,400).

PREFACE.

Scope of the volume. This is a book of American roads, for men who travel on the bicycle. Its ideal is that of a gazetteer, a dictionary, a cyclopædia, a statistical guide, a thesaurus of facts. The elaborateness of its indexing shows that it is designed less for reading than for reference,—less for amusement than for instruction,—and debars any one from objecting to the multiplicity of its details. No need exists for a weary wading through the mass of these by any seeker for special knowledge. The information which he wants can be found at once, if contained in the book at all; and the pages which do not interest him can be left severely alone.

Assumptions for a special class of travelers. In reporting my own travels, I have assumed that the reader (as a bicycler who may plan to ride along the same routes) desires to know just what I was most desirous of having advance knowledge of, in every case; and I have tried to tell just those things, in the simplest language and the most compact form. I have accounted no fact too trivial for record, if it could conceivably help or interest wheelmen when touring in the locality to which it relates; and I insist that no critic, save one whose road-experience makes him more competent than I am to predict what such tourists want to know, has any right to censure me on this account, as "lacking a sense of perspective." My power to please these particular people, by offering them these microscopic details, can be proved by experiment only; but I object in advance to having any one meanwhile misrepresent me as endeavoring to please people in general. "The general reader" may justly demand of the critic that he give warning against a writer-of-travels, as well as against a novelist or verse-maker, who is so precise and exhaustive as to be tedious; but a chronicler who avowedly seeks to be precise and exhaustive, in compiling a special sort of gazetteer,—and who disclaims any desire of restricting its scope to points which are salient and notably significant and universally interesting,—may as justly demand of the critic that he do not condemn the work "because unsuited to the general reader."

Fair warnings for "the general reader." As regards the latter all-powerful personage, I recognize that "his money is as good as anybody's"; and I intend, incidentally, to sell him a good many copies of the book; but I am bound that he shall buy it with his eyes open, if he buys it at all, and shall have no pretext for pretending that I catered to his taste in preparing it, or relied upon his patronage in making it a success. I aim, rather, to pique his curiosity by proving that profit may be gained, in defiance of him, from the support of a world of readers whose existence he never dreamed of; and I expect that, whenever his curiosity forces him to pay me tribute, in order to study the manners and customs of those readers who inhabit this new "world on wheels," he will be civil enough to remember the motive which induced his expenditure, and to refrain from reviling me as having baited him in by false pretences, or failed to give him his money's worth. As regards "the general reader," then, I say: "*Caveat emptor!* Having paid up, let him shut up! If I welcome him to my show, it is avowedly for no other reason than that his coin may help fill the yawning chasm at my banker's. I have not planned the performance to please him, nor have I varied my ideal of it one iota to avoid the danger of his derision. I shall be glad, incidentally, to win his good-will; but, if his ill-will be aroused instead, I protest against his proclaiming it in such way as to obscure this truth: that what I chiefly aim to win is the good-will of the 3000 wheelmen who have subscribed to my scheme in advance, and of the 300,000 wheelmen whom those subscribers represent."

Attempts at verbal attractiveness. "Well-written and readable beyond the common" was the verdict which the reviewer of the *Times* passed upon my opening chapter, when it first appeared, in a magazine, four years ago; but I have not endeavored to make any of my regular touring reports "readable," to the uninitiated, save only the one called "Straightaway for Forty Days." This, as a description of the first time in the earth's history when its surface was marked for as much as 1400 miles by the continuous trail of a bicycle, seemed worthy of exceptional treatment, by reason of the chance it gave for impressing the imagination of the unconverted with the peculiar charm, and the magnificent possibilities, of "wheeling large." I do not assert that my actual description possesses any such power,—but simply that, in this one case, I did endeavor to formulate my enthusiasm. The 305th page, in this description, has literary force enough to bring back clearly, before my own mind, the strangest scene in my long tour; and so, without asserting that other readers should accord it the graphic quality, I mention it as the only page on which I have in fact attempted to do any verbal scene-painting.

Amusement and instruction for non-cyclers. As regards my two extraneous chapters (pp. 407-472), "the general reader" is quite as likely as the cycling reader to be amused by what I have said there concerning the dear dog that I loved and the queer house that I live in; while, as regards my statistics of roads, they necessarily have value to thousands of people who know nothing of the joys of cycling. Each year finds a larger number of Americans seeking recreation by pedestrian and equestrian tours, and by carriage-drives across long stretches of country; while even the "horsey" intellects of hackmen and teamsters (and their fashionable imitators who laboriously exhibit themselves on "tally-ho coaches ") may have power to recognize some statements in this book as worth incorporating into their stock of stable knowledge. Indeed, as was said in the preface of "Roughing It," by Mark Twain, "information appears to stew out of me naturally, like the precious ottar of roses out of the otter." Were cycling destined to immediate disappearance, this volume (the only existing one of its kind) would none the less deserve a place in every American reference-library, as a veritable colossus of roads.

Simplicity of literary ideal. As regards my style of expression, though I may not have mastered the difficult trick of calling a spade a spade, I have at least used every effort to master it, from the day in 1860 when I first took up the pen; and I have striven to win nothing else of the literary art. The putting of ideas into written form has ever been to me a painful process, which I have sought to shorten as much as possible. I have always kept quiet unless I had something to say; and, though this rule may not always have made my actual words seem to other people worth the saying, it has certainly prevented me from being classed with "the mob of gentlemen who write with ease." Chatterers, for the mere pleasure of listening to the noises of their own mouths, may perform an acceptable function in amusing folks who are too stupid even to chatter; but that function is not mine. I have about as little liking for "literary men" as has the elder Cameron of Pennsylvania, and am often tempted to apply to them the same damnatory adjective. In fact, I hardly know of a class of fellow-humans whom I like less,—except "the political machinists" of the Cameronian type, and perhaps, also, "the athletes" and "sporting men."

The bicycle's slowness its charm for the elderly. My book aims to be practical rather than "literary," and my desire to see it serve as an effective instrument for "setting the world on wheels" forces me to be very explicit in showing that I am as different a person as possible from the "author" who is presumably conjured up in the minds of most men by the first sight of its title. I am not "an athlete," and have never attempted anything difficult upon the bicycle. Whatever tours I have taken with it,—whatever pleasures or advantages I have gained from it,—may be readily taken and gained anew by any man of average strength and activity. Whether or not I may be believed to resemble Goldsmith's more distinguished "Traveler" in being "remote, unfriended, solitary," it is certain that I resemble him in being "slow." The restless rush for the cemetery, which the English-speaking men of to-day seem absorbingly anxious to reach "in advance of all foreign competition," is a race I have no share in. If my book were big enough to momentarily block the progress of the generation now on the down-grade of life, I would wish it might in that moment say to them : "Look here at the bicycle! It is a slower and more comfortable vehicle than the hearse, into which you are all trying to crowd yourselves, with such unseemly haste ! "

The selling of 30,000 books less notable than the pledging of 3000 subscribers.

Hence I say that my longest tour on the wheel shrinks into insignificance beside this novel *tour de force,*—this strange showing of a world-wide brotherhood which gives advance-supporters to an unknown American book, not only in every State and Territory of the Union, but 400 of them outside it: in Canada and Great Britain, in Australia and New Zealand, in Continental Europe, in Asiatic Turkey, Persia and Japan. Whether or not I shall reap the expected reward for this exploit (by pleasing these 3000 strangers so well that they will quickly force a sale of 30,000 books for me), experiment only can decide; but I wish now to record the opinion that, if I do reap such reward, it will not seem to me so phenomenal a proof of the peculiarly personal power of cycling enthusiasm as does this preliminary exploit itself. I wish, too, that before any critic hastens, off hand, to condemn this expectation as a colossal conceit, he will carefully consider whether, from his knowledge of the human animal's indisposition to pledge money for anything unknown, my scheme for selling 30,000 books, by a simple appeal to the friendly sentiment of 3000 strangers, is really so unbusiness-like and unpromising and unreasonable, as was my first step for proving the substantial sympathy of those 3000.

Business necessity of my personal revelations.

I have a right to insist that that solid phalanx of supporters shall never be ignored in the judgment of any one who assumes fairly to judge the book which has been produced by their encouragement. While declaring that so great a phalanx could not have been summoned, by the mere push of a pen, in behalf of any other sport than cycling, I will not affect a mock-modest belief that even this phalanx of cyclers could thus have been summoned, in the absence of a prevailing opinion that there was a man behind the pen. I feel, therefore, that I ought not to be censured or ridiculed, because, as a mere matter of business, I devote considerable fine type, in Chapter xxxviii. (pp. 701-733), to telling them who this man is. Unless denial be made in advance that I have any right to persuade these people to serve me freely as book-agents, my mere attempt to placate them, by showing the sort of person they are serving, cannot be condemned. I insist that I am not trying there to exhibit myself to other people; and that "the general reader" is not bound there to search in pursuit of something else. If he be curious to study "the growth of an idea" which has (by imperceptible gradations, and in spite of my hatred of publicity and "business") led me into a scheme whose success now demands that I strive to make myself the most notorious inhabitant of the "wheel world," he can find the full details there given; but he must remember that I do not assume his curiosity in them, and do not give them for any other than a purely practical purpose. If I am to sell 30,000 books without resorting to the book-stores,—without granting discounts to cycling tradesmen or premiums to private agents,—without paying much advertising money to the wheel papers and none at all to the general press—it is plainly incumbent upon me to tell my prospective assistants exactly what I want them to do, and exactly why I hope for their help in victoriously violating the traditional rules of the book-business. The gist of my endeavor is to ensure conviction that the three years demanded by this book have been spent solely in their interest,—that I have constructed it with absolute personal independence and honesty:

> "My motives pure; my satire free from gall; chief of my golden rules I this install:
> '*Malice towards none, and charity for all.*'"

Typography and proof-reading.

It is due to my printers to say that, as they have obeyed the contract calling for close adherence to copy, even in the smallest details of punctuation, I alone am responsible for variations in "style." My excuse for these, is, not simply that the original act of writing has extended from '79 to '86, but chiefly that the electrotyping itself has extended through nearly two years. So, as my book has grown farther and farther beyond the limits first set for it, I have resorted more and more to abbreviations and condensed forms of expression. The proportion of fine type, too, has been vastly increased, and the indexes of names have been unpleasantly "jammed," in a similar effort to reduce the bulk. Even "Mr." has been banished, as not worth its room. By two personal readings of the proofs,

I have been able to "fill in" nearly every line which most books would have wasted in blanks; and, as my excellent proof-readers have perused each page four times, I think that few purely typographic errors can have escaped their well-trained eyes. As the eyes of a great majority of my other readers have not yet been dimmed by forty years' usage, I trust that even my finest type will not prove trying to them, for all of it is clear-cut and has been carefully put to press.

Suggestions to reviewers. | "The mob of gentlemen who write with ease" reviews which censure and short notes which tease, in the "literary departments" of journalism, will not think me inconsistent, I trust, in presenting them with the book, or with specimen chapters thereof, even while proclaiming that its chief significance is not "literary." It has been said of old-time that "the title, publisher's name and price of a new book or pamphlet, when clearly printed in a public journal, form alone a very valuable notice, both for reader and for author"; and I therefore hope that the reviewers whom I hurl my work at may be willing to advertise it thus briefly, even though they say nothing more. Such simple statement of fact will be accepted by me as fully covering every obligation in the case ; but, if more be said, I have a right to ask that regard shall be paid to my own theory of my work. The theory may be called bad and the work bad, but I may not be fairly called to account for not working on some other theory. For reasons by no means "literary," I think many reviewers may find my facts suggestive and my opinions provocative of comment ; but I expect from them merely "the sort of attention which is always bestowed upon a man who knows what he wants and shows that he means to have it."

Three hopes for the future. | The editor of a moribund magazine, to whom I once tried to sell the manuscript of my Kentucky chapter (in the humble hope that he might, by printing it, help hasten the deserved death, which soon happened), said, when he remailed the pages : "Though not without merit, they have a little too much of the Anabasidic flavor of *Enteuthen exelaunei stathmous pente* to interest the average reader." The remark was an eminently truthful one, and it offers me a fair excuse for saying that, as I am quite unambitious in regard to posthumous remembrance, my ghost will be quite content in case this present "Story of the Ten Thousand" shall last as long as Xenophon's. Nevertheless, as a living modern man, I shall be vastly disappointed if I fail to make more money from it than did that ancient Grecian from his immortal chronicle. Besides this prospective profit, there are two things which I hope for : first, that I may always keep my private life and my family name "out of the newspapers"; second, that I may always live "on the Square."

KARL KRON.

WASHINGTON SQUARE, N. Y., May 4, 1887.

Subscribers who receive copies of Preface and Contents-Table (whereof I print an extra ed. of 10,000, as an adv. of the book) are invited to distribute the same among their cycling acquaintances and other possible purchasers. I shall account it a special favor if they will show the book itself to local librarians and hotel-keepers, and will supply me with the addresses of wheelmen who are likely to be interested in my circulars and specimen pages. Publishers of catalogues and price-lists in the cycling trade are invited to insert therein the following free adv.,—on the theory that they will help their own business by helping the sale of such a book :

TEN THOUSAND MILES ON A BICYCLE. By Karl Kron, author of "Four Years at Yale, by a Graduate of '69." Cloth bound, gilt top, heliotype frontispiece, 41 chapters, 908 pages, 675,000 words, elaborate indexes, no advertisements. Mailed on receipt of money-order for $2. by the publisher, KARL KRON, *at the University Building, Washington Square, New York City, D.* Analytical contents-table, descriptive circulars and specimen pages sent free.

An electrotype of same size as present page, giving names and prices of all American cycling books and papers now in the market, will be freely supplied by me to any publisher who is willing to print from it. A proof will be mailed on application. I will also freely send proofs of any pages which any one may wish to reprint, without cutting into his own book for the "copy."

TITLES OF THE 41 CHAPTERS.

"*Ten Thousand Miles on a Bicycle*" (908 pages of 675,000 words ; pub. May 25, 1887 ; price $2) is characterized as "*A Gazetteer of American Roads in Many States ; an Encyclopædia of Wheeling Progress in Many Countries.*" Of its 20 local indexes, the chief one . gives 8418 references to 3482 towns ; and its chief personal index gives 3126 references to 1476 individuals. There are 1555 subjects catalogued in its general index, with 3330 references, and its table-of-contents shows 857 descriptive head-lines to principal paragraphs. An idea of the book's general scope, and of the regions and subjects to which it gives greatest prominence, may be gained by inspecting the titles of its 41 chapters, which stand as follows:

ON THE WHEEL (essay) — AFTER BEER (verse) — WHITE FLANNEL AND NICKEL PLATE — A BIRTHDAY FANTASIE (verse) — FOUR SEASONS ON A FORTY-SIX — COLUMBIA, NO. 234 — MY 234 RIDES ON " NO. 234 " — AROUND NEW YORK — OUT FROM BOSTON — THE ENVIRONS OF SPRINGFIELD — SHORE AND HILLTOP IN CONNECTICUT — LONG ISLAND AND STATEN ISLAND — COASTING ON THE JERSEY HILLS — LAKE GEORGE AND THE HUDSON — THE ERIE CANAL AND LAKE ERIE — NIAGARA AND SOME LESSER WATERFALLS — ALONG THE POTOMAC — KENTUCKY AND ITS MAMMOTH CAVE — WINTER WHEELING — IN THE DOWN EAST FOGS — NOVA SCOTIA AND THE ISLANDS BEYOND — STRAIGHTAWAY FOR FORTY DAYS — A FORTNIGHT IN ONTARIO — FROM THE THOUSAND ISLANDS TO THE NATURAL BRIDGE — THE CORAL REEFS OF BERMUDA — BULL RUN, LURAY CAVERN AND GETTYSBURG — BONE-SHAKER DAYS — CURL, THE BEST OF BULL-DOGS — CASTLE SOLITUDE IN THE METROPOLIS — LONG-DISTANCE ROUTES AND RIDERS — STATISTICS FROM THE VETERANS — BRITISH AND COLONIAL RECORDS — AUSTRALASIAN REPORTS — SUMMARY BY STATES — THE TRANSPORTATION TAX — THE HOTEL QUESTION — THE LEAGUE OF AMERICAN WHEELMEN — MINOR CYCLING INSTITUTIONS — LITERATURE OF THE WHEEL — THIS BOOK OF MINE, AND THE NEXT — THE THREE THOUSAND SUBSCRIBERS — DIRECTORY OF WHEELMEN — THE LAST WORD (verse). These chapters cover 800 pp. of 585,000 words ; the PREFACE and ADDENDA, 33 pp. of 27,000 words ; and the INDEXES, 75 pp.

"*Ten Thousand Miles on a Bicycle*" has been produced at an expense considerably in excess of $12,000 (representing a cash outlay of $6200, and four years' all-absorbing work). It will not be exposed at the bookstores, but an ultimate sale of 30,000 copies will be enforced by the unpaid efforts of the 3000 "co-partners " whose subscriptions combined to cause its publication. In more than 150 of the 852 towns represented on the subscription list, volunteer agents of this sort have consented to serve regularly as depositaries. A circular containing their names will be mailed on application. The chief agencies are as follows : **New York,** 12 Warren st., 313 W. 58th st., 49 Cortlandt st. ; **Boston,** 79 Franklin st., 509 Tremont st., 107 Washington st. ; **Baltimore,** 2 & 4 Hanover st. ; **Buffalo,** 585 Main st. ; **Chicago,** 291 Wabash ave., 222 N. Franklin st., 108 Madison st., 77 State st. ; **Cincinnati,** 6 E. 4th st. ; **Cleveland,** 1222 Euclid ave. ; **Indianapolis,** office of *Wheelmen's Gazette,* Sentinel Building ; **Newark,** Broad & Bridge sts. ; **New Orleans,** 115 Canal st. ; **Philadelphia,** 811 Arch st. ; **Portland, Or.,** 145 Fifth st. ; **St. Louis,** 310 N. Eleventh st. ; **San Francisco,** 228 Phelan Building ; **Washington,** 1713 New York ave. Booksellers wishing to fill orders from their customers will be allowed a deduction of 25 c. on each volume purchased at these places (merely to cover the cost of handling), but there will be no other "trade discounts," nor will the book be mailed to any one for less than $2.

The volume is bound in dark blue muslin, smooth finish, with beveled edges and gilded top (size, 8 by 5½ by 1½ inches ; weight, 2 pounds), and is not disfigured by advertisements. Its only ornament is a photogravure portrait of the distinguished bull-dog (b. 1856, d. 1869), to whose memory the entire work is dedicated, and whose biography forms its most readable chapter. Copies will be sent for $2, post-paid to any post-office, or express-paid to any office of the American Express Co. and many connecting expresses which allow the 15 c. mail-rate.

Requests for forwarding the volume " on approval " (to be paid for subsequently or returned, — a month's inspection thus costing but 20 c.) can be granted only by the Publisher, " KARL KRON, AT THE UNIVERSITY BUILDING, NEW YORK CITY, D."

accredited with this result in the case of the women on the boats, but the fiery beverages dispensed at the lock-houses possibly have something to do with it in the case of the men. Even that mild decoction known as "bottled sarsaparilla," or "root beer," which is presumably kept on hand only to accommodate the children of the fleet, is given a peppery addition by the bar-keepers of the canal.

Of the numerous novel experiences I have met with in the course of a hundred miles of tow-path touring, the earliest was the most exciting, because of its suggestion of a tragic termination. I had passed many of the boat-pulling teams from the rear without a suspicion of trouble, but the very first pair of mules that I met face to face suddenly whirled about, and, tripping up their driver with the tug rope, sent him rolling over and over down through the weeds and brambles of a thirty-foot embankment. I shouted to the man to inquire if he was hurt or if he needed my help, but he answered me not a word. The force of life-long conviction that there existed only one responsible source for all the evils in the world—namely, his mules—could not be upset by any such slight tumble. Getting his shaken body together, therefore, and scrambling up the bank, he utterly ignored my existence or connection with the case, but poured forth a torrent of the most profoundly complicated cursing into the capacious ears of his team, simultaneously belaboring their well-tanned sides and quarters. The captain's wife, however, took a less mystical view of the matter. Recognizing in me the responsible cause of the mules' misbehavior, she leveled against me a tirade of righteous though somewhat incoherent indignation and abuse. The point of it was that I was liable to fine or imprisonment merely for having a vehicle on the path, as I must well know from the warning sign-boards of the bridges, if haply I had ever learned to read; that if the mules had seen fit to commit suicide by jumping into the canal or plunging down the bank, I should have had to pay the price thereof; and that, in general, only the extreme and unusual mildness of her disposition caused her to graciously refrain from springing ashore and dragging me off to jail forthwith. Thereafter, on the tow-path, I deferentially dismounted in the face of all approaching mules, though their drivers often persuasively shouted, "Come on, cap'n! Don't stop for these damned mules! They can't get away with me. I'll risk 'em. I'll stand the damage." The remarks and comments of the people on the boats were almost always good-natured, generally respectful, and rarely uncivil or sarcastic, even when designed to be jocular and to exhibit the smartness of the speaker. One form or another of "Wheredyecumfrum, judge?" and "Howfuryergoin', major?" were the invariable inquiries, which "Schenectady" and "Buffalo" satisfactorily settled. I here call to mind the quaint observation of a certain tall humorist at the helm, who was inspired by the presence of no other auditor than myself when he shouted, "I say, general, I wish I had one of them big, old-fashioned, copper cents; I'd make you a present of it." Much richer than this was the caution deprecatingly administered to me (in a tone of friendly confidence, as

garment used as an undershirt. As for one's white flannel knee-breeches, by the time their waistband gets shrunk beyond the buttoning point, the breeches themselves become worn out and may wisely be torn into rags for the polishing of the nickel plate.

Breeches, shirt, undershirt, drawers, socks and shoes, in addition to those worn by the rider, can be tied up tightly together in a roll, with comb, hair-brush, tooth-brush, sponge, soap and vaseline; and around this in turn can be rolled his coat. Stout cords have seemed to me more satisfactory than leather straps in securing this roll to the handle-bar, or in slinging it over one's shoulder when coasting was to be indulged in. Straps always let the roll sag down too far on the brake, while by careful tying of good strings it can be kept well on top of the handle-bar, though the strings have to be tightened occasionally to check the sagging. An excellent device for preventing this is the Lamson patent " bicycle shawl-strap," of which I made satisfactory trial on my latest tour. The wires of this contrivance are so small that it can readily be put in the pocket or slung over the shoulder with the roll to which it is attached, whenever one desires to have his handle-bar free. In dismounting at noon to sit at a hotel table, one's coat may be easily assumed without disturbing the inner roll. I do not insist that this coat shall be made of white flannel, since it is not to be worn on the bicycle, but the lighter and shorter it is the better. A linen duster and a flannel jacket made without lining have in turn served me well. When the day's ride is ended, I take a sponge bath, apply vaseline to any bruised or sore spots, assume new clothes throughout and arrange to have the damp clothes I have been riding in properly dried during the night for use in the next day's ride.

My wish always is in planning a tour to send my valise ahead of me where I may meet it at the end of the second or third day, but it is often impracticable to arrange any meeting of this sort when one starts out on an unexplored path, and in my last tour, which was an all-quiet one along the Potomac, I was five nights as well as five days away from my base of supplies. I suffered no special inconvenience, however, though my outfit was the simple one before described, with the addition of a razor and a third undershirt. I have never experimented with " M. I. P." or other bags, which are designed to encumber the backbone or handle-bar or axle of the bicycle, and I never intend to. There seems no sense in handicapping one's wheel with the weight of a bag (letting alone its ugly appearance, and the awkwardness of climbing over it) when the coat or shirt which necessarily forms a part of the baggage will answer all the purposes of a bag. The necessities of touring are confined absolutely to the articles which I have named, and those can surely be carried more compactly and comfortably in a roll than in a bag. The luxuries of touring are innumerable, and nothing less than a valise, sent by express from place to place, can keep the bicycler supplied with any appreciable amount of them. A good wheelman, like a good soldier, should be proud to go in light marching order, carrying in compact form the things that he really needs, and

2

almost every conceivable beverage that comes within reach. Water, ice-water, soda-water, mineral-water, lemonade, milk, chocolate, sarsaparilla, root-beer, lager, shandygaff, ale, porter, half-and-half, cider, and light wines,—all these "drinks" I swallow in great quantities, when heated by riding; and I also delight in chopped ice, water-ices, ice-cream, melons, lemons, oranges, apples, and all sorts of juicy fruits. Solid food is of small consequence to me on a hot day's ride, but drink I must have and plenty of it. "Drink as little as possible"? Well, I *should* smile! Rather do I drink as much as possible, and thank Mother Nature betimes for the keen physical delight implied in the possession of so intense a healthy thirst simultaneously with the means of gratifying it healthily! Your little riding-rules may do well enough for babes and sucklings of the tricycle, Dr. Richardson; but don't you presume to thrust them upon a six-thousand-mile bicycler like *me!* How I wish that you, or some other abstemious Fellow (of the Royal Society, London), had tried to trundle a tricycle behind me for fifty miles through the blazing sands of Long Island on that historic "hottest day of seven years"! Perhaps then you would have adopted my theory that thirst, under such circumstances, is one of Nature's warning signals which it were dangerous to disregard. Perhaps, again, you would have preferred pertinaciously to die for your theory, even at the risk of being buried with Truth at the bottom of one of the numerous wells which I that day drank dry! I'm sorry to appear uncivil, but my rage at your repressive rules *must* be given vent, and so I finally break out into rhyme in this way :—

> Just hear the roar, "Two-Thirty-Four,"
>   Of all these learned buffers,
> Who say they think 't is wrong to drink
>   When raging thirst one suffers!
> But you and I know that 's a lie,
>   And so I shout out gladly :—
> " Drink all you can, my thirsty man,
>   Nor choke in saddle sadly!
> Don't ever fear good lager-beer,
>   When there 's no water handy;
> Drink pints of ale, milk by the pail,
>   But never rum nor brandy!
> Drink half-and-half, or shandygaff,
>   Or lemonade, or cider;
> Drink till your thirst is past its worst,
>   Then mount, a freshened rider!
> Keep fairly cool (that is the rule),
>   Curse not, nor fume, nor worry;
> (My ' fume ' joke means tobacco smoke);
>   Nor take risks in a hurry;
> Nor tear your shirt while on a spurt;
>   Nor clothes while in a snarl don;
> Just make no fuss; just be like us—
>   ' Two-Thirty-Four ' and Karl Kron."

XVII.

KENTUCKY AND ITS MAMMOTH CAVE.[1]

THE Blue-Grass region of Kentucky, so celebrated for its beauty, never had a better reason for feeling proud of its good-looks than on the opening week of summer in 1882, when I for the first time cast my eyes upon the same. May had been almost continuously damp and rainy until its very close, so that every sort of vegetation seemed as fresh and luxuriant as possible. The foliage of the trees—which do not often form thickly-interlacing "woods," but stand out alone in their individual majesty, as if some magnificent land-scape-gardener had designedly stationed them there to form the symmetrical landmarks and ornaments of an immense park—was brilliantly verdant; and the tall grass, which gives its peculiar name to that section of the State, shone, if I may say so, with the bluest green imaginable. Great fields of grain, also, waved beneath the breeze, in graceful emerald undulations, up and down the soft slopes of the hills; and whitewashed fences "far along them shone " in the summer sunlight. Outside the towns and villages the houses were numerous enough to keep the tourist assured that he was traveling in a settled country; but they were so neat and trim, and withal so scattered, as readily to har-monize with the fancy that their inhabitants must be salaried "keepers of the Blue-Grass Park," instead of ordinary farmers, who tilled the soil simply for the sake of securing such profit as they could wrest from its reluctant grasp. The time for sowing had gone by, and the time for reaping had not come. There was no bustle or activity in the fields,—not " a shadow of man's ravage " anywhere. Nature was doing all the work; and a blessed atmosphere of peace, prosperity, and contentment seemed to pervade the landscape. For purposes of spectacular display the Blue-Grass Region was at its best; and not again in a dozen years would a bicycler who sought to explore it in sum-mer-time be likely to be favored with as cool and comfortable temperature as generally favored me during the eight days while I pushed my wheel 340 m. among the Kentucky hills.

A dutiful desire to " help represent the East " in the third annual parade of the League had caused me to sojourn in Chicago for the last three days of spring, during which I made trial of its streets and park-roads to the extent of 75 m.; and then I took train for Cincinnati, in company with the club-men of that city returning from the parade, in which their new uniforms of green vel-veteen had played so picturesque a part. None of the numerous bicyclers from various localities whom I talked with in Chicago had planned to prolong

---

[1] From *The Wheelman*, October, 1883, pp. 30-37 (" The Hills of Kentucky ").

offered the inducement of half-rates, if we would stop over for a day or two and help "open the season" of his as yet unpeopled establishment; and it may be added that several of the lesser hotels previously patronized had immortalized our visit by opening new registry books, emblazoned as to the title-page with "Tour of the Portland Bicycle Club," beneath which legend we placed our precious signatures.

I had hardly believed that the fascination of "riding in a regular body together" would retain its hold on the tourists in such a place as Mount Desert, where the plan of jogging about in twos or threes or solitarily, according to individual whim, seemed so much more in keeping with the character and spirit of the place; but the captain was inexorably bent on taking a regular ride; and not a man could I find to join me in rebellion against him. His decision was, after a brief inspection of the map, that we must attempt what is known as "the 22-m. drive"; and though it might perhaps be fairly assumed, on general principles, that the roads of an island distinctively famous for its rocks and crags could not be safely accepted as favorable for bicycling, except on better evidence than the beliefs and guesses of a lounger in a "summer-resort hotel,"—the rest of the party acquiesced in the decision as unquestioningly as if it had related to an afternoon's spin along a familiarly-known macadamized track, like the one overlooking the Hudson from New York to Tarrytown. So, at a quarter before 2 o'clock, the devoted ten wheeled out from the seclusion of the Grand Central Hotel, and started southward, with gay and hopeful hearts,—the carriage of the artist bringing up the rear. Six hours and ten minutes later, the specified circuit of 22 m. was completed. The appointed task of getting the bicycles "around the drive" had been accomplished; not one of the pleasurers had shirked a single rod of it; and though most of them were badly bruised, all were at least sufficiently alive to be conscious of unbroken bones. Yet these men were the *élite* of the thirty-five, so far as touring was concerned, for a similar number of equally good riders could not have been selected from the remaining twenty-five, nor a similar number of better riders from among ten times as many average bicyclers. Not one of them was weak or inexperienced or ill-mounted on the wheel; and not one of them failed to get tremendously tired before half the distance was gone over. It was by all odds the most memorable trip of the entire tour. Its hardships and exasperations made it in many respects unique, for probably no similar set of tourists ever suffered so much in so short a time, as a suitable reward for their foolishness. A graphic picture of the character of the roads, and of the afternoon's sport, may be vividly presented to the minds of all bicyclers by the simple record: "Six bent handle-bars, out of a possible ten!"

The road, though rough and hilly, was fairly ridable at the start, for, when a stop was made for water, at the end of 1 h., 4 m. had been covered, and one intermediate rest had been indulged in. The pace seemed to me much too fast for comfort, however, and I gradually dropped to the rear,—

The white flannel of my riding-shirt, which the rain had been moistening for hours, was not to be dried even by the white heat of this thousand-mile triumph; but the glow of this was certainly great enough to make the next hour's riding very vivid in my memory. I wheeled through no less than 5 m. of mud in that interval, though the rawhide bearings on the axle had now grown so soft as to make it revolve with great difficulty; and then I tramped through the darkness (7 m. in 2 h.) to the end at Port Jervis,—encountering at first continuous shallow puddles upon a smooth surface which would have been ridable by daylight, and afterwards stretches of soft and sticky mud. The picture presented at the closing in of night,—just before I dismounted, and resolved that I would take no more risks in reaching my base-of-supplies, however tiresome foot-progress thither might prove,—impressed itself more lastingly upon my mind than any other of the many curious and attractive scenes encountered on the forty days' journey. It was at a canal-lock in a sharp bend of the mountains, where a water-fall rushed and gurgled, and a bridge afforded a mimic stage upon which the snail-paced mules seemed to be posing themselves in a sort of ghostly fashion, as their great shapes loomed up with vague outlines against a background of mist. The yellow lights of the lower boats glimmered fitfully down the canal, and the red and green lanterns of the Erie cars and switches flashed a fierce response from the opposite shore, as the trains thundered around the bend. The gathering gloom and darkness seemed almost palpably to increase with every turn of the wheel, as it slipped silently along through the mud, carrying me nearer to this strange scene; and the shadowy summits guarding the river's defile could be imagined as coming nearer together, as if bent on the grim joke of closing the gap against me. Somehow, the situation suggested the Vir-gilian lines with which the shipwrecked Æneas so nobly voiced his gratitude to the tender-hearted Dido. Somehow, those lines brought up the memory of my magnanimous bull-dog, and made me wish that dear old friend were alive again, in order that I might tell him how great an inspiration the thought of his indomitable perseverance had been to me, in marking the thou-sand-mile trail. Somehow, I felt called upon, in the white heat of my triumph, —as I proudly pushed my spattered bicycle down the muddy path of glory which seemingly led but to a misty grave,—to do homage to his blessed ghost. And so, at the top of my voice, I shouted to the tops of the mountains:

> " *In freta dum fluvii current, dum montibus umbræ*
> *Lustrabunt convexa, polus dum sidera pascet,*
> *Semper honos, nomenque tuum, laudesque manebunt,*
> *Quæ me cumque vocant terræ.*"

Only one fall was experienced by me in the entire 618 m. between Syra-cuse and Staunton, and that happened just before noon of the final day, when I was within less than 30 m. of the finish. In grinding against a rut, the front wheel was somehow pulled out from under me towards the r., while I sat down heavily towards the l., exactly as in a case of slipping on the ice.

20

XXX.

LONG-DISTANCE ROUTES AND RIDERS.

CONFIRMATION has already been given—in the shape of foot-notes to my touring reports, showing the swifter average advance made by other riders on the same routes—of the fact insisted upon in the Preface, that such reports instructively exhibit what anybody of ordinary physique can easily do. I have said that this book would seem much less likely to gain acceptance, as a valuable contribution to human knowledge, if it recorded the exploits of an athletic or exceptionally strong and vigorous traveler, rather than the common-place experiences of a man-of-no-account, who regulates the speed and the distance of his riding by the simple rule of getting the most possible pleasure from it. As cumulative evidence in the same line of argument, I offer the present chapter to prove that my capacity to take pleasure thus, in laying down a long bicycle-trail, is by no means exceptional. There are plenty of other men who enjoy this particular form of "conquering the earth" just as heartily as I do; and several of them have indulged in such amusement much more extensively than myself. Those whose stories I here group together are fairly representative cases; and though the first one is likely to forever stand unique in history, the number of less-notable long-distance tourists will surely increase with each advancing year. Some parts of my introduction to Chapter XXXI. might serve also as a suitable preface to the reports now given.

Thomas Stevens (b. Dec. 24, 1854) rightly holds the place of honor on this record. He has already made a straightaway bicycle trail of 8000 m.,—an incomparably longer and more difficult one than any previously in existence,—and he will extend it during 1886, until it completely encircles the globe, unless he gets killed on the way. Leaving the Pacific ocean at San Francisco, April 22, 1884, he pushed the bicycle 3700 m. before reaching the Atlantic at Boston, August 4; and resuming his trail, on the other side, at Liverpool, May 2, 1885, he extended it 4300 m. to Teheran, the capital of Persia, September 30, where he halted again for the winter, to prepare himself for the third and most desperate stage of his dangerous round-the-world adventure. A native of Great Berkhamsted, Hertfordshire, England, he emigrated to America at the age of 18, and went immediately to join a brother who had settled w. of the Mississippi. From that time (1871) he never recrossed the river until the bicycle brought him to it, 13 years later. Much of this period was given to farming and ranching in Missouri and Wyoming (his parents still carry on a farm near Kansas City); but for two years he was employed in the rolling mills of the Union Pacific r. r., at Laramie City, and he also engaged somewhat in out-door "railroading," kept a small store for a while, and turned his hand to a variety of things such as offer a livelihood to an enterprising emigrant in a new country. Having a desire to vary this sort of life by "seeing more of the world," the notion occurred to him that the saddle of a bicycle might be made to offer a practicable outlook. Hence his decision to attempt the ride from ocean to ocean, in the belief that the incidents of so novel a journey might be formulated into an attractive book, whose publisher would supply funds for continuing the trail across Europe to Con-

XXXI.

STATISTICS FROM THE VETERANS.

BASHFULNESS has been defined as "vanity turned wrong-side-out," or a sort of mental awkwardness resulting from the belief that one's little errors and defects of behavior are closely observed by others. In fact, however, not much philosophy is needed to convince a man that the self-absorption of those others prevents them from noticing his faults, just as inevitably as it prevents them from recognizing his merits. They have no energy to waste in keeping a careful watch upon any one who is not of extraordinary consequence. To assume their disapproval, therefore, is hardly more modest than to assume their approval; for the basis of each assumption must needs be the notion that one's presence is of that exceptional importance which has power to stir them from their usual unobservant attitude of profound indifference. My object in mentioning these things is to make clear what I mean by the theory that the admitted difficulty of procuring personal statistics is probably due to the fact that most men are either boastful or bashful. The former hate to lay aside the long-bow for the pen, and to reduce their glittering generalities to exact statements, with dates and details, which may be investigated. The bashful men, on the other hand, hate to publish the simplest facts about themselves, out of dread lest the act be taken for boastfulness. They are afraid that the whole world will halt from its customary business, in order to point the finger of scorn at them for presuming to put on record such personal details as might, in the case of a very famous man, attract the whole world's interest. It is hard to disabuse them of this silly notion, and to make them realize that the interest of statistics is a purely scientific and impersonal one. It is *because* they are of no possible account, as individual atoms, to the world at large, that their stories, when grouped together, make an interesting aggregate which is of value to the world. However little we may care for the doings of "an average man," as such, "*the* average man" is a personage who claims some share of the sympathy of all of us; and it is the function of personal statistics to help define and materialize him. When I ask John Smith, and Tom Brown, and all the rest, to let me print their birthdays alongside their wheeling records, it is not from a belief that these dates have any personal interest outside the small circle of each man's acquaintance; but because of their statistical value, when aggregated, in helping determine the average age at which a man is most active on the wheel.

It would not be strictly true for me to say that I have spent more time and energy in persuading thirty cyclers to prepare for this book brief and un-

XXXII.

BRITISH AND COLONIAL RECORDS.

GREAT BRITAIN possesses at least a quarter-of-a-million wheelmen. Indeed, some guessers insist that the real number is twice as large, though I am not aware that any attempt has been made at a careful estimate. Yet only two dozen of this vast multitude have consented to answer my call for personal statistics. Hence, while some of these seem very remarkable, I do not pretend to assume that a still more extraordinary lot might not be collected in that country,—if the collector were powerful enough to get hold of every privately-kept wheeling record which is now hidden there. I simply assert that I got hold of all I could, and that I print all I got hold of. I offer these figures for just what they are worth in each individual case, and I hope no writer in the English press will be so unfair as to make sneering or censorious remarks against any of my contributors. Those whose records are small are by no means trying to pose before the American public as distinguished long-distance riders. My invitation was to *all* foreign wheelmen of a statistical turn of mind, that they favor me with a summary of their personal memoranda. "The average man" is just as heartily welcome to a place in this chapter as the exceptional man. I am grateful to all who have consented to stand here, but the degree of my gratitude to each is measured by the amount of trouble which he may have expended in supplying me with his personal story, and not by the amount of miles included in it, nor by the amount of interest it may presumably have to readers in England. My introduction to the previous chapter applies in good part to the present also, and should be carefully considered by whomsoever the impulse seizes to say something satirical about any of the men mentioned here.

The first place in this group seems properly to belong to the only man I ever heard of as having an authentic year's record of 10,000 m. on a bicycle. This is E. Tegetmeier, a member of the Belsize B. C. and a resident of the Finchley suburb of London, whose report to me (May 3, '84) is dated at the office of the *Field*, 346 Strand. I infer that he is a regular writer for that paper, and assume that he is about 30 years old ; and I have somewhere seen the printed statement that his father is also an enthusiastic cycler : " From a wheelman's point of view, England may be regarded as possessing unequaled facilities for locomotion. Scarcely a mile of country but is intersected by a road of some kind, and although many are what we here call bad, few in their normal condition are unridable. With these advantages, English riders are not only able to show better results, as far as distances go, than those less favorably situated, but they derive a degree of pleasure from the pursuit commensurate with the smoothness of the roads they travel upon. During '83, I was enabled to devote considerable time to bicycling, and this may account for my riding a distance about three times greater than my previous yearly average. Living near London,—about 7 m. due n. of Charing Cross,—I am fairly well situated for riding. In going out for a day's run, I generally take a northerly course, as by that means

CONTRIBUTORS' RECORDS.

XXXIX.

THE THREE THOUSAND SUBSCRIBERS.

THE following persons have each subscribed $1 to ensure the publication of this book, and they are authorized to persuade as many other persons as possible to buy copies of it at $2.00. each. Numerals signify the order of enrollment upon the subscription-list, and town-names show where other details may be found by consulting the alphabetized lists of the Geographical Directory (XL.), in which the States stand as follows : Me., N. H., Vt., Mass., R. I., Ct., N. Y., N. J., Pa., Del., Md., Dist. of Col., W. Va.,Va., N. C., S. C.,Ga., Fla., Ala., Miss., La., Tex., Ark., Tenn., Ky., O., Mich., Ind., Ill., Mo., Ia., Wis., Minn., Dak., Neb., Kan., Ind. Ter., N. Mex., Col., Wy., Mon., Id., Wash., Or., Utah, Nev., Ariz., Cal. After these may be found Canada, England, the various countries of Europe and Asia, and the colonies of Australia. Italics are used in referring to all these regions outside the U. S. Foreigners are reminded that Baltimore is in Md., Boston in Mass., Brooklyn in N. Y., Chicago in Ill., Cincinnati in O., Philadelphia (shortened to " Phila.") in Pa., San Francisco in Cal., St. Louis in Mo., Washington in D. C., and that the name of the State must always be added to any address in the U. S. The only exception to this is the chief city of all, because (as it has the same name with the chief State of all, and lies within its borders) a duplication of " New York " is not necessary.

Aaron, Eugene M., Philadelphia	108, 2216-29	Aekison, J. D., Oakland, Cal.		3238
Abadie, E. R., New Almaden, Cal.	2012	Affleck, Robert, Gateshead, *Eng.*		2784
Abbott, Edward G., Diss, *Eng.*	2939	Aiken, W. H., College Hill, O.		1933
Abel, P. L., Riverside, Cal.	2065	Albee, E. D., Wakefield, Mass.		102
Aborn, Geo. P., Wakefield, Mass.	1848	Albright, H. S., Orwigsburg, Pa.		3362
Abrams, Edwin H., Croton Falls, N. Y.	3271	Aldrich, James, Spencer, Mass.	3152,	3153
Acker, W. Wallace, Norristown, Pa.	2551	Alexander, A., Liverpool, *Eng.*		2904
Adams, C. Franklin, Bordentown, N. J.	2274	Allen, Add S., Summit Point, W. Va.		1437
Adams, C. M., Mansfield, Pa.	1782	Allen, jr., Chas. W., Cincinnati, O.		1305
Adams, D. C., Plainfield, N. J.	1338	Allen, F. H., Brattleboro, Vt.		1565
Adams, D. C., Randolph, N. Y.	86	Allen, N. G., Athens, N. Y.		29
Adams, E. C., Battle Creek, Mich.	2863	Allerton, jr., O. H., Pittsburg, Pa.		2958
Adams, Edwin W., New York	75	Alley, Chas. K., New York		1683
Adams, F., Newark, N. J.	2486	Allison, Geo. F., Oswego, N. Y.		89
Adams, Frank M., Rockville, Ct.	333	Allison, J. G., (Galveston, Tex.)	·	518
Adams, Horace A., Willimantic, Ct.	756	Allison, Robt., Greenock, *Scot.*		3079
Adams, J. Fred, Haverhill, Mass.	245	Alm, H. A., Minneapolis, Minn.		2811
Adams, J. Howe, Philadelphia, Pa.	573	Alter, C. H., Homestead, Pa.		2115
Adams, J. H., Yarmouthville, Me.	2646	Alvord, C. E., Detroit, Mich.		665
Adams, L., Eastbourne, *Eng.*	2584	Alvord, Jas. Leslie, Philadelphia, Pa.		1369
Adams, R. G., Henderson, Ky.	2324	*American Hotel*, Allentown, Pa.		1265
Adams, Walter H., Worcester, Mass.	3158	*American House*, Calais, Me.		2090
Adams, W. E., Melbourne, *Vict.*	1710	*American House*, Indiana, Pa.		1899
Adams, William, Brooklyn, N. Y.	1671	Ames, E. H., Titusville, Pa.		1302
Adcock, A., Hobart, *Tas.*	3214	Ames, F. V., S. Abington Station, Mass.	1289	
Adelphi Library, Easthampton, Mass.	3201	*Amis House*, Pine Bluff, Ark.		2725
Adriance, J. R., Poughkeepsie, N. Y.	490	Amory, R. G., New York		1388

DIRECTORY OF WHEELMEN.

The names of the 3000 subscribers, which have just been exhibited alphabetically, are here repeated geographically. They are grouped under residence-towns, which are alphabetized by States; and the order of these, from Maine to California, is given at the head of the previous chapter. Libraries, hotels and clubs are italicized, and are named in advance of private subscribers. The double asterisk (**) denotes insertion in "Trade List of Agencies where this book may be bought or consulted"; which list forms the conclusion of the present chapter, and which agencies belong for the most part to dealers in bicycles, who are otherwise designated by the single asterisk (*). Clergymen are marked by †, lawyers by ‡, physicians by ¶, dentists by ‖ and druggists by §; while small-capitals are used as follows: LC, League consul; LCC, League chief consul (the president of a State Division); LR, League representative; LS, League secretary-treasurer (of a State Division); L applied to a club means that all its members belong to the League; L applied to a hotel means that the League recommends it; TC and TCC mean consul and State consul, respectively, of the English "C. T. C."; WC, WCC and WR mean consul, chief consul and representative, respectively, in the Canadian Wheelmen's Association; o means a non-rider and N a non-member of club. Capital letters designate club officers thus: B, bugler; C, captain; F, flagman (color-bearer); L, lieutenant; P, president; S, secretary; T, treasurer; and they are used as follows in the title-lines (the town's name being understood when no other is given): B. C., bicycle club; C. C., cycle club; T. C., tricycle club; W. C., wheel club; W'l'n, wheelmen. The parenthesis, when around a club's name, means that those grouped below are presumed to be members; when around a man's name, it means that he has left the town or club; when around the official letters, it means that he has left the office. As official terms are all the while ending, by resignation or limitation, the parenthesis should doubtless be used in many cases where the "ex" has not been called to my notice; while, on the other hand, many active officers are left unmarked because of my ignorance as to their election or appointment. Likewise in regard to club-membership, the mistakes must be numerous, as so large a proportion of my subscribers have neglected to inform me of their status. In the short lists, where a single club is supposed to have a claim on all names not excepted by "N" or "o" or the parenthesis, I probably have failed to make exceptions enough; while, in the large towns, where the club-members and unattached are grouped in separate alphabets, it is almost certain that several of the former should be wrongly classed among the latter. In fine, I do not ask any one to accept this Directory as a piece of perfection. I the rather warn all concerned to be reconciled in advance to its inevitable shortcomings and errors. Yet, with all its faults, it represents an enormous amount of painstaking; and I therefore trust it may be admired by some, in the same spirit which ensured praise to the performing dogs of Dr. Johnson's time—"not that they danced well; the wonder was they danced at all."

MAINE.

Augusta: (*Kennebec County W'l'n*),
 Augusta House, C. S. Hichborn.
Bangor: (*Pine Tree W. C.*, Oct. 22, '83),
 James Crosby, W. R. Roberts, VP,
 Geo. O. Hall, C. J. H. Ropes, †N,
 O. B. Humphrey, ‡L, W. F. Stone,
 Charles A. Lyon,* F. C. Weston.
Belfast: J. Louis Pendleton,
 Geo. T. Read,* Fred J. Stephenson.

Brunswick: *Bowdoin College Library.*
Calais: (*Calais B. C.*, 1885),
 American House, by D. M. Gardner,
 Frank H. Moore, S.
Dexter: W. A. Small.
Fairfield: James O. Whittemore.
Lewiston:
 A. F. Nutting, Elmer I. Thomas.
Lubec: *Cobscook Hotel,* by T. J. Lincoln.
Paris: Will. L. Perham.

In the following list of towns named in this book, those which the " U. S. Official Postal Guide " designates as money-order offices are put in full-faced type ; and the star (*) marks such as are county-seats. Towns outside the United States have their countries given in italics. A numeral higher than 764, shows that one or more subscribers to the book are catalogued on the specified page ; and the numbers 609, 610 refer always to the names of subscribing hotels.

THE following list is designed to give the family name of every person mentioned in this book, and also of many who are alluded to without being named. References to such allusions are enclosed in parenthesis. Quotation-marks cover pseudonyms and names of fictitious persons. The star (*) points to birthdays. The list contains 1476 names and 3126 references.

TEN THOUSAND MILES

ON A BICYCLE

By KARL KRON

AUTHOR OF "FOUR YEARS AT YALE, BY A GRADUATE OF '69"

———————

MAILED BY THE PUBLISHER ON RECEIPT OF MONEY-ORDER FOR TWO DOLLARS PAYABLE AT STATION D.

———————

PUBLISHED BY KARL KRON

THE UNIVERSITY BUILDING, WASHINGTON SQUARE

NEW YORK

1887

Comparing the 675,000 words in this book with the 220,000 in my " Four Years at Yale " (728 pp., $2 50), I see that the price, at same rate, would be $7.50 ; while, at rates of T. Stevens's book (517 pp. of 230,000 words, $3), or " Gen. Grant's Memoirs " (1232 pp. of 300,500 words, $7), the price would be $11.75, or $15. The pages of any single chapter will be mailed for 25 c.

LAUDATION AT LONDON.

The Greek Kalends and Karl Kron's book were by many assumed to be synonymous, but the hope deferred has at length been fulfilled, and we are in possession of what may truly be called the first classic of cycling literature. Consisting of 900 pages, well and closely printed, the book offers a store of information which we shall not exaggerate by describing as simply marvelous. To the wheelmen of the world it appeals, its interests being in no way circumscribed by the limits of the American Continent.

To review this book is difficult, to find fault with it well-nigh impossible. It is what it purports to be, a description of ten thousand miles traveling by bicycle in the New World; and we venture to say that the reader who conscientiously examines its wonderful collection of facts and fancies will rise from his perusal with a knowledge of America, her roads and scenery, which no other book in existence will afford him.

There is many a noble thought nobly expressed in this book, with its bold originality of style and daring impudence of advertisement and egotism. Karl Kron is well read and entirely free from superficialism, a searcher after truth and a merciless prober of what he considers offenses. He is also possessed of a vein of smart American humor, which illuminates the dry text of his book from beginning to end. In places, such as the inimitable chapter devoted to his bull-dog "Curl," he soars to a pitch which reminds the reader very forcibly of Mark Twain and Max Adeler; and the cyclist who loves his dog will read this chapter over more times than once. To "Curl," whose noble and expressive features act as frontispiece, the book is dedicated, and there is a certain pathos in the selection.

"Ten Thousand Miles on a Bicycle" teems with valuable information, supplied in witty phraseology, and as a work of standard reference and exhaustive interest is likely to remain for many a day unrivaled. In addition to a literary taste, the book is distinctly appetizing from the mingled acridity and simplicity of its style. It is a really wonderful work, which we have no hesitation in saying will be the greatest work on cycling the world has seen. Beside its far-reaching interest, literary style and completeness of detail, the English work to which we have referred above ["Cycling," in the Badminton Library Series] sinks into insignificance; and in recommending our readers to buy the book, we suggest it not only to men who buy cycling literature as a matter of course, but also to the large division which reads no more than it can avoid. This is a good book, written and compiled by a clever man, and we hope it will be blessed with a very large circulation.— *Wheeling, London.*

An American paper (the *Athlete,* of Philadelphia) says that the general English verdict on Karl Kron's book is against it. This is not so. The book is a good book, well worth the money, and its only hostile critics are two men, one of whom has compiled a very onesided English book, while the other, it is rumored, is about to produce another. We believe this latter will be good, but common modesty should have prevented both men from laying themselves loose on poor Karl Kron.— *Wheeling, London.*

(P)

A FREE ADVER.

TEN THOUSAND MILES ON A BICYCLE. By Karl Kron, author of "Four Years at Yale, by a Graduate of '69." Cloth bound, gilt top, photogravure frontispiece, 41 chapters, 908 pages, 675,000 words, elaborate indexes (10,468 titles and 22,806 references), no advertisements. Mailed on receipt of money-order for $2, by the publisher, KARL KRON, *at the University Building, Washington Square, New York City, D.* Analytical contents-table, descriptive circulars and specimen pages sent free to any applicant by postal-card. (Publication was made May 25, 1887.)

I urge that every man who in any way makes money from the cycling-trade ought to freely advertise and push the sale of this book, simply as a scheme for increasing his trade ;—and that he ought to give such incidental help, not only to this book, but to all other books and pamphlets of cycling, and to all the cycling journals. Whether a given one of my agents may be influenced by this personal motive of helping his own business, or by the broader motive of winning new converts to cycling as a gratification of sentiment, or by a simple desire to see me reap some reward for what I have risked and suffered in building a more elaborate literary monument than any other sport can boast of,—he at least must be credited with expecting no payment from myself.

JOURNALISM.—The following is a complete list of the 16 cycling papers now published in America (May 4, '87), arranged in order of their age, with date of first number of each, names of editors and publishers, and places of issue. The weeklies are marked " w." and the monthlies " m."—the former's price being $1 and the latter's 50 c., unless otherwise shown : *Bicycling World*, w., Nov. 15, '79; C. W. Fourdrinier and J. S. Dean; B. W. Pub. Co., 12 Pearl st., Boston, Ms. *Wheel*, w., Sept. 25, '80; F. P. Prial, 23 Park Row, N. Y. *Wheelmen's Gazette*, m., Apr., '83; H. E. Ducker, Springfield, Ms. *Canadian Wheelman*, m. ($1), Sept., '83; J. S. Brierley; C. W. A. Pub. Co., London, Out. *Bicycle South*, m., Dec., '84; H. P. Seiferth; Hunter & Genslinger, 116 Gravier st., New Orleans, La. *Star Advocate*, m., Mar. '85; E. H. Corson, East Rochester, N. H. *L. A. W. Bulletin*, w., July 2, '85; A. Bassett; Ex. Com. L. A. W.; 22 School st., Boston, Ms. *American Wheelman*, m., Aug., '85; L. S. C. Ladish; A. W. Pub. Co., 108 N. Fourth st., St. Louis, Mo. *Bicycle*, m. (12 c.), Apr., '86; L. P. Thayer, West Randolph, Vt. *Pacific Wheelman*, w., Sept., '86; Crandall Bros., 339 Bush st., San Francisco, Cal. *Bicycle Herald & Evangelist*, m. (15c.), Sept., '86; H. A. King ; King Wheel Co., 51 Barclay st., N. Y. *Minnesota Division*, m., Nov., '86; E. C. Smith, Winona, Minn. *Wheelmen's Record*, w., Jan. 6, '87; G. S. & P. C. Darrow; W. R. Co., 25 Sentinel Building, Indianapolis, Ind. *L. A. W. Pointer*, m., Apr., '87; J. A. Hinman; L. A. W. P. Pub. Co., Oshkosh, Wis. *Wheel News*, w. (70 c.), Apr. 1, '87; N. L. Collamer, 47 St. Cloud Building, Washington, D. C. *Oregon Cyclist*, Apr., '87; F. T. Merrill, 145 Fifth st., Portland, Or. No price is attached to the last-named, nor notice as to when the future numbers will appear ; but, as it is "entered at the post office as second-class matter," such numbers seem to be intended. It has 22 pp., of standard size,—letterpress and adv. alternating.

As regards this brief adv. of the American press, I urge that it ought to be given free insertion not only in every American book and pamphlet devoted to cycling, but in every trade-catalogue or price-list which any American cycle dealer may issue. "Intelligent selfishness." and "the law of reciprocation" may both be said to demand this policy (as I explain on pp. 653, 718); but I believe the only catalogues of '87 whose makers have yielded to my many printed and written arguments for granting such slight favor to the press are those of the Gormully & Jeffery Co., and A. G. Spalding & Brother, both of Chicago.

(C)

www.ingramcontent.com/pod-product-compliance
Lightning Source LLC
Chambersburg PA
CBHW030837270326
41928CB00007B/1096